INFORMATION MANAGEMENT IN GOVERNMENT

UTPAL K. BANERJEE

CONCEPT PUBLISHING COMPANY
NEW DELHI

First Published 1984

Utpal K. Banerjee (1935-)

Published by

Naurang Rai
Concept Publishing Company
H-13 Bali Nagar
NEW DELHI-110015 (India)

Printed by

Asia Composer
at Sunil Printers, Naraina
NEW DELHI-110028

To
My
Parents

PREFACE

The book is intended to cover both the current status (state-of-the-art) of information management in government and a workable proposition towards a meaningful framework for information systems at the national level. The readers who would profit most from the book are users of government information: Central and State government administrators, managers in public utility systems and public sector enterprises, on the one hand, and executives and decision-makers from private industries and business houses who have to interact so often with the government sources for eliciting various information. General readers—pertaining to public policy, government affairs, communication, statistics, and other socio-economic areas—will find in the book glimpses of a rich tapestry, containing facades of a vastly variegated machinery handling information and being gradually rationalised in terms of information processing facilities.

The book is largely based on the author's own experience in government spanning 17 long years which provided opportunities to handle information in many ministries and to help in creating a computer-based data-bank for the Ministry of Industry. This also involved participation in a national team working for the proposed National Informatics Centre, heading its project for suggesting national information systems in three sectors: industry, social science and technology development. The book also draws upon the author's involvement with many courses and seminars organised by Indian Institute of Public Administration, New Delhi; Administrative Staff College of India, Hyderabad; the Indian Institutes of Management, Ahmedabad, Bangalore and Calcutta; All-India Management Association, New Delhi; LBS National Academy of Administration, Mussoorie; and Department of Personnel and Administrative Reforms, Cabinet

Secretariat, New Delhi; and has gained particularly from many fascinating questions asked by the considerably knowledgeable participants in those forums.

Some earlier versions of the material used in the book were published to elicit public response to them, viz., "Sources of Public Information" in *Labour and Management Studies*; "Commodity Codes for Industrial Information", "Information System for Industry", Information System for Science and Technology", and "Computer Control for Socio-Economic Information" in *Economic Times*; "Data Bank for Industrial Planning" in *ISI Bulletin*; "Operational Research and Government" in *Journal of the LBS National Academy of Administration* and "Computer and Information Management Concept" in *Management Engineering*. While the above material has been extensively edited and enlarged for the purposes of the book, the remaining material has not been published anywhere. For the two appendices, the author is thankful to Mr S. Ramanathan, Secretary, Department of Chemicals and Fertilizers, and Mr R. Ganapathi, Secretary, Department of Mines for their speedy clearance, and to Mr Ramaswamy R. Iyer, Secretary, Economic Administration Reforms Commission for suggesting their inclusion in the first place.

Any views expressed and errors committed are entirely the author's own.

NEW DELHI
March 1983

UTPAL K. BANERJEE

CONTENTS

LIST OF FIGURES

LIST OF TABLES

1

OVERVIEW

1.1 General

The prevailing notion that a government suffers from a surfeit of information is largely true. There is, in general, a plethora of reports and returns which reach various departments of a government. Some of these reports often contain information which is duplicated in others. Coordination in matters of collection of information and elimination of redundancy are not often realized in practice.

What is more serious, use of information for actual decision-making is, at times, either tardy or altogether lacking. Simon (1977) outlined traditional and modern techniques of decision-making, as summarised in Table 1.1.

Programmed decisions need an information-base of repetitive kind for using modern methods of operational research and computer processing. These decisions are usually of an operational nature and to meet needs for short-term periods. On the other hand, non-programmed decisions need an information-base of mainly one-time kind. The point that ought to be stressed is that both kinds of decision-making need a solid foundation of information.

The Government of India has a large number of ministries and several departments under Cabinet Secretariat. With the increasing complexity of today's administration and with the expanding pattern of covering a large number of subjects and application-areas under the government umbrella (as departmental activities or under public utility systems), the need for efficient marshalling of data and analysis of information cannot be over-emphasised.

TABLE 1.1 : **Traditional and modern techniques of decision-making**

Type of Decisions	Decision-Making Techniques	
	Traditional	Modern
Programmed		
Routine, repetitive decisions Organization develops specific processes for handling them	1. Habit 2. Clerical routine: Standard operating procedures 3. Organization structure: Common expectations A system of sub-goals Well-defined informational channels	1. Operations Research: Mathematical Analysis models Computer simulation 2. Electronic data processing
Non-programmed		
One-shot, ill-structured novel, policy decisions Handled by general problem-solving processes	1. Judgment, intuition, and creativity 2. Rules of the thumb 3. Selection and training of executives	Heuristic problem-solving techniques applied to: (a) training human decision makers (b) constructing heuristic computer programmes

A number of government departments have made attempts to study the information systems prevailing in their organisations and using them systematically for purposes of monitoring and decision-making. The work of Sub-group of the Advisory Committee on Management Accountancy in Government of the proposed Management Information System (MIS) for the Department of Chemicals and Fertilisers and the sub-group of the Working Group on Review and Redesigning of MIS for the Ministry of Steel and Mines can be cited a serious efforts towards devising MIS in the government. Relevant extracts from their reports, submitted in 1978 and 1981 respectively, are reproduced in Appendices 'A' and 'B' at the end of the book. The formats devised are regularly used up to the Secretary's level in these departments and have proved quite useful.

1.2 The objective

The present study attempts to survey the available sources of public information, to appreciate the framework under which ministries and departments operate both at the Centre and in the States (Chapter 2). Since development of industry is a specific responsibility undertaken by the government, the study attempts a look at the schemes of classification and codification for industrial information (Chapter 3) and the (Nation) of a databank for industrial planning at the Central Government level (Chapter 4).

As large repetitive data are needed for structured decision-making, use of computers is inevitable. The study, therefore, surveys the scene of computer-aided information processing for government departments (Chapter 5). Similarly, operational research techniques are important in analysing complicated situations which abound in restrictions, conflicts and priority-schemes of both pre-emptive and non-pre-emptive kinds. The study, to that extent, looks at some of the current applications of operational research which have already found a place in our government's working (Chapter 6).

Once the state-of-the-art is surveyed, it is necessary to look towards an integrated framework under which national-level information systems can grow and flourish. Through association with the team to negotiate for UNDP-aided programme for National Informatics Centre (NIC) in Delhi, the author had an opportunity to suggest information systems for industry, social sciences, and science and technology. Since these have considerable academic as well as practical interest, the study attempts to look at some outlines of such information systems which may be of help to government information planning (Chapter 7, 8 and 9).

Also, in view of the all-pervading importance of computers in information management, the study examines a few information management concepts in relation to computers (Chapter 10). Thereafter, specific projects are mooted for the use of computers for providing control and operator guidance in the field of socio-economic information (Chapter 11). Finally, the study endeavours to lay down a blueprint for information management planning with special reference to industrial information (Chapter 12).

In brief, the main objective of the study is twofold :

(a) to survey the existing ground on information management in the government ; and
(b) to explore new ideas for more effective and integrated information systems at national level.

1.3 Computing needs of Central Government

The concept of a national informatics centre (NIC) came into being in the early seventies to link up all the departments of the Government of India in the form of a computer network for an information base for the central government. The aim was to have a large, centrally operated data bank at the third-tier level which would have a number of decentralized information bases (developed on minicomputers) at the second-tier level. Evidently, the first-tier information basis would be the local information centres all over the country.

In pursuance of the above, the NIC linked up nearly a dozen departments of the Government of India up to May 1977. In fact, the NIC was in the process of connecting 50 to 60 minicomputers, one in each department of the Government of India, to a large $3.5 million computer which would act as the host system. It also developed competence in the hardware and software inter-connections. Twelve minicomputers were to be connected to their front-end HP 21 MX system within the following few months. Between IPAG and NIC, there were 40 post-doctoral specialists in Electronics and Computer Science and as many M. Techs. This strength was expected to double by the end of the financial year 1977-78. The NIC has established a thorough credibility as is evident from their obtaining in 1977 a $1 million software/firmware export contract from the USA.

The position did not change materially in the following two years. By May 1979, the computing needs of the Central Government departments and ministries located in Delhi were proposed to be met through: the computer systems of the National Informatics Centre (NIC), under the Department of Electronics; the Government Computer Centre of the Department of Statistics; and the Computer of the Planning Commission. Some bulk data on industries were being maintained by the Planning Commission for their needs, and the new Inter Data 8/32 computer installed there in February 1978 has enabled expansion and speeding up of this effort. The Director General Technical Development (DGTD) processed "monthly production data" relating to 97 industries, covering about 1400 large-scale industrial companies registered with the DGTD, on the computer system of the Government Computer Centre. During 1979, DGTD increased the monthly production data to cover about 184 industries, thereby processing information relating to approximately 2,900 companies, which would comprise approximately 80 per cent, by statistical weight, of the large-scale industrial sector. A Burroughs 3800 computer system was selected for installation at the Government Computer Centre of the Department of Statistics. This system has now been installed, replacing the Honeywell-400 computer used for the past decade. The NIC provided assistance to the office of the Development Commissioner, Small Scale Industries (DCSSI), in developing a similar information system for small-scale industrial units.

It was proposed to locate minicomputer terminals in various government departments/organizations of the government of India in Delhi and inter-link them to the large computer system of the NIC by means of communication links. Five minicomputer terminals were installed and became operational, and another 10 such terminals were located during 1979 and afterwards. Of these, four terminals were used to develop information systems relating to industries. NIC installed and commissioned in August 1980 a large host computer, Cyber 170/720 system of the Control Data Corporation, USA, with the assistance of the United Nations Development Programme (UNDP). The system consisted of a dual central processing unit, 196K word memory (60 bit/word), 2.5 billion bytes of disc storage, nine magnetic tape drives, two line printers, two card readers, one batch terminal, three network processing units, 30 terminals and one system console (DOE, 1980-81). This is the biggest computer in the country and is already earmarked for further expansion in 1983-84. Through the NIC network, it is now possible for different decision-making bodies of the central government to have access to various data banks distributed across a number of departments/organizations, on a need-to-know basis.

By the end of 1979, computerization services were given to 18 departments/organisations of the government. Supplementary regional facilities at a minimal level were established by 1981 at the NIC Cells in Bombay, Calcutta and Madras. Similar regional facilities were established in Calcutta during 1980, and in Chandigarh, Pune and Roorkee afterwards. These projects provide regional availability of computer services to all as well as computer network infrastructure for sharing of information between various departments and organizations, thereby avoiding duplication of effort.

Up to 1981, mini-computer terminals were fully commissioned at eight user locations, namely, National Council of Educational Research and Training, National Institute of Health and Family Welfare, Shastri Bhavan, Nirman Bhawan, Sardar Patel Bhavan, Indian Council of Social Science Research, Office of the Registrar General (Census) of India, Indian National Scientific Documentation Centre (INSDOC) and an optical document reading facility at UPSC. Steps were initiated for the installation of terminals at Krishi Bhavan, Udyog Bhavan and North/South Block (DOE, 1980-81).

National Informatics Centre (NIC), as per the Planning Commission's charter, had the responsibility to assist the user Government departments/ministries and autonomous organisations in the development of computerised information systems.

To achieve this end, NIC established an intracity computer network in Delhi, by connecting six minicomputer terminals to the host Cyber computer system being leased telephone lines and radio (VHF) frequencies. With a view to build up an intercity network, NIC also successfully conducted the Delhi-Ahmedabad satellite data communication experiment, using APPLE satellite (DOE, 1981-82).

To assist the various government ministries/departments in analysing the performance data to take policy decisions, 50 information systems have been developed by 1982. The development status of the first 16 information systems is given in Annexure I (DOE, 1978-79) for illustrative purposes.

The IX Asian Games 1982 were possible to be staged in India with the cooperation and participation of many government ministries/departments. Computerised information systems played a unique role in this endeavour, a summary of which is presented in Annexure II (as culled out from the literature distributed by the IX Asian Games authorities).

1.4 Industrial and technology policy for minicomputers and micro processor-based systems

By mid 1979, the Department of Electronics recognized that minicomputer/micro-processor-based systems could bring significant cost reductions, design simplifications and better flexibility in industry apart from finding a wide range of applications in a number of other areas of the economy. The minicomputer/microprocessor industry would, therefore, be one of the major thrust areas in the field of computers. The government, therefore, decided that the development of the industry would be on the basis of the following policy framework :

Based on capability, size and structure of the system as well as type of application, minicomputers and microprocessor-based systems could be classified into the following usage categories :

(i) Dedicated applications :
OEM (Original Equipment Manufacture) options for specific functions on a real-time basis with nominal peripherals.

(ii) Standard on-line applications;
(OEM option with peripherals and software).
(iii) Major on-line applications ; and
(iv) Stand-alone systems.

The following guidelines would be applicable for approval of proposals for the manufacture of these systems : The major objectives in the development of the minicomputer/microprocessor industry would be on setting up of systems engineering companies which are not necessarily engaged in the manufacture of central processing units (CPUs) or peripherals. Manufacturers of processors of peripherals would, however, also be permitted to produce minicomputer systems. For dedicated applications, e.g., direct data entry, accounting/ invoicing machines, data acquisition systems, type-setting applications, and dedicated controllers, medium and small-scale entrepreneurs with a technical background would be preferred. For requirements of on-line and stand-alone applications, units from the organized sector would be considered. Qualified individuals/groups abroad wishing to return and invest in minicomputer-related industrial programmes would be actively promoted.

While examining applications for industrial licences and small-scale approvals, a detailed scrutiny would be undertaken to ensure that the applications areas in which the minicomputer/microprocessor system was to be used were in tune with national priorities. The industrial licensing policy would also continue to be restrictive in areas where labour displacement is likely to be involved.

Foreign technical collaboration for high performance peripheral units would be permitted on a selective basis. Electronics being an industry which thrives on sophistication, in exceptional cases where it was demonstrably in the interests of quality and sophisticated electronics development in the country, foreign technical collaboration would be permitted; otherwise, no foreign financial or technical collaboration would be permitted for companies wishing to make minicomputer systems. Foreign brand names would be permitted to be used for the explicit purpose of promotion of export sales.

Indigenous brand names should be evolved for the domestic market.

To facilitate programmes for the systems engineering of minicomputers, industrial capacity for the production of a standardized range of peripherals and CPUs would be built up on an OEM basis, so that there was free indigenous availability at reasonable prices of the basic building blocks for minicomputers and microprocessor-based systems. In this regard, peripheral units, semi-conductor elements involved in CPUs and consumables, would be standardized to the maximum possible extent and licensed and approved companies would need to configure their systems around these standard building blocks.

Until indigenously produced peripherals and CPUs were available, efforts would be made to import certain preferred components, CPUs and peripherals on a stock-and-sale basis to obtain price advantages. However, wherever system/companies/users are in the definite need of acquiring peripherals/processors outside this range, the Department of Electronics will recommend ad hoc import clearance after review.

The performance of the units licensed and approved to make minicomputers and microprocessor-based systems would be reviewed periodically (annually to begin with) and expansion of capacity approved on the basis of these reviews.

All pending applications would be scrutinized by the Government and duly disposed. The viability of the applicants in terms of their R&D facilities, capability to maintain standards and quality, current infrastructure and future potential would form the basis for such scrutiny. Fresh applications would be called through a Press Note, only after the pending applications were decided.

Qualified individuals and groups abroad wishing to return and invest in minicomputer-related industrial programmes would be actively promoted. Foreign technical collaboration for high performance peripheral units would be permitted on a selective basis. Electronics industry, being an industry which thrives on sophistication, in exceptional cases where it is demonstrably in the interest of the quality and sophisticated electronics development in the country, foreign technical collaboration could be permitted.

1.5 Indian languages and computers

An interesting offer made by the Government was to use Indian languages on computers. To make such usage, appropriate input and output units were needed by way of hardware, and in addition, software has to be developed for coding, text processing, translation and programming. Electronics Corporation of India Limited (ECIL) made preliminary efforts in using Indian languages on computers on this basis and succeeded in generating Devanagari and Telugu characters on display screens. While they used a dot matrix printer for 3-line printing of text in an Indian language, 3-tier printing was necessary by having to provide for upper and lower *matras*. They also developed a FORTRAN compiler to process texts in Hindi or Telugu. Concurrently, awareness of the feasibility and potential of using Indian languages on computers was created through several promotional measures taken by the Department of Electronics, one of which was a symposium on "Linguistic Implications of Computer-based Information Systems" ogranized by the Department of Electronics at New Delhi in November, 1978. The question of commercial exploitation of the computer system would depend on the demand for such products.

1.6 Scope of study

The present study is *not* in the nature of a text-book on management information system nor is it a treatise on computer-based systems design and development. Nor this study is a conceptual exercise divorced from practical moorings.

The study is intended for both Government administrators and general readers who are interested in understanding the role of information in the running of Government and its interplay with decision-making under fairly specific objectives.

1.7 Suggestions

While the NIC has made a very laudable effort to establish an integrated information system at the Central Government level, there are a few pitfalls which should perhaps be avoided in its future operation :

(a) The NIC should ideally serve as a policy-making body

which can give guidelines to different ministries and departments for designing and implementing their own information systems. In other words, its role of being a service bureau should be reduced due to sheet complexity of such a task and unpractical nature of achieving governmental information systems by the efforts of single executive agency.

(b) The NIC should also concentrate on monitoring the implementation of information systems by various ministries and departments within specified guidelines laid down by the NIC in consultation with the users. At the same time, the departments and ministries should be free to design, develop and implement their own information systems either with in-house expertise or by outside consultancy agencies.

(c) In consequence of (b) above, there would be an automatic growth of both in-house efforts and outside consultancy expertise in the country. This would be much healthier than the NIC having to employ its own systems analysts and programmers who are not likely to have always a thorough management knowledge of different ministries and departments and who cannot, therefore, deliver the goods within promised time schedules.

ANNEXURE I

FIRST 16 INFORMATION SYSTEMS DEVELOPED BY NATIONAL INFORMATICS CENTRE (1979)

Sl. No.	Name of the Information System	User Agency	Status
	1	2	3
1.	A. Customs and Excise Information System	(a) Directorate of Statistics & Intelligence (DSI) (Customs & Central Excise) and Customs Houses at major port towns.	The information contained in the Bill of Entry (Import Data, has been computerized using latest techniques of data base management system. This facilitates a variety of reports on import statistics for the customs houses and All India Consolidated Reports for the Central Board of Excise and Customs.
		(b) DSI (Customs and Central Excise)	The data contained in RT-12 on production, clearance and revenue of 37 excisable commodities has been computerized in the form of a data base. This helps in the generation of various types of reports for monitoring and analysis work.
	B. (Import/Export) Licences Information System	CCI & E	Feasibility study has been conducted. A computerized Information System is being developed to generate statistical reports for utilization of import/export licences.
2.	Finance Information System		
	(a) Accounts Information System	Controller General of Audit and Accounts	Software packages have been developed for consolidation of major headwise accounts based on pay and account system of the Government of India. Also, the detailed headwise expenditure, progressive expenditure, etc., have been computerized.

(b) Budget Information System	CGA and Budget Division of Department of Economic Affairs	Software packages have been developed for grant directory, monitoring of expenditure and revenue receipts, appropriation of account and finance accounts.
(c) MIS for Bureau of Public Enterprises	Bureau of Public Enterprises	Computer programmes have been developed for accounts of public sector undertakings.
(d) Loan Information System	Various ministries/ departments funding the State Governments, public sector undertakings	A software package has been developed which tabulates the defaults in repayment of loans, interests due and defaults thereof, penal interest leviable on such defaults, etc.
(e) Information System for Monitoring Finance Position of Companies	Department of Company Affairs	To monitor the financial and legal aspects of the companies, a computer-based MIS is designed. The computer-oriented card layout and file design are finalized.
3. Economics Information System	Industries and Mineral Division of Planning Commission; Bureau of Public Enterprises	The industry-wise information system for production, capacity, as well as other information like inventories and profitability of respective industries have been developed. Reports providing details on these aspects are being continuously supplied to IMD, Planning Commission. The normalized socio-economic index data bank has also been developed to provide relative socio-economic information.
4. Water and Irrigation Information System	(a) Central Water Commission (CWC)	All the system development to produce the water year book is tested and put on production. Other programmes for analysis are also put on production.

ANNEX. I—*contd.*

1	2	3
	(b) Ganga Basin Water Resource Organization (GBWRO)	An information system has been developed for GBWRO, software packages have been developed and implemented to produce various reports for GBWRO.
5. Rural Development Information System	Department of Rural Development (Ministry of Agriculture)	A software package has been developed and implemented to produce monthly as well as quarterly reports for all the 74 districts under Drought Prone Area Programme.
6. Energy Information System	Central Electricity Authority (CEA)	The following software have been developed for the OMI Directorate of CEA. (i) Monthly performance report of all power stations in the country ; (ii) The daily generation report of all the power generating units of all the power stations in the country ; and (iii) Interactive programmes for analysis which utilize the data base created for the above reports.
7. Fertilizer and Chemical Information System	Ministry of Chemicals and Fertilizers	Feasibility study for this system has been completed. A preliminary structure of data base has been designed and the implementation work is in progress.
8. Minerals and Metals Information System	(a) Indian Bureau of Mines	The feasibility study for locating a terminal at Indian Bureau of Mines, Nagpur, has been conducted.
	(b) Bharat Aluminium Co. Ltd.	A project of statistical analysis of geological data has been carried out.

9. A. Industry (Small Scale and Standards Information System)	(a) Small Scale Industry Development Organization	The computer programmes have been developed for analysis of data relating to Rural Industries Programme and computation of monthly production index. The development of data base for the registration of small-scale industries is in progress. The questionnaire for collecting data from leather industries has been designed.
	(b) Indian Standards Institution (ISI)	The data base for ISI standards and licences has been developed and implemented. The computer programme has been developed for generating a keyword index for standards for ISI Handbook 1978.
B. MRTPC Information System	MRTPC	A feasibility study has been conducted and the projects for computerization are studied.
10. Construction Information System	Ministry of Works and Housing	The development of an urban and regional information system has been taken up.
11. Patents Information System	(a) Patent Offices (b) Industries	A software package for the retrieval of bibliographic information from INPADOC patent data tapes has been developed.
12. Education Information System	(a) Ministry of Education, Social Welfare and Culture	A set of computer programmes has been developed to process the data about schools and school attendance. Programmes are also developed to analyse literacy data collected at household literacy survey which is conducted under the National Adult Education Programme.

ANNEX. I—*contd.*

1	2	3
	(b) NCERT	A software package to examine the answers of candidates for National Talent Scholarship has been developed and implemented.
13. Social Sciences Information System	Indian Council of Social Science Research	The data base carrying detailed information about social scientists in the country has been developed. The codes for specialization of social scientists have been standardized and created on tape. Also, programmes for processing data on "Privileges of Scheduled Castes and Scheduled Tribes in Haryana State"—an ICSSR project—have been developed.
14. Health Information System	National Institute of Health and Family Welfare	The feasibility study to look into the computerization needs of the Institute has been conducted. The computer programmes have been developed for analysis of data on population. The data base design for storing the information needs of the National Documentation Centre has been finalized.
15. Manpower Information System	(a) UPSC	The work regarding reorganizing UPSC examination system is almost finalized. The UPSC will utilize the facilities being set up by NIC for optical page scanner.

	(b) Bureau of Public Enterprises	A Personnel Selection Information System for the upper four slots of executives in public enterprises is in the process of development. The coding of the information is about to be completed and the sample data has been tested on already developed computer programmes.
16.	Transport Information System	Central Road Research Institute	A feasibility study is in progress.

ANNEXURE II

COMPUTERISED ASIAN GAMES INFORMATION SYSTEMS DEVELOPED BY NATIONAL INFORMATICS CENTRE (1982)

The IX Asian Games held in November-December 1982 at New Delhi were the largest ever staged. About 5000 competitors participant in 21 different sports spanning about 215 events. Most of these events were organised in a system of several heats, elimination rounds and finals. These events and matches were conducted as per detailed international rules and regulations on the number of participants, dates and times of draws, order of lanes, knockout and league principles. The conduct of the games involved an enormous amount of organizational effort in building the stadia and housing complex; finalising competitor particulars; draws of matches/heats; scores, result sheets; accommodation and other particulars. All these activities required and generated a large amount of information which would be impossible to handle by manual methods. Information about participants, officials, invitees, schedules, results of current, and past games were all of interest to the various organisers of the games and to the national and international press.

Recognising the importance of all this information and the need for its timely dissemination, a computerised system was installed under the National Informatics Centre, Electronics Commission who carried out the task of design, development and implementation of a computer network and the Computerised Asiad Information Systems (CAIS). The computerised system for ASIAD 82 covered the following aspects :

(a) Past Asian, Olympic and Commonwealth results ;
(b) Current Asiad results ;
(c) Accreditation and accommodation ;
(d) Village resident status ;
(e) Stadia construction monitoring ;
(f) Personnel selection ;
(g) Ticket accounts consolidation.

To facilitate the use of these systems interactive terminals were installed at the Asian Games primary complexes. Jawaharlal Nehru main stadium, Indraprastha stadium, Talkatora Swimming Pool Complex, Asian Games Village Complex, and ten other stadia. These terminals were linked to a host computer through P&T leased lines and VHF. The NIC network provided a versatile enquiry service on various aspects of the results of previous games, current Asiad results, accreditation and accommodation details. All queries were handed over to the NIC terminal operators in a free format written form.

Sports in general, and the Asian Games in particular, generated interest in a wide cross-section of people. The extent of interest was of the nature of (a) casual curiosity of a typical newspaper reader to keep abreast of current events or (b) keen inquisitiveness of a sports fan to facts and figures related to sportsmen and results of a single sport or (c) bibliophlic range of sportscasters and sports journalists looking for statistics and stories or (d) selective specificity of the organisers and officials involved in the conduct of the games.

The scope of the query system covering the first three data bases and their sample queries are described next.

(a) Results of previous games

A wide range of queries on past Asian Games, Commonwealth and Olympic games based on any combination of the five attributes—event, game, year, winning country and medal position were covered. Each of these attributes could be specified with a number of distinct values or a range of values or with lower or upper bounds. The answers to queries contained full details of event, game, year, winning country, medal, name and performance details (wherever applicable). This information was based on the details furnished by Special Organising Committee (SOC) for the Asiad.

Sample free format queries

1. Give the details of medals won by India in Men's Hockey in Asian Games ;
2. Give the Men's 100m sprint gold medals in the last three Asian Games ;

3. Give the performance of India, Pakistan and Korea in Football in the past Asian Games ;
4. When did Japan win the first Olympic gold?
5. Which Indian wrestlers have won medals in the last two Asian Games?

(b) Result information system (RIS)

This system covered processing of scores/results on the 21 sports held in the IX Asian Games. These 21 sports did not cover the demonstration games. The processing involved the following :

(i) Daily summary of results, stadiawise (at NIC HQ) ;
(ii) Broadcasting of current results where NIC terminals are installed;
(iii) Summary of results ; records, set, medals tally—countrywise, sportwise;
(iv) Query on current results.

Each sport involved various score/result sheets which provided detailed and consolidated information. The score/result sheets were for all heats, elimination/final rounds. The enquiry services covered both current results and the detailed schedules of draws of matches/heats. This was based on the information provided by SOC. Queries in free format written form, using any combination of the attributes were accepted by the system under the following attributes :

Sport/event ; Venue ; Date ; Country (Team events) ; Competitor/Back/Athlete No ; Match/bout/heat No./semi-finals/finals; Final position.

The answers gave details of results or schedules depending on the query. After each event was over, queries on Asiad 1982 results were answered in a similar manner as for the past games.

Sample free format queries

1. Give the results of the heats of men's 200m sprint held on a particular date ;
2. With whom is India next scheduled to play in Football?

3. In which stadia are the Malaysians competing today?
4. Winners of 100m sprints for men ;
5. Results of matches played between country *A vs.* country *B* in a given sport/game ;
6. Record set in the current Asiad, if any (with information on latest world/Olympic records, etc.) ;
7. Medal tally position—countrywise/eventwise/daywise—as of date.

(c) Accreditation and accommodation details

This System provided information on all participants, officials, judges and authorised visitors. The information consisted of personal particulars such as ID number, name, category of person, function, event(s) participation, date of birth, accommodation, arrival and departure particulars. For competitors, other relevant information regarding their past performance were made available. This system provided a master list of all personnel in various sequences—countrywise, categorywise, etc. To the personnel information accommodation, details were appended. The enquiry services covered all the accredited personnel, who have been issued ID cards and whose ID No. and other particulars were present in the checklists. This query service was available for retrieval to authorised officials of SOC at the primary complexes. Queries could be specified as explained earlier in a free format using any combination of the following attributes :

Name ; ID No. ; Country ; Sport ; Event ; Function ; Accommodation ; Back No. ; Sex ; Date of birth ; Date of arrival ; Date of departure.

Answers to these queries were either complete or selective fields of personal information covering the above attributes. Outputs also included past performance and bio-data wherever applicable.

Sample free format queries

1. How big is the Japanese contingent?
2. In what Athletic events are the Malaysians taking part?
3. How many Indonesian competitors are staying in the village today?

4. What is the weight of the Korean boxer with Back No. 10.
5. How many women gymnasts are there with age below 20 years?

REFERENCES

Herbert, A. Simon, *The New Science of Management Decisions*, Prentice-Hall, Englewood Cliffs, 1977.

DOE (Department of Electronics), *Annual Reports*, 1978-79, 1980-81, 1981-82, Government of India, New Delhi.

Computerised Asiad Information Systems, Executive Agency, National Informatics Centre, IX Asian Games, Delhi, 1982.

STATE-OF-THE-ART

2

SOURCES OF PUBLIC INFORMATION

2.1 Introduction

Statistical sources of information have long been known to be of use to planners, decision-makers and researchers as long as their efforts are based on a precise data base. In a country geared to the efforts of developing its socio-economic structure, it is important that such statistical information are not merely available, but are also authentic. As considerable data flow into the hands of government and public systems in India, some care has been taken to let them be duly collated, summarized and disseminated in published forms for general purpose use.

In this Chapter, we describe the functions and organization structures of various public agencies and departments of the Government, both Central and State, which compile and publicize various kinds of socio-economic information.

2.2 Background

The progress after World War II in the statistical systems has been remarkable, with their expansion in all respects—theory, methodology, application and geographic coverage. It is almost without precedent in history. This fact was noted in the forty-first session of the International Statistical Institute in Delhi in December 1978, while the following problems about availability of reliable and accurate information and the scientific analysis of data vital to a developing economy were being highlighted :

(a) Although statistics on agriculture were of both high quality and adequate nature, it was necessary to make them more comprehensive, so that needs for better production and means to secure improvement in the village economy could be assessed ;

(b) More information was required on cottage and village industries, unorganized trade, transport and services to create better employment opportunities, and to improve the efficiency of artisans and non-agricultural workers ;

(c) Long delays in obtaining the requisite information were to be avoided, by a judicious combination of EDP systems and traditional systems for tabulation in the statistical system.

The lack of correct and up-to-date information has often been the scourge of the existing social, economic and political environment, and insensible restrictions on the free flow of information have hindered progress. Programmes for ending mass poverty, illiteracy and unemployment, and for improving quality of life are today matters of high priority and demand very dependable and comprehensive statistics. In order to study and recommend the information system in our Government, it is necessary to study first its sources and dissemination mechanism.

2.3 The linkage model

All flows of Government information are essentially two-way processes—there is a well-defined environment from which finished reports on raw data are captured for the Government and there is a Government agency which, as recipient of the above data and reports, serves as the centre for disseminating aggregated information to the interested environment. This may be exemplified for DGTD as presented in Figure 2.1.

In this diagram, medium and large-scale industry form the environment from which monthly and annual production reports are originated as prescribed formats and sent to the DGTD. The latter, in turn, consolidates the firmwise position on its computerized data bank and prepares industrywise summaries for wide dissemination. The following points are worth observing :

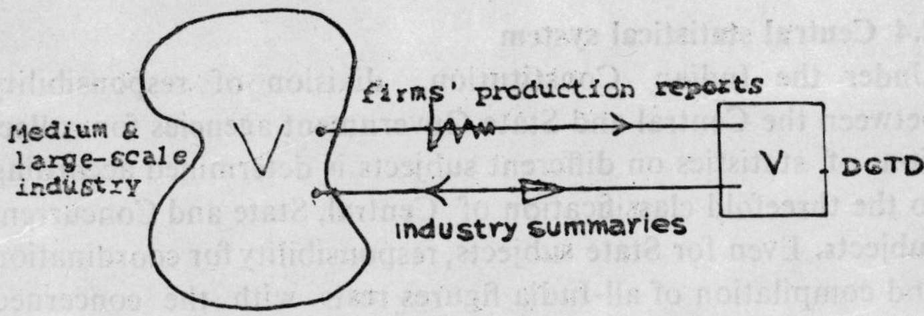

FIG. 2.1 : *Two way flow of government information*

(i) the firm must observe regularity in sending their returns and accuracy in what is contained in the returns in order that the DGTD is posted with timely and reliable data, and is able to consolidate them for industry's use. Any lapse in this chain means only incomplete or delayed industrial information which are not, therefore, worth while ;

(ii) industry summaries preserve confidentiality for each firm's own data and yet serve as useful indicators, by giving average performances and norms, to interpret the industry's health and specify its ills. Each firm can, then, assess its own norm and performance against a similar but wider backdrop.

The above two-way processes of consolidation and dissemination maintain a delicate balance which is recognized to be so important as to merit legislation for being statutorily ensured. In fact, action in this regard is on to make furnishing of production data obligatory so that the above aggregative and interpretative function of the DGTD could continue unimpaired by lack of proper data. It is, by the way, interesting to note that in this well-balanced data collection and information dissemination machinery, there has to be consolidation and reduction in variety in being aggregated by the DGTD(V) whereas the industry summaries have to be amplified in scope and application to make sense to the large number of firms who make use of them (V). This also follows from a general law of requisite variety from cybernetic sciences with far-ranging applicability in other areas.

2.4 Central statistical system

Under the Indian Constitution, division of responsibility between the Central and State Government agencies for collection of statistics on different subjects is determined according to the threefold classification of Central, State and Concurrent subjects. Even for State subjects, responsibility for coordination and compilation of all-India figures rests with the concerned Central agencies. This is presented in Figure 2.2.

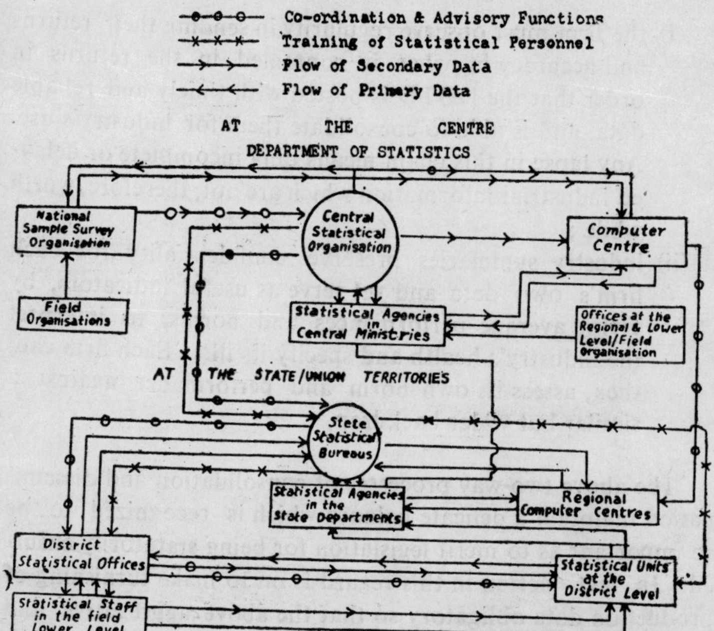

FIG. 2.2 : *Statistical System in India*

Within the above framework, a central statistical organization takes care of the preparation of national accounts, and processing and analysis of industrial statistics, apart from statistical standards, training and coordination (Rao, 1976). The organization, started in 1951 with headquarters in Delhi, has an elaborate set-up under a director with a number of joint, deputy and assistant directors and supporting staff in a pyramidal structure. Its industrial statistics wing at Calcutta replicates this structure, albeit in a smaller form.

The annual white paper on national accounts statistics, issued by the above organization, contains detailed estimates of the national product at current and constant prices. The base for constant price at 1960-61 was updated to 1970-71 recently. The white paper also contains estimates of prime consumption expenditure patterned on the System of National Accounts (SNA) from the West. Although the issue for 1973-74 was printed in 1976, the early estimates and the latter issues for 1974-75 onwards have been considerably expedited and are gradually being made up-to-date.

Comprehensive statistics on the production, employment and capital structure of the factories registered under Sections 2(m) (i) and (ii) of the Indian Factories Act, 1948, are compiled and published in 10 volumes. The summary results are issued in advance in the form of a general review. For instance, the general review for ASI 1970 was published in 1975 while summary results for ASI 1973-74 for the entire factory sector were released in 1976, with the detailed results for 1970-71 processed for printing. Starting from the detailed data for 1973-74 onwards, the whole process has been considerably hastened up.

The above organization, apart from arranging regular training courses in official statistics and related methodology for statistical personnel in India and abroad, also maintains a close liaison with the statistical wings in the different ministries at the Centre and in the States, and also with specialized international agencies like the UN statistical office and the international statistical institute. Such international contacts help maintain and develop uniform concepts and definitions, and also ensure coordination among the various statistical disciplines in the country.

There is a computer centre under the control of the central statistical organization, with the responsibility of data processing for Central Government organizations and public sector undertakings. The Centre had a Honeywell-400 computer which has now been replaced with a large fourth generation computer Burroughs-3800.

2.5 State statistical systems

The importance of statistics and economic analysis for planning and policy purposes at State level was recognized early and such State organizations as the bureau of economics and statistics in Andhra Pradesh (A.P.) and elsewhere made a beginning in 1954. The needs for sophisticated statistics for the various sectors of the economy are met with as illustrated below for the A.P. bureau :

(a) The system of agricultural statistics and crop estimation surveys has stabilized over the years with timely high-quality estimates on the area and production of crops, say, within two months of the ending of a season ;

(b) With wide coverage in the field of prices, fortnightly reviews on the prices of essential commodities, monthly reviews on the index number of wholesale prices of essential commodities and monthly consumer price index numbers for industrial working class are released regularly ;

(c) Such sophisticated statistics as the estimates of State income, per capita income, capital formation in the State Government sector, local bodies and State public sector undertakings, etc., are collected and compiled ;

(d) In association with the National Sample Survey Organization, half the samples are covered by the bureau in a national sample survey, providing estimates of employment, underemployment and unemployment, household consumption expenditure of various sections of the population, the capital, inputs and outputs in the non-registered industrial sector, and so on ;

(e) Such All-India schemes as agricultural census (1977) are conducted by the bureau for obtaining the size distribution of operational holdings in the State, along with the landuse, cropping pattern, irrigation pattern and tenure status on holdings of different sizes ;

(f) Another All-India scheme of economic census (1977-78) for all non-agriculture State establishments has been conducted to provide basic information on the unorganized industry sector for income estimation and programme formulation purposes ;

(g) In order to disseminate basic statistics periodically to administrators and policy-makers, the bureau has started a monthly review of economic conditions in the State, a monthly review on the index numbers of industrial production and a monthly review on the agricultural situation ;

(h) Planning cells have been established in all district offices of the bureau to assist in small units for collecting regularly employment data as well as conducting ad hoc surveys on employment ;

(i) The bureau has conducted a comprehensive census of Government employees (1976) for information on the tenure status, nature of occupation, pay-scale, and so on. This information, since computerized with the help of the Administrative Staff College of India has been found very useful by different user departments.

2.6 National Sample Survey

This multi-subject and multi-purpose survey (NSS), perhaps ranking amongst the largest in the world, collects socio-economic data from probability samples on a continuing basis. Each NSS extends over a year and takes up single or double-subject inquiries, using stratified two-State sampling design and covering a sample of 9,000 villages and 500 urban blocks, with households or persons as basic entities. Around 100 classificatory characters or attributes are collected from about 1.5 lakh households or 7.5 lakh persons on the following range of socio-economic subjects :

(a) *Decennial* : (i) demography, health and family planning ;
(ii) assets, debt and investment ;
(iii) landholdings and livestock enterprises ;

(b) *Quinquennial*: (i) employment, unemployment, rural labour and consumer expenditure ;
(ii) self-employment in non-agricultural enterprises ;

(c) *Triennial* : Special surveys.

NSS primary data conforms to standard concepts and definitions, and it is usually possible to generate comparable data using suitable conversion procedures. Further, the data are multi-classificatory and collected as per predetermined codes. Also, the data requirement by users is of standard bivariate frequency distributions, means or ratios. In general, the estimates can be obtained using AND, OR and NO Boolean operators. Since the primary data relates to a probability sample, the aggregate values of a characteristics has to be estimated at stratum, region, State or national level. In order that estimates have a particular precision, choice of sub-population levels for particular geographical regions is necessary.

NSS data banks have been recommended by some authorities (Rao, 1978) in order to enable the multi-classificatory and multi-variate. NSS data play a dynamic role of generating secondary data; to meet unanticipated user requirements; and to ensure efficient and economic retrieval of information. The following subjects are listed for a primary data bank :

(i) employment and unemployment (person data) ;
(ii) consumer expenditure (household data) ;
(iii) non-agricultural enterprises (enterprise data) ;
(iv) population, births, deaths and migration (person data) ;
(v) landholdings (household data) ;
(vi) special surveys on weaker sections of population, irrigation, electricity, etc. ;
(vii) village data built from listing schedules of various NSS rounds ; and
(viii) regional data, storing estimates of socio-economic characteristics from various NSS rounds.

For macro-studies, cross-section and time-series data worked out for various sub-populations and combinations of attributes will be useful.

2.7 Other information sources

(a) *Registrar-General of India*

He is responsible for census data, generated from decennial census operations, on literacy, religion, sex, migration, occupation structure, industry classification, residential status, mother tongue, and so on. In 1979—the International year of the Child—an All-India infant and child mortality survey was undertaken covering nearly 8 lakh households, for generating about 65 output tables.

(b) *Reserve Bank of India*
Apart from controlling the banking credit and other operations, this organization conducts rural credit survey, cost-benefit studies, field studies, banking facilities studies, determination of norms, assessments and valuation, and so on.

(c) *Commissioner of scheduled castes and scheduled tribes*
He is responsible for all data connected with these castes and tribes, e.g., representation in services, educational development, eradication of untouchability, protective legislation, allotment of land to landless labour, and so on.

(d) *Directorate of Economics and Statistics, Ministry of Agriculture*
They are responsible for such data as cultivation cost of principal crops, agro-economic research coordination, crop-estimation surveys, ad hoc agricultural and livestock census, market intelligence on crop arrival, sale price, etc., assessment and evaluation of intensive agricultural district programmes, and so on.

An illustrative and near-exhaustive list of Government information sources, drawn up by the author, is presented in Table 2.1.

2.8 Central and regional data archives
Since the Indian Council of Social Science Research (ICSSR) is responsible for catering to the research needs of all the disciplines falling under the rubric of social sciences, the enormous task of its data acquisition and organization was allocated to its data archive, with its first priority to acquire data sets created by ICSSR-funded projects and to organize data produced by official agencies. ICSSR-funded projects

TABLE 2.1 : **Government information sources**

Information and Source	Publication
1	2
Industry	
(a) Ministry of Industry and Civil Supplies :	1. Industries Development and Regulation Act ; 2. Guidelines for Industries.
(b) Directorate General of Technical Development :	1. Annual Report of D.G.T.D. ; 2. Hand Book of Indigenous Manufacturers of Engineering Stores ; 3. Hand Book of Indigenous Manufacturers of Chemical and Miscellaneous Stores ; 4. Hand Book of Industrial Data.
(c) Development Commissioner, Small Scale Industries :	Small Industries at a Glance.
(d) Central Statistical Organization :	1. Annual Survey of Industries ; 2. Monthly Statistics of Production of Selected Industries of India.
(e) Office of the Textile Commissioner, Bombay :	Indian Textile Bulletin.
(f) Coffee/Board :	Indian Coffee Statistics.
(g) Tea Board :	Tea Statistics.
Agricultural and Livestock	
(a) Directorate of Economics and Statistics, Ministry of Food and Agriculture, New Delhi :	1. Estimates of Area and Production of Principal Crops in India ; 2. Indian Agricultural Statistics, Vol. I and II ; 3. Indian Livestock Statistics ; 4. Bulletin of Food Statistics ; 5. Sugar in India ; 6. Indian Forest Statistics.
(b) Institute of Agricultural Research Statistics :	Statistical News Letter and Abstract.
Fisheries	
Central Inland Fisheries Institute :	Annual Report of the Central Inland Fisheries Research Institute.

TABLE 2.1—*contd.*

1	2
Minerals	
(a) Indian Bureau of Mines, Nagpur :	1. Indian Mineral Year Book ; 2. Mineral Statistics of India ; 3. Directory of Principal Mines of India.
(b) Publications and Information Directorate, CSIR :	Mineral Wealth of India.
Irrigation	
Central Water Commission :	1. Irrigation Statistics of India ; 2. Water Year Book.
Meteorology	
(a) Director of Agricultural Meteorology :	Annual Report on Agricultural Meteorology.
(b) Deputy Director General of Observatories :	1. Indian Daily Weather Report ; 2. Weekly Weather Report ; 3. Monthly Weather Report ; 4. Aerological Data of India ; 5. Seismological Bulletin.
Banking	
Reserve Bank of India :	1. Reserve Bank of India Bulletin ; 2. Report on Currency and Finance.
Cooperative Movement	
(a) Reserve Bank of India :	1. Statistical Statements relating to Cooperative movement in India ; 2. Review of Cooperative movement in India.
(b) Department of Cooperation :	Cooperative movement in India—Important statistics.
Joint Stock Companies	
Department of Company Affairs :	1. Annual Blue Book on Joint Stock Companies ; 2. Quarterly Blue Book on Joint Stock Companies.

TABLE 2.1—*contd.*

1	2
Trade	
(a) Department of Commercial Intelligence and Statistics Calcutta :	1. Monthly Statistics of the Foreign Trade of India—Vol. I (Exports and Re-exports) ; 2. Monthly Statistics of Foreign Trade of India, Vol. II (Imports) ; 3. Indian Customs Central Excise Tariff, Vol. I and II.
(b) Ministry of Commerce :	Import Trade Control Policy, Vol. I and II.
Railway	
Directorate of Statistics and Economics, Ministry of Railways :	1. Monthly Railway Statistics; 2. Indian Railways.
Civil Aviation	
Office of the Director General of Civil Aviation :	Hand Book of Civil Aviation Statistics.
Tourism	
Department of Tourism :	Indian Tourist Statistics.
Post and Telegraph	
Directorate General of Post and Telegraph :	The Detailed Annual Report.
Labour	
(a) Labour Bureau :	1. Indian Labour Journal; 2. Trade Union India.
(b) Directorate General of Employment and Training :	
Transport	
Census of Central Government. Employees, Transport Research Division :	1. Basic Road Statistics of India; 2. Indian Posts and Shipping Statistics ; 3. Indian Transport Statistics.
Wholesale Price	
Office of the Economic Adviser, Ministry of Industry and Civil Supplies :	Index number of wholesale prices.

TABLE 2.1—*contd.*

1	2
Retail Prices	
Central Statistical Organization :	Retail Price Bulletin.
Direct Tax	
Directorate of Inspection, Ministry of Finance :	All India Statistics of Direct Taxes
Indirect Tax	
Central Excise, Ministry of Finance :	1. Statistical Bulletin ; 2. Central Excise Statistics ; 3. Indian Custom Tariff.
Education	
Ministry of Education :	1. Education in India, Vol. I and II ; 2. Education in States ; 3. Selected Educational Statistics.
Public Health	
Central Bureau of Health Intelligence :	1. Annual Report of Directorate General of Health Services ; 2. Health Statistics of India.
Housing	
National Building Organization :	Journal of National Building Organization.
Planning	
Planning Commission :	1. Five Year Plan Reports ; 2. Annual Plan Reports.
National Income	
Central Statistical Organization :	Estimates of National Product.
Electricity	
Central Power Commission :	Power Supply Position in the country.
Population	
Registrar General of India :	Census Reports.

were inventorized early and the following data sets were also acquired, amongst others :

(i) optimum utilization of educational expenditure in Gujarat ;
(ii) impact of electoral process on Harijans and Adivasis of Gujarat (1971) ;
(iii) a study of mid-term elections (1969) ;
(iv) communication links and pattern of political participation ;
(v) economic change and political attitudes in rural Rajasthan ; and
(vi) electoral data for all elections to State assemblies (1952-67), as received from Prof. Myron Weiner of MIT, USA.

These apart negotiations with Government agencies to preserve their data holdings and make them accessible to social scientists for analysis resulted in the acquisition of the following data sets, among others :

(i) Registrar General of India :
one per cent sample of 1971 census data ;
(ii) Reserve Bank of India :
sixth follow-up of rural credit survey (1963-66) ; cost-benefit studies for tubewells in Punjab (1966-67) ; field study to assess benefits from construction of wells and pump sets (1967-68); a study of banking facilities; and a study of determination of norms, assessment of repaying capacity and valuation of hypothicated property (1969-70).

The ICSSR data archive acquired SPSS (Statistical Package for Social Sciences) programme package for use at computer centres in Delhi University; Physical Research Laboratory, Ahmedabad; and elsewhere to meet the data processing needs of social scientists, apart from developing other general purpose software.

There are a number of general-purpose social science data archives of machine-readable data in the West. On the lines of Roper Public Opinion Research Centre (1946), International Survey Library Association (1964) and the "Zentralarchiv" in the school of Economics and Social Sciences of the University of Cologne (1960), several national and international bodies like the Council of Social Science Data Archives and Social Science Research Council serve the needs of social scientists. Alongside central data archives, Sardesai (1974) recommended regional data archives as depositories of a specified number of re-usable studies at institutions and universities which were engaged in research in social sciences. Activities of a regional data archive could comprise the following :

(i) to give data and tabulation for research purposes ;
(ii) to give adequate publicity of its activity through its own as well as central archive bulletins ;
(iii) to develop systems of storage and retrieval ;
(iv) to import training to research staff in EDP operations ;
(v) to acquire additional data sets ; and
(vi) to encourage secondary analysis, both within the organization and with outside researchers.

2.9 Bibliographic data bank

National bibliographic data banks (NBDB) have been proposed (Bhatia, 1978) as a cooperative venture for efficiently operating exchange of information, especially in developing countries where universities and other institutions of higher learning and research do not often possess well-equipped libraries and laboratories. Such a data bank helps in the collection of bibliographic information—describing and providing clues to the location in libraries of documents in print and non-print form—composed of records for books, documents, periodicals, microfische, microfilms, tapes, etc., and providing approaches to them.

A beginning for the NBDB is possible through the ICSSR data archive and the Indian National Scientific Documentation Centre (INSDOC), with the latter maintaining Union catalogues of periodicals. In a computerized form, the NBDB can provide multiple approaches and provide services in the fields of cooperative acquisition, cataloguing and reference, and then disseminate indexing and abstracting lists to all the interested organizations by providing selective dissemination of information (SDI). Convenient linkages are also feasible with such international indexing and abstracting services as MEDLARS, Chemical Abstracts, Physical Abstracts, Social Science Abstracts, and so on.

The latter opens up further possibilities of establishing contacts with international information services, such as Development Science Information System (DEVSIS), United Nations Information System in Science and Technology (UNISIST), Science and Technology Policies Information Exchange System (STPINES), and so on. These services are based on the cooperation of participating countries and the NBDBs of different countries can be interlinked for mutual benefit. Technological possibilities for such linkages were visibly demonstrated by the on-line data transmission demonstration held in Bombay in 1976, where the author, with other Indian scientists, was provided fruitful access to the data bases at the European Space Agency Information Centre at Frascati near Rome.

2.10 Data base for planning

An interesting final thought can be offered on the strong database needed as a prerequisite for updating the administrative, political and statistical fabric of the planning concept. Poland, China and Japan, who have been resorting to planning techniques, have efficient and dependable statistical machineries. Japan has a terminal-oriented computer system to feed the communication base while China's large manpower-based system has been computerized over the last five years. Multinationals in the West, resorting to rolling plan, have invariably well-equipped EDP systems—with one organization having 128 national branches and 18 billion dollar annual budget, preparing the rolling plan every January-end within 15 days.

An information and monitoring system has to be visualized for the Centre, for each of the 23 States and Union Territories, for each of 350 districts, for each of 5,500 blocks and ultimately for each of approximately 5.75 lakh villages. This entails a huge organization to ensure the following :

(a) the rolling plan would shift the base annually, with a timely and comprehensive comparison between targets and achievements ;
(b) the planning would be done annually at the prevailing prices, with fresh constant prices worked out every year;
(c) New technical coefficient would be worked out every year, to provide the backbone of models involved in the planning exercises, viz., macromodels, input-output analysis and material balances.

The strong data base needed for operating the "rolling plan" concept and carrying on the above updating exercise has an inevitable implication of computer-based information system at higher echelons and an efficient data-collection and transmission system at the village and block levels to serve as king-pins in a multi-disciplinary area-planning perspective. The management of the whole data-base needs a well-formulated scheme (with implication of manpower and computer) whose design, development and implementation remains to be seen.

2.11 Conclusion and overview

The foregoing attempts to describe the background of establishing statistical information systems in India and the two-way process of both collection and dissemination of data with the Government as the focal point. The Central and State statistical systems are looked at in some detail, and the functions of the National Sample Survey, Registrar General, Reserve Bank, Commissioner of SC & ST and the Directorate of Economics and Statistics are given along with a comprehensive list of public information sources. The following main limitations are revealed :

(a) The delays in obtaining the requisite information continue to beleaguer the government and the process of dissemination of information is often too tardy to retain their relevance for planning and decision-making ;
(b) The sources of information on cottage and village industries, unorganized trades, transport and services are still far from satisfactory ;
(c) The data archives conceived so far are based on somewhat arbitrary collection of information from disparate

sources and the all-important aspect of selectivity is missing from these schemes ;

(d) The planning in India, currently envisaged to be done on a "rolling" basis, needs a far better statistical data-basc than is available at the moment.

All the above factors are capable of improvement. Particularly at input-ends, attention to only chosen items of data would enable a quick collection machinery to work smoothly. Sources for unavailable data need some organizing ability and identification of appropriate agencies. As regards data archives and a timely updated statistical base for plans, it is imperative to think in terms of computerization, for which sufficient skill and resources are already available in the country. An enlightened approach to statistical information system (Banerjee, 1979), it is hoped, will emerge sooner than later to tackle and solve meaningfully the above issues.

REFERENCES

Prakasa Rao, A.S., correspondence with author under DO No. R-11015-1/74-ITD of 15 March, 1976.

Rao, G.D., "Data Bank for Socio-Economic Data of NSS", Paper for Computer Society of India Conference in Calcutta, February 1978.

Sardesai, D.B., "Social Science Data Archive—Emergence of New Institutions in India", in *Artha Vijnana*, Vol. 15, no. 4, December 1974.

Bhatia, Mohan, "Information System—sources, Dissemination Mechanism", in *Economic Times*, 15 September, 1978.

Utpal K. Banerjee, "National Information System for Social Sciences", 2 parts, in *Economic Times*, 6 & 7 July, 1979.

3

COMMODITY CODES FOR INDUSTRIAL INFORMATION

3.1 General

There have been several national attempts to standardize codes for commodities and services pertaining to Indian industries. These have followed the pattern of international classifications, such as international industry classification, international trade classification and Brussels trade nomenclature. Except for trade classification, attempts were seldom made to evolve an all-India standard codification for industrial commodities.

An attempt was made through an inter-ministerial working group, of which the author was the chairman, to evolve an all-India standard codification for industrial commodities. The principles followed for this classification were closely based on international classification for goods and services (ICGS). The allocation of codes followed a two-digit pattern for groups, sub-groups, classes and sub-classes. The rationale, advantages potential for further expansion and limitations of the above approach on standardization for commodity codes are explained in this chapter.

3.2 International standard industrial classification

Commodity codes are a statistical tool for pigeon-holing a wide variety of statistics where the units of observations are goods and services. Data on output, certain costs, prices, marketing, etc., of goods and services are of interest to many organizations including government agencies, business firms and economists and also to the international community. Collection of such data is a continued activity of these organizations and institutions.

At present much data are collected in accordance with data classification schemes, with the result that it is difficult to collate these sets of data and make a useful analysis of the same. Much of the time has to be spent on making two or more of data comparable.

An important classification scheme is the international standard industrial classification (ISIC) which is a four-digit scheme prepared by the United States sometime in 1966 for classifying all economic activities under various industries groups. Based on ISIC, national industrial classification (NIC-70) was evolved in 1970 to cover at a four-digit level important industries and groups of industries in the Indian context.

The main feature of the ISIC and of NIC-70 has been to recognize the fact that outputs of one industry can often be inputs to another. Thus, output of the aluminium industry serves as the raw material for transmission towers in the power industry. This input-output relationship is important when individual establishments have to catalogue statistical data for various industrial activities. Another feature is that goods which are typical or primary outputs of one industry are in many cases also produced by establishments belonging to other industries. To illustrate, benzene produced by steel plants is a coke-oven by-product and, therefore, should be classified under the group covering coke-oven by-products. But benzene is also produced as a petro-chemical and should, therefore, find a place under the petro-chemical group. To obviate this difficulty of classifying a particular item under two or more industry groups, such items are classified under the industry group which is responsible for bulk production of that item. This ensures a unique classification of each item, no matter if it is produced by two or more industries. Lastly, parts which are clearly identifiable as peculiar to or for the use of a particular machine or apparatus (or with a group of machines or apparatus) falling within the same ISIC industry group are classified in that industry group. If there is no specific reference to these parts, they are to be classified in the same sub-class as a machine or apparatus for which they are specialised items.

3.3 International schemes

There have been attempts made on an international basis to evolve data classification trade-wise. These are particularly suited to internal commercial activities, import and export activities, and so on. In India, such activities relate to functions broadly grouped under the Ministry of Commerce. Standard trade classification has been evolved in India to cover such activities based on the international trade classification pattern. Another internationally well-known trade classification is known as Brussels Trade Nomenclature (BTN). As both international trade classification and BTN have purposes which do not ideally cover industrial information of an input-output nature, they are not discussed further in this paper.

There have been a few indigenous attempts for classifying industrial information other than the above. For instance, the Department of Economics in the Bombay University is known to have attempted an industrial commodity classification which follows broadly the current international practices but are not specifically linked with NIC-70. Similarly, a few Central Ministries in the Government of India have their own classification pattern for industrial commodities which do not relate to NIC-70 or any such scheme, but are often evolved to meet the specific needs of each ministry. As a result, there is no standardisation whatsoever in the commodity codes evolved and utilised separately by these Ministries.

The need for common commodity classification has long been felt not only in India but also in many advanced countries like the USA, the UK, etc. This was emphasized in the Presidential address to the American Economic Association by Prof. Wessily Leontief. He emphasized the need for common classification in the following terms:

> The shift from casual empiricism that dominates much of today's econometric work to systematic large-scale factual analysis will not be easy. The spectacular advances in computer technology increased the economists' potential ability to make effective analytical use of large sets of detailed data. What is, however, urgently needed is the establishment, maintenance and enforcement of coordinated uniform classification system. Incompatible data are useless

data. How far from a tolerable, not to say ideal state our present economic statistics are in this respect, can be judged by the fact that because of differences in classification, domestic output data cannot be compared, for many goods, with the corresponding export and import figures. Neither can the official employment statistics be related without laborious adjustments to output data, industry by industry. An unreasonable high proportion of material and intellectual resources devoted to statistical work is now spent not on the collection of primary information but on a frustrating and wasteful struggle with incongruous definitions and irreconcilable classification.

The statistical commission of the United Nations Economic and Social Council has prepared over the last three years a draft international standard classification of industrial commodities termed as international classification of goods and services (ICGS). The ICGS has a specific role to play in overcoming the difficulties mentioned by Prof. Leontief. Although the latter's comments were made in the context of the American economy, his observations are nevertheless true for other countries as well. Keeping this is view, the ICGS has been circulated to the national statistical offices of different countries for their comments. The final classification is likely to emerge after the 19th session of the Statistical Commission of the United Nations Economic and Social Council.

The ICGS is essentially an extension of the ISIC to cover various products and services falling under each industry or industry groups. This has been achieved by extending the ISIC to a eight-digit code. Essentially ICGS classification brings from the 157 industry groups defined in the ISIC at the lowest level of four-digit classification. Thereafter, ICGS consists of 1123 six-digit classes of industries, 705 of which are further divided into 2660 eight-digit sub-classes. The remaining (1123−705) or 418 six-digit classes are not further divided so that there are a total of (2660+418) or 3078 undivided categories of goods and services, within which each goods and service has a specific place according to its industrial origin.

The ICGS lays emphasis on the goods and services in their own right and do not make the manufacturing establishment as the statistical unit, as used in the annual survey of industries published by the Central Statistical Organization under the Ministry of Planning. The ICGS is also related to a number of other international classifications such as the Standard International Statistical Classification (SISC), the International Standard Statistical Classification of Aquatic Animals and Plants (ISSCAAP) both produced by FAO, etc.

3.4 Indian scheme

It was felt that difficulties due to multiplicity in different commodity classification schemes could be obviated if we in India could evolve a common commodity classification on the lines of the ICGS with the following objectives in view :

(a) to use the rationale in the ICGS which reflects the latest thinking in industrial classification ; and
(b) to provide a common base to various government agencies in India for goods and services of industrial origin.

The above objectives were discussed in various inter-ministry and inter-departmental forums and Central statistical organization convened a meeting in June 1974 with a view to evolving a common commodity classification for use by various government agencies in India. A working group was set up under the chairmanship of the author with a view to evolving such a classification. Representatives from different organizations, such as CSO, DGTD, DGSD, P & T Department, Department of Company Affairs, Department of Electronics, Ministry of Defence, Ministry of Agriculture, Railway Board, and other Ministries and departments were members of the working group from the beginning or coopted from time to time.

This group was asked, to start with, to adopt the present NIC-70 as a base and extend it to six or eight-digit level so as to cover major industrial commodities looked after by various organizations in the country.

As a first step, it found necessary to consider the changes that ought to be made in NIC-70 in order to make it more rational, comprehensive and up-to-date. Several meetings have been held in Delhi and it has been possible to thrash out some of the points regarding the rationalization of NIC-70 so that it incorporates all important industries and industry groups, and do not reflect individual commodities at the four-digit level. For instance, the solvent extracted oils and inedible oils which were hitherto being classified under the chemicals division were brought under food groups as per practice followed in the ICGS. Similarly, it was agreed to open a separate group for industrial gases which were hitherto scattered over two groups relating to manufacture of inorganic and organic chemicals. A number of other far-reaching changes were agreed to be made to NIC-70 to make it meaningful, an important one being complete overhaul of the electronics' classification, and inclusion of such new categories as medical electronics and mass entertainment electronics.

At the next stage, work relating to the extension of NIC-70 to cover industrial commodities (products and sub-products) was undertaken with the following aims: (a) To ensure comprehensiveness of NIC-70 at four-digit level for each industry and industry groups ; (b) To cover individual commodities at the six-digit or a digit level, following the general principles of the ICGS ; (c) To ensure that the coverage at six-digit or eight-digit level caters for the need of the government and other agencies ; (d) To allow Ministries and departments to come over to the national commodity classification, derived as above, on a tentative basis even while the work is on, so that advantage can be taken early of a common commodity classification as far as possible ; (e) To allow other Ministries and departments, which cannot come over to the common commodity classification for one reason or the other, to build up a concordance between their current systems and the common classification system. This will help them in not upsetting their existing classification system which might have been implemented already but will also facilitate referencing from one system to the other.

The work made considerable progress and was scheduled currently for completion. It was significant that almost all departments in the Ministries found the above aims acceptable and decided to correlate with it. In fact, the working group collected the list of industrial commodities from different Ministries and departments to consider their incorporation in the common commodity classification. Further, the working group also gathered information on the current commodity classification schemes in vogue or in preparation in various Ministries and departments, so that transition to the common system, or coordination between the existing system and the common one, are facilitated to a large degree.

Three important features of the above standardization of commodity codes were as follows : (i) Only significant items at product or sub-product level are to be taken up so that the level of aggregation meets the needs of the users as also the capability of generating statistical data. (ii) Up-to-date knowledge about "state of the art" in any industry is to be taken into account. This has affected the commodity classification for the electronics industries, the tyres and tube industry, the heavy engineering industry and a few others. (iii) The commodity classification is to be done in such a scientific manner that eventual computerisation of statistical information under these commodity codes is possible without any hitch.

It was appreciated by the working group that once the principles for evolving common commodity classification are clear and the aims are properly kept in view, a large amount of the work in the actual pigeon-holing of the commodities under the digital slots can best be entrusted to individual members of the working group. This part of the job is now on. To give an example the DGTD has already finalized the commodity classification of products and sub-products falling under 40 industries which have been initially earmarked by them for a computerized information system. This work is being further extended by the DGTD to cover other industries which are to be incorporated in the computerized information system later on.

Two special points emerged in the work for the standardization of commodity codes as follows: (a) Along with the commodity classification there is a need for standardization in the commodity nomenclature. This is to ensure that the same nomenclature is used for a specified commodity by all concerned. For instance secretariat for industrial approval (SIA) issues licences for industrial commodities for which various reports and returns are sent by the licencee units to their administrative ministries. If the commodity names are standardized, any confusing distinction between, say "raw material for paints" and "lead oxide" will not arise; (b) In addition to standardization of commodity nomenclature, there is a further need for suggesting standard accounting units. For instance, the production capacity of a crane-producing concern can be expressed in terms of either the number of cranes or the tonnage of cranes or the monetary values of the cranes. If there is no standardization in the accounting unit, it will be difficult to follow the progress made by the above concern from year to year in the plethora of different units used from one year to another.

An endeavour was made to keep in view the above points to make the commodity classification comprehensive and acceptable to different authorities.

3.5 Extension

There is considerable scope for extension of this classification as a number of vacant slots are available for accommodation in the new class of products even at a four-digit level. The same is also true at the six-digit and eight-digit level because the allocation of codes follow the same basic principles of a two-digit pattern for classes and sub-classes under each major industry or industry group. Further, there are only a little over 3000 categories into which all goods and services have to be classified. This is clearly inadequate as about 5000 commodities have been listed separately in the trade classification alone. Further, extension of this classification is inevitable if it has to be used for any industrial statistics application.

As is quite obvious evolution of commodity codes by individual government and private agencies is the first step of sophistication before developing an information system. At the second level of sophistication, the need becomes apparent of matching the individual commodity codes among the different organizations so that inter-change of information is feasible in a machine-readable form. At the third stage of sophistication the standardization of commodity codes should not merely be applicable to Government agencies and others within India, but also to international agencies which store valuable industrial information and are in a position to cooperate with India in the venture of building an industrial information system. The present attempt at standardization of commodity codes, in keeping with the principles of the ICGS is a vital step in the right direction. This will enable India in not merely achieving standardization within the country but also to remain in step with the international developments in the field.

3.6 Conclusion

To summarise, there have been various attempts both national and international, to evolve and use commodity codes for industrial information. There has been a crying need for standardizing the commodity codes so that in a country like India where various Government agencies and others are involved in managing affairs of industrial commodities, there can be a consensus in the devising and application of commodity codes for industries. With this need in view, steps have been taken to evolve standardized commodity codes as an extension of NIC-70 so that a national commodity classification is available to various Government agencies as early as possible. As these codes are in consonance with the international practice, considerable advantage will be reaped by the standardization both within the country and abroad. While there is still scope to extend the classification to accommodate new products, this is by no means a disadvantage, since the fundamental base is being laid on scientific lines.

4

DATA BANK FOR INDUSTRIAL PLANNING

4.1 General

Industrial Planning in India ensues from the Industrial Policy Guidelines issued by the Government of India in 1956 and 1978, as amended from time to time. Among the basic objectives, balanced growth of industries for the ultimate industrial uplift of the country, subservience of profit motivations to the broader social interests, curb on the growth of monopolies, and gradual self-sufficiency in all fields by a phased process of import substitution have received unmistakable emphasis from the Government as the goals of industrial planning.

The apex body responsible for industrial planning remains the Planning Commission. Under its Member (Industry), industrial situations are reviewed, existing and upcoming capacities assessed, and targets set for long-term fulfilment. Not merely the administrative ministries but also representatives from industries are associated with these exercises. The Department of Industries is responsible for the growth and advancement of all the scheduled industries listed in the Industrial Development and Regulations Act (IDRA), 1953.

Based on the criteria of total investment and capital equipment, distinction has been made between the small-scale industries, on the one hand, and large and medium ones on the other. While the small-scale industries are under the charge of the Small Scale Industry Development Organization (SIDO), the Directorate General of Technical Development (DGTD) is responsible for the large and medium industries on an all-India basis. By their sheer number and variety small-scale industries occupy an extremely large spectrum and planning has to be more extensive than intensive. The reverse is true for industries borne on the lists of the DGTD where intensive help can be given to the industries before, during and after licensing. Recognizing the latter as a necessary instrument for planning and control, the DGTD exercises its functions in assessing large and medium industries. The support that the DGTD provides to the industries is of three kinds:

(a) Infrastructural support regarding raw material, furnace oil, special steel, coal, coke, cement, etc.;
(b) Entrepreneurial support to the industrialists as the information on capacity existing and desirable in different areas of the country; and
(c) Technological support to provide indigenous or foreign know-how on technology in consultation with the Council of Scientific and Industrial Research (CSIR).

This involves a decision-making process, requiring timely availability of accurate and authentic information. The DGTD has a vast reservoir of data which is tapped for conversion into meaningful information for planning, check and review, and for timely assistance to ensure maximum utilization of capacities in stimulating growth. Considering, however, the extreme diversification of industries as well as the growth which has taken place and in order that maximum advantage can be taken of data through less laborious process, it was decided to introduce a computerized information system in the DGTD under the author.

4.2 Objectives of management information system

In order to take up the question of data bank for planning of industries looked after by the DGTD, the author had to face many problems regarding objectives of Management Information System (MIS) to be catered for by the data bank dealing with industries, codification and classification of data, structuring of output analysis, availability of input documents and data, reliability of information and, not the least, feedback provided to the industrial units. These questions are dealt with *ad seriatim*.

The objectives of Management Information System for the DGTD were visualized as follows:

(i) to build up industry profiles and to provide for computerization of production data for industries selected on the basis of: (1) their importance to economy, (2) weightage of output, and (3) mass consumption items concentrating on industries dealt with by the Ministry of Industry and Civil Supplies in the first instance;

(ii) to provide information for forward and coordinated planning (with due and proper consideration for various inputs) for a periodical industrywise review at Secretary (Tech. Dev.) and other levels with the Federation of Indian Chambers of Commerce and Industries (FICCI), Association of Chambers (ASSOCHAM) and other manufacturers' organizations and industries. In pursuance of this objective, meetings were held by the Secretary (TD) with the FICCI and Associated Chambers in June-July, 1975. It was intended to follow up such meetings on a six-monthly basis at Secretary (TD) level and at less intervals by other officers;

(iii) to review production trends and constraints against monthly and quarterly targets of production for selected industries;

(iv) to provide information to various departments of the Government on growth profiles and capacity utilization of various industries; and to provide feedback information to the State Governments on selected industries on a half-yearly basis according to this format decided;

(v) to facilitate adequate forecasting of raw material requirements and other inputs to help in advance planning for the latter on an integrated basis based on progress made in implementing establishment of new capacities;

(vi) to plan foreign exchange release based on foreign exchange requirement of industries;

(vii) to create a suitable technology data bank which will provide information on indigenous availability of technology, its analysis, approvals and nature of foreign collaborations, assimilation and absorption of technology in order to provide an industrywise technological picture including export of technologies; and

(viii) to give a feedback to selected industries on a quarterly industrywise basis on (a) capacity utilization, (b) production performance, (c) export performance, (d) reasons for shortfall in production, and (e) foreign exchange release.

4.3 Development of a data bank

It was appreciated that the fulfilment of the objectives stated earlier and, in fact, further development of these objectives to cover other information activities could be developed only in a progressive manner. It was necessary to build up an industrial data bank from scratch and to keep it updated periodically from the input documents.

There could be various approaches possible to build up such a data bank, an important one being based on control theory. This approach utilized a constant comparison between the standard norms according to which industrial activities ought to be performed, and performance indicators which told us as to how the same activities were being actually performed in practice. A model of this approach is presented in Fig. 4.1.

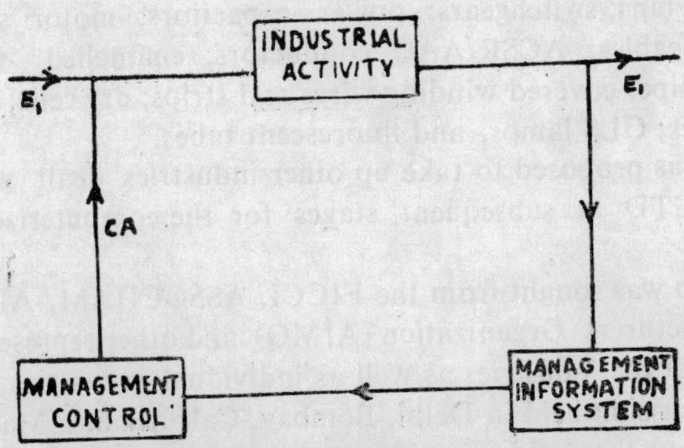

FIG. 4.1 : *Flow of industrial activities*

Special features of the model were:

(a) Standard norm for activity i(E_i)

(b) Performance indicator for activity i(E_i*)

(c) Management Information System to report on the feedback (FB) which was a function of (a) and (b), and

(d) Management control to take corrective action (CA) which, in turn, was a function of (c).

In other words, the model visualized that a continual endeavour was made to keep track of the performance indicators for all important industrial activities and these were used for a constant comparison with the standard norms which are preset for the same activities. Such comparison over a period of time would help in identifying the health of industry.

Keeping Fig. 4.1 in view, the industries selected for first stage of the computerized data bank in the DGTD for industrial planning were the following:

Cement; paper; newsprint; caustic soda; soda ash; calcium carbide; auto tyres and tubes; PVC resins; synthetic detergents; soap; rayon tyre cord; nylon tyre cord; industrial gases; milk products; nitrogenous fertilizers; phosphatic fertilizers; aluminium; commercial vehicles; tractors; scooters; bicycles; ball and roller bearings; industrial fasteners; razor blades; machine tools; electric motors; transformers; stampings and laminations; electric fans; switchgears; power capacitors; motor starters; power cables; ACSR/AAC conductors; enamelled winding wires; pipe, covered winding wires and strips; dry cells; storage batteries; GLS lamps; and fluorescent tubes.

It was proposed to take up other industries dealt with by the DGTD at subsequent stages for the computerized data bank.

Help was sought from the FICCI, ASSOCHAM, All India Manufacturers' Organization (AIMO) and other representative bodies of the industries as well as individual industries during the discussion held in Delhi, Bombay, Calcutta and Madras to thrash out these objectives for the data bank and to arrive at mutually agreed structuring of the input formats, the data for which would be willingly provided by industries after realizing their importance as well as utilization. What is more, help was also sought for agreed schemes to codify and classify the data for the proposed data bank.

4.4 Product code

To start with, each industrial unit belonging to the selected industries and borne on the DGTD's list was given a unique 11-digit code. The first-four digits of the code were the standard census enumeration of States and their districts. This standardization was decided upon after consulting SIDO so that transfer of an industrial unit from the DGTD's list to the small-scale industry sector or *vice versa* would still not require change in the first-four digits of its label. The next three digits were used to provide a serial number to the industrial unit and the remaining four digits (out of a total of 11) were left blank to cater to the future expansion in the code with utmost flexibility. Similarly about 200 major products of the selected industries were provided with a product code each. This was a nine-digit code and identified the major group of industries, specific industry, specific major product for a specified industry and other details, where relevant. The diagrammatic representation of the code is shown in Fig. 4.2.

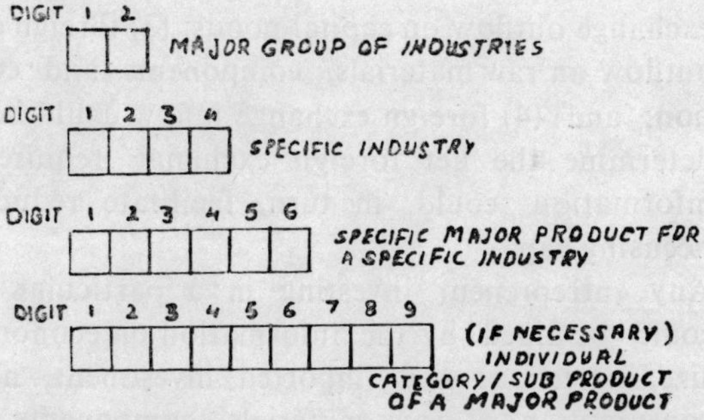

FIG. 4.2 : *Diagrammatic representation of a product code*

For example, the first-two digits corresponding to "Basic metals and alloys industry" are 33. If in this industry "pig iron" is manufactured, then the next two digits are 02. If in addition, "a foundry grade" is given to the pig iron produced then the next two digits may be 02. Thus the code given to pig iron which belongs to basic metals and alloys industry with a specific foundry grade may be 330202. The remaining three digits of the product code may be used when need arises as indicated in Fig. 4.2.

4.5 Product and factory profiles

Based on this codification scheme, product and factory profiles provide information on the industries covered by the DGTD. Practically all the information on product profile is maintained on a yearly basis. The factory profile, on the other hand, is to be updated monthly or quarterly as the case may be. Information from factory profile and other sources is to be used to update the product profile once a year.

The following is the rationale behind the current designs of the product and factory profiles:

(a) The demand figures, which are classified into export and internal demands could provide the basis for setting the target of production. The information on the target of production could be used along with the information on targeted production, actual production and actual installed capacity to determine the targeted installed capacity;

(b) Information on (1) capital goods (CG) costs for maintenance, replacements and modernization; (2) foreign exchange outflow on capital goods; (3) foreign exchange outflow on raw materials, components and collaboration; and (4) foreign exchange inflow could be used to determine the net foreign exchange required. The information could, in turn, facilitate reducing the licensing gap.

(c) Any entrepreneur investing in a particular industry could be aided by the information on economic plant size, indigenous and imported investment, norms of consumption of raw materials, components, spares, energy inputs, infrastructure inputs and norms of employment.

(d) Information on technology used, substitution by phased manufacturing programme and substitution by conservation of raw materials could be used as guidelines for the industry.

(e) Information on the existing policy on collaborations and approval terms and conditions of the past collaborations could be used to facilitate the approval on collaborations. Accordingly provisions have been made to include approval terms and conditions of past ten collaborations in the designs of the product profile.

(f) Information on the category of the industry, details of the last few capital goods licences, norms for capital goods requirements and total capacity covered under previous capital goods licences could be used to facilitate the approval on capital goods licences. Accordingly provisions have been made in the design of the product profile.

(g) Information on current import policies of end-product, import policy of important raw materials, norms of consumption and average consumption could be used to issue raw material licences and as such provisions have been made in the design of the product profile.

(h) Information on (1) statewise, and (2) major productwise capacities and production for an industry could be used to study problems of distribution and as such provisions have been made for factory profile.

These are only a few of the possible uses of the information on the products and factory profiles. The uses of information as currently made available in the product and factory profiles could only be extended and not reduced. The design of product and factory profiles is flexible enough to incorporate, at a later date. The possible changes in terms of content, context and equipment to handle large-scale data systems.

4.6 Output analyses

The following output analyses have been decided upon with the help of Indian Institute of Management, Calcutta (IIMC), from the product and factory profiles on half-yearly basis for each of the selected industry:

(a) Industrial target-setting,
(b) Industrial licensing,
(c) Capital goods,
(d) Raw material,
(e) Collaboration, and
(f) Statewise distribution of capacity.

Besides, detailed information on individual products for an industry is also to be obtained from the data bank.

The programming of the output report has been taken in hand and action initiated to inform units in the selected industries about their codes and classification for rendering reports according to the new production return given in the Guidelines for Industries 1975-76. However, the information pertaining to personnel, maintenance and other features which show little variation from month to month will be required to be given on a six-monthly basis as has been agreed with the various associations. The system handed over by the IIMC has been further developed and formats for input data for reporting have been devised. The industrial units will be asked to submit returns in the revised form in the line with instructions for the industry.

4.7 Production analysis

This fulfils the first objective set out for Management Information System for the DGTD. While the second and fourth objectives are policy activities, the next important objective is the third one regarding production trends and constraints. To fulfil this objective, production analysis have begun for the 40 selected industries indicated earlier. Such analyses cover, on a statewise basis, the licensed or registered capacity, installed capacity, days of work (with shifts per day and hours per shift), factory booking, planned production, actual production (including that for export), capacity utilization percentage, production per manhour or machine hour, average cost per unit of production, production for export, stocks at the end of the month, number of days required for produced stock, production detail for individual sub-products, order book position (opening and closing balance), orders received, cancelled and fulfilled during the month, average number of employees, expected duration of drop in employment and reasons for perceptible drop in employment. Based on the computerized output reports on production statistics, the statewise summaries could be readily compiled for the Northern, Eastern, Western and Southern Zones, and discussions will also be held on a zonal/statewise basis between the Secretary (TD) and the State Secretaries of Industries.

4.8 Infrastructural analysis

It is significant that the entire information used in this analysis is available from existing production data. The form for production return, however, has been streamlined in the Guidelines for Industries 1975-76 to make it more logical and quantitative, and less descriptive. An important feature of this rationalization is to obtain, in the coming years, data on production bottlenecks for individual items, such as special steel, coal, coke, furnace oil, power, water, cement, etc. In keeping with the fifth objective of the DGTD organization, these data are planned to be collected as, say, power required, received and consumed. For an item like power, one could then aggregate the required power on a statewise and districtwise bases and this information could be collated with the small-scale industry sector as well. Again, power received can be totalled on a statewise basis and after adding the small-scale sector to it, one could do something for apprising the authorities on the power available situation for the purpose of current and potential industrialization of that State. Lastly, power consumed would similarly lead to determination of industrial averages for a major product and thus could help in setting up norms of consumption on an all-India basis for power needed by that product. The scope of infrastructural analysis is thus far-reaching in consequence.

4.9 Capacity analysis

Another important activity initiated from the data bank is to carry out analysis on the follow-up action taken after industrial units are issued licences for creation of new capacity or expansion of existing capacity. "G" form is the necessary input document for this purpose and has been completely rationalized in a logical and quantitative manner, and incorporated in the Guidelines for Industries 1975-76. In its current format, it is still of great use to the Secretariat for Industrial Approval (SIA). It is proposed to analyse licences issued since 1971-72 to date to find out to what extent action is in progress for obtaining capital goods and raw materials, acquiring land and so on. In addition, analysis will be made to single out the defaulting units which have been sending either incomplete returns or none at all.

4.10 Foreign exchange allocation and raw material planning

A future activity, already initiated, according to the sixth objective of MIS, relates to the analysis of foreign exchange allocation sourcewise and major productwise. These data are available in the office of the Economic Adviser and, once analyzed, can help to obtain insight into the foreign exchange distribution pattern in the past and assignment of priorities in the future.

Another activity, planned already according to the fifth objective of MIS, relates to analysis on raw material planning. With the liberalization of licensing for import of raw materials help has to be sought from the office of the Chief Controller of Imports and Exports (CCI&E) on the figures for actual import, apart from the consumption of raw material for a major product. After linking this with production figures for the same major product, it should be possible to formulate industrial averages of consumption of crucial raw materials per unit of production for any major product. Fitted against the norms of consumption for such raw materials already available with the administrative ministries or the DGTD, these industrial averages will throw interesting sidelights on the behaviour pattern for consuming imported raw materials. Similar analyses can then be easily extended to scarce raw materials as well.

In regard to technology data bank in keeping with the seventh objective of MIS, the DGTD will work out the design of requirements for storage and retrieval of technical information on the aspects covered by the objectives, and bearing in mind the other inputs from other sources like the Indian Investment Centre, Department of Science & Technology (DST), Bureau of Public Enterprises, etc.

4.11 Feedback on selected industries

A very significant feature of the data bank is to decide on a feedback to the selected industries and to States as visualized in the eighth and last objective for MIS. The significance of this lies in the fact that the suggestion emanated from the dialogue with the industries. Actual inception of this activity will depend on the inflow of data from the revised formats of the "G" form and production return. It is planned to give this feedback the widest possible circulation through the Indian

Trade Journal, the Newsletter from Indian Investment Centre and other widely circulated media of publicity.

4.12 Input formats and data reliability

As regards availability of input documents, the DGTD holds a large amount of data collected and held over a long time. Some of these input formats have been mentioned earlier and the following included amongst others:

(a) Application for industrial licences,
(b) Letters of Intent followed by industrial licences,
(c) Application for capital goods imports,
(d) Application for raw material import,
(e) 'G' form,
(f) Production returns, and
(g) Other data available with the Development Officer of DGTD and the Economic Adviser.

It is interesting to note that the production return, which is one of the important sources for periodic information, is collected so far on an entirely voluntary basis. It is quite possible to make furnishing of this return obligatory. But the fact, however, remains that furnishing of reliable data depends very much on the willing cooperation from industrial units at which source all data originate, and it has been promised by the industry.

This brings us to the important question of reliability of data, which is the one and only basis behind any policy activity, as contemplated in the second and fourth objectives of MIS. In order that the periodic high-level reviews for any industry and the corrective measures sought to be taken are of any meaning, there must be an enlightened data base. In the dialogue with industries in Delhi, Bombay, Calcutta and Madras, opportunity was taken to highlight this point and also to stress the fact that feedback to the industries on an industrywise basis (and not on an individual unit basis, to preserve the sanctity of individual unit's data) will make sense only if the industrial units supply reliable data to the Government in the first place. It is most encouraging that industrial representatives saw the validity of both these arguments and promised enthusiastic cooperation to make the data bank a success for industrial planning.

4.13 Conclusion

It is necessary to stress the point that the structure of any data bank has to depend on both the needs for it by the users and on the capability for generating data by the industrial units. By an intensive process of in-house consultation within the DGTD, SIA, EA's (Economic Adviser) office and the CSIR, it has been attempted to ensure that data are put to data bank only at a level of aggregation where they are useful to the Government agencies (including Planning Commission), and are not too detailed on any account. The balance on the latter aspect can be struck by consulting the representatives of the industries who are the only ones to ensure that collection of data is not too detailed to frustrate attempts at collecting them. This attempt, one is glad to observe, has also been fairly successful.

The data bank for industrial planning has now been initiated but there is a long way to go before it could be perfected in any sense of the term and could meet the diverse needs of the Government. At the moment, certain selected needs only are meant to be satisfied, but the day is not far off when the data bank can be linked with the proposed National Informatics Centre at Delhi and will be far more useful.

5

COMPUTERS AND GOVERNMENT

5.1 General

The computer has been a phenomenon with us only for the past three decades. The concept of inter-linked electro-mechanical circuits, for performing computations, however, dates back to the last century, when Prof. Charles Babbage in England had already visualized the idea. And although asked to produce only a simple calculating machine, Prof. Babbage went ahead to work on his Difference Machine and Analytical Machine with the typical Oxbridge dedication. This alarmed the Establishment. Consequently, the financial grant was stopped and Babbage died a broken man. The concept, however, remained and, with the building of the first digital computer at the M.I.T. and Harvard in 1948, informational power was in our hands.

An interesting analogy has been drawn between three decades of nuclear power and those of informational power. The nuclear era had begun with the explosion of an atom bomb in Hiroshima in 1945. At present, we are trying to control the fission-fusion process augmenting much greater nuclear energy. Purely in terms of physical power, the process of transition has not been without its hazards. Steam had made it possible, with the industrial revolution, for the factories to produce cheap goods by being concentrated in one place. But this led to unemployment among the traditional craftsmen and brought in monotonous labour. Only of late, gas and electricity have come in a portable form and mobile energy sources have introduced controllable power into our offices, shops, homes and vehicles so that physical power has become a clearly positive and constructive factor in our civilization.

Almost comparable to the vastly enhanced physical power, with nuclear fusion round the corner, the informational power afforded by the digital computer has also introduced a qualitatively new factor in our civilization. The informational power is less visible, less audible and less tangible than physical power and has introduced into our lives something essentially new and extremely potent. Some simple and direct applications of the new power did result in the automation of long and routine procedures which formerly required the eyes and brains and hands of many men. But fortunately the main potential lies, and has been recognized as such, in carrying out complex analyses involving very large and repetitious data which can lead to applications in planning and control. The latter is conducive to efficiency in any organization and can lead to its strengthening and expansion requiring yet more brains and hands.

5.2 The image and the work

To those who have been affected by computers, what is the image that the new power has? To some, the computer is a super-humanly fast, accurate, methodical and tireless worker. To others, especially those concerned with preparing procedures for computers to execute, such a worker is also *illiterate* (without any understanding of our universal languages), *perversely literal* (greatly sensitive to misuse of even commas and full-stops), devoid of initiative (not moving to work without being specifically asked to), and so *high-salaried* that one must strive continuously to keep it running out of work. To yet others, the new power has lightning-like, *infallible* intelligence. In reality, none of these images is wholly true. Confining ourselves to digital computers and their common applications, we can call the new power as the capability of carrying out several hundred thousand elementary instructions per second and storing them at will, with almost nil possibility to commit any error for billions of calculations.

How does one specify the programs or the routine of instructions for being executed by computers? Typically, the elementary instructions are written in special-purpose languages sequenced very tightly and then interconnected by miniscule logical bonds as to constitute informational granite. These characteristics explain why the new informational power applies to large and repetitious applications, and render it unresponsive to subtle guidance or precise control by men. Does that not sound similar to one that can be written about the present-day technology of nuclear power?

Digital computers have been advancing quite dramatically in their speed, accuracy and tireless working methods through a number of phases. The 50s marked the transition, along with the electronic industry, from vacuum tubes to transistors. This immediately gave rise to an improved performance, compactness and reliability, and was heralded as a change-over from the first to the second generation of computers. In the 60s came the integrated circuits (IC) where sub-assemblies for whole units became only minor parts of really integrated systems, giving rise to the third-generation technology. The present decade has been the advent of large-scale integration (LSI) and microprocessors, and the availability of hundreds of active elements in a small space has opened the floodgates to new design approaches. The fourth generation of computers, several times faster, have a far greater accuracy, are certainly more capable of withstanding hundreds of hours of ceaseless work and—to cap it all—have catapulted downward in pricing. Today, in fact, computer is about the only commodity whose phenomenal increase in power and efficiency have been matched by an equally traumatic fall in its price.

5.3 The Indian scope

It is only now that India has started taking advantage of this world situation. Having made an early beginning in a computer being made and installed in Calcutta with the joint collaboration between the Indian Statistical Institute and Jadavpur University, the country seems to have let the new information revolution slip by. In May 1977, there were in all 391 computer systems installed in the country, the vast bulk of which belonged to the second generation. IBM then had 154 computers, ICL 42, ECIL (a government-owned firm) 87, DEC 31, HP 14, Honeywell 12, Rayad 11, Burroughs 6, Varian 5, CII 4, Interdata 4, Computer Automation 3 and others 18. By January

1980, there were nearly 600 computers and increasingly third, and later, generation technology.

The encouraging feature has been that, apart from the use in education, research and scientific organizations, the Indian business world had quickly caught on the new informational power and, having been pegged down early with smaller computers, started clamouring for the third-generation machines. Slowly the scene has been changing, and the Government has started permitting the business and industry to go beyond the limited use in routine data-processing of mostly accounting nature. The process of installing large computer systems with tremendous capability of complex data-acquisition, instantaneous processing and immediate usefulness for being retrieved for live decision-making is becoming the reality of the day.

At the national level, certain computer-based projects have been thought of to catalyze development in the national economy by reaping the benefits of information revolution. The more important of such projects are National Centre for Software Development and Computing Techniques at Bombay; National Informatics Centre at New Delhi; and National Centre for Computer-Aided Design, Kanpur. Creation of these centres of excellence is expected to serve as focii for computer activities in the four corners of the country, besides providing specialized assistance to all organizations needing it.

5.4 Computer in Government

Almost all vital aspects of social welfare—health, education, energy, communication and transport, to name just a few—are under the control of the State or its agencies in India. This imposes a heavy responsibility on the Government departments, both at the Centre and in the States, to initiate and implement measures which would ensure a rapid socio-economic growth, and that the benefits of such measures reach the lower strata of society. The administrative machinery tends to slow down owing to enormity of data that it has to deal with and difficulties in retrieving specific information at short notices. Furthermore, the process of decision-making is getting more and more complex.

Computers are finding increasing use in Government

departments essentially on account of their ability to store vast amounts of data, retrieve them quickly, conduct a variety of analytical exercises with ease, examine a host of alternatives, and present factual reports in a summarized fashion. All this could significantly speed up the tasks of senior administrators—planning, directing, coordinating and controlling. Owing to their versatility, computers have been used in varied fields from missile flight control to treasury accounting, flood control to inventory management.

At national level, the Indian Railways have the largest number of computers and are in the process of further acquiring several third-generation computers. Movement of their rolling stocks on a national network of tracks is monitored on computers. Their future planning is for a massive computerization at Railway Board, zone, division and lower levels, starting from on-line real-time wagon movement and flight control, and passenger reservation systems, upto a number of batch-processing applications involving materials management, financial planning and control, and production management. Theirs is one of the most ambitious fields of computer applications in India today. Indian defence services use the latest computers for a variety of purposes, including planning (with operations and intelligence), administration (with financial budgeting, personnel training and health), logistics (with food and transportation), and production control purposes. Some typical examples are trajectory evaluation ; planning of management responsibilities in terms of departmental levels ; statistical applications for army vehicles ; inventory problems including imports and high lead-times ; production scheduling for naval dockyards ; and personnel management system for career planning, placement and training. All the steel plants have their own computers to optimise their production and inventory stocks. Shipping, Civil Aviation and Banking are among the several other areas benefiting from computerised applications. Police administrations all over the country have adopted computers to assist them in crime detection. They have ambitious plans of developing a national hook-up of computers to benefit from police information across the country.

State Governments, too, have not lagged behind and are

adopting computers as an aid to efficient administration. A few State governments have already set up their data processing centres and several others are in the process of acquiring their own computers.

Availability of indigenously manufactured computers in the country has substantially contributed to the use of computers in administration. Some of the areas where computers have found wide adoption are briefly discussed below :

Planning department

The department plays a pivotal role in formulating annual plans and monitoring the progress of all developmental projects. It has to coordinate the activities of different departments and executing agencies to provide the thrust for planned growth. The department has to deal with an enormous volume of information coming from various on-going project-data on physical progress, financial, status, spill-over expenditure, etc. Corrective measures have to be initiated to ensure timely completion of projects.

Computers assist in monitoring project-wise progress and identifying critical areas calling for attention. Performance statistics and variance reports are generated. The data base, regularly updated with progress of work, serves as an aid to plan formulation. Once plans are finalised, computers assist in projecting manpower and other resource requirements. Thus, computers can provide substantial aid in all aspects of the department's work-plan formulations monitoring and evaluation.

Finance department

Computers are ideally suited for a wide range of applications in the Finance Department due to their speed and accuracy in numerical computations. Computers can assist in budget formulations, tax administration and treasury accounting.

The Department has to deal with a stupendous pile of data on receipts and expenditure, classified under thousands of account-heads, emanating from various State treasury offices. Further, this has to be reconciled with the figures available with the Accountant-General's office. Manually handled, this effort could significantly delay the consolidation and reconciliation work. Several State Governments are taking the assistance of computers in tackling the problems of treasury accounting. Tax management is another area where computers are used. Sales and Entertainment taxes provide a big chunk of the State revenue and, as such, call for close monitoring to ensure effective collections and to check tax-evasion. Keeping records of important dealers on the computer and processing their advance payments can greatly facilitate generation of tax assessment, balance recovery statements, tax refund reports, statutory reports to the Central Government, cases of tax evasion, etc. Computers assist in building a data base of commodity revenue, prices, income, dealers, production and trade statistics which would aid in tax planning. In the case of entertainment tax, details of all cinema houses can be held on computers to keep track of daily sale of tickets and tax due from feature and advertisement films.

Other areas which can benefit from computerized accounting and monitoring are the administration of excise duty and other State taxes, and also in maintaining records of land holdings and land revenue.

Bureau of economics and statistics

In several States, the bureau is entrusted with the task of conducting socio-economic surveys and analysing the data collected to help the administration formulate policies. Population census, agricultural census, economic census, industrial census, National Sample Surveys, opinion surveys, price statistics, etc., are the major areas of the work of the Bureau.

Speed and accuracy are the primary reasons for the use of computers in analysing the data collected during the surveys. Forecasts on agricultural and industrial production, formulation of price indices, demographic statistics and analysis of other specific surveys are easily possible on the computers. Data so collected can be conveniently retained as data bank over long periods to undertake studies in trend analysis.

Agriculture and irrigation

The agriculture department has to deal with data on rainfalls, area under different crops, irrigation, number of wells, etc., in each village. Based on these the department forecasts crop productions and plans for the supply of seeds, fertilizers, pesticides, etc., and evolves policies on credit facilities to farmers. The department also conducts several agronomic and agro-economic surveys to help formulate policies. Computers can assist in production forecasts, procurement and distribution planning for chemicals and fertilizers, and procurement of outputs. The yearly data can be retained for historical purposes and also to undertake trend analysis.

Computers can significantly assist the Irrigation Department in management of on-going projects in terms of their physical progress, cost control, manpower planning, stores accounting, materials management, inventory control, etc. Management of water resources both surface and underground – is also assisted through computers.

Public works department

The PWD looks after the maintenance of roads and bridges, construction of buildings for Government departments and other public works. The main areas where computers can assist in the functions of the department are stores accounting, materials management, project monitoring and requirement planning. As in the irrigation department, on-going projects can be effectively monitored for physical progress and cost control. Timely completion of projects would check cost escalations.

Transportation department

Almost all states have road transport corporations to plan and provide for transportation facilities. Due to complexity of their operations, computers have been widely used by several such Corporations in areas like spare-parts management and maintenance scheduling. Computers can also assist in optimization of bus routes, tariff fixation, forecasts of future traffic loads and requirements planning.

Health department

Implementation of various health programmes—curative (medical), preventive (public health) and promotional (family welfare)—is carried out by the Directorate of Health and Family Welfare. Monitoring performance of hospitals in terms of utilization and cost is aided by computers. Planning for hospital services requires a vast amount of data on community health needs, existing hospital services and their utilization, population characteristics and environmental factors. Computers greatly assist in building a data base for hospital services planning.

In the area of disease control, computers are assisting in identifying factors causing spread for epidemics like malaria. This helps in monitoring and controlling such diseases.

Education and social welfare department

Several States have adopted computers in examination results processing at high school and intermediate levels to handle the work connected with the several lakhs of students appearing for such examinations annually. Accuracy and speed of processing enables faster publication of results and creates confidence in the results. Analysis of the socio-economic background of the students has also been attempted on computers to help formulate policies. In the area of social welfare, various surveys are conducted to study the conditions of a community or a group, like tribal communities, backward classes, etc. Computers assist in analysing the data collected and this greatly assists in welfare measures being formulated.

5.5 The future

It is interesting to speculate whether the full realization of the information revolution will await the widespread distribution of the power of information processing, when an organization will no longer ask for a whole computer, but only a wall-socket or a portable computer in offices, shops, homes and vehicles. This seems to be also fast becoming a reality in the West. As distinct from this mini-computing network, such world giants as IBM are planning seriously to launch a $400 million venture by the Eighties called Satellite Business System (SBS), in partnership with Comsat and Aetna Life & Casualty, whose versatile new satellite communications will enable customers to forge celestial links connecting their offices and plants—and to make far more extensive use of their computers and other office equipment.

Whether India goes the West's way remains to be seen. The

need here is for the kind of informational power provided by the present-day computers, the power to follow, rapidly and accurately, procedures that have been pre-specified in detail. Man, however, triumphs over his slowness ("restricted channel capacity") and forgetfulness ("limited memory storage") by his infinite flexibility in changing situations and through self-instruction. Man-computer interaction is, therefore, essential to effective use or exploitation of computers and the facilities for interaction should be developed as close as proves desirable.

6

OPERATIONAL RESEARCH AND GOVERNMENT

6.1 General

Operational Research originated during World War II in the U.K. It was very much a government-sponsored affair since it was the then Prime Minister, Sir Winston Churchill, who called a group of gifted scientists from all walks of life including the universities and formed an inter-disciplinary team to look into the complicated problems of war which baffled Generals, Admirals and Air Marshals and discovered the solutions. Sir P.M.S. Blackett, Nobel Laureate in Physics and working in the University of Manchester, was placed as the head of this team which, in common parlance, came to be known as Blackett Circus. The Circus performed some miraculous feats in the special preserves of the professional soldier who had not imagined a scientist to be his likely competitor before. In fact, the deadly accuracy and efficiency achieved in some of the solutions in naval problems related to the detonation on depth charges against German U-boats, protection given to the mercantile fleet by the naval convoys and saturation bombing against the German industrial belt in Ruhr. The Government was naturally elated and the birth of Operational Research as a war-baby took place among bullets and bombshells. Another immediate problem tackled by this new science was to narrow the gap between visual detection of enemy aircraft and interceptions by own fighters after a timely take-off from the ground. That was the story behind how radar was created for surveillance of the air.

Operational Research, even after war was over, was a thriving science in the U.K. By then, the U.S.A. had found this new inter-disciplinary application of scientific approach to the real-life problems as immensely useful and went ahead with a multi-pronged attack of the new science on not merely the problems of defence and government, but also the problems of industry, commerce, education, health and a host of others. Operational Research in the West, particularly in the U.K., the U.S.A. and Canada, has become so much part of the life, that these techniques are applied down to the problems of garbage disposal of local self-government. The applications did not remain confined to the government or defence alone. It has been estimated that twenty largest enterprises in the world have all on Operational Research department each so that there is a built-in capability of the new science available to these big houses all the time.

6.2 Basic structure

Operational Research (O.R.), in its broadest applications, is understood to be research of study in depth into operations or activities of an organization. The nature of the organization is not important for carrying an investigation of an Operational Research kind. Only functions and activities of the organization come for deeper probe than the organization itself. Operational Research ensures that in studying the performances of the organization, certain specific objectives are kept in view which are consonance with the overall objectives of an organization. As long as these objectives are precisely defined to take into account, the structure or content or even control aspects of an organization need not be kept in view.

The main emphasis in Operational Research is on the scientific investigation of the inter-disciplinary kind. The development here has followed three mainstreams :

Classical Operational Research

This refers to the mathematical and statistical techniques of a general nature which was supplied by the O.R. scientists during the war and immediately thereafter solving problems.

Technical Operational Research

It relates to the battery of techniques developed since the war to solve problems which are encountered by government, industry, business and defence in common. These techniques include mathematical programming which can obtain extremely precise solutions as to what is best for an organization with regard to its given objectives. This approach is called optimization.

Contextual Operational Research

This applies to techniques which are devised in the context of specific problems for deriving solutions. These techniques cut across the barriers of different disciplines and draw liberally from Psychology and Sociology, Information Theory and Industrial Engineering.

It is, however, not always common that the O.R. techniques are applied in the above compartmentalized form. Most often there is a mix of techniques which are applied to solve problems.

6.3 Problems of applying operational research

The actual application of Operational Research solutions by the policy-making levels in the Government (as also in industry, business and defence) is naturally an important aim of any O.R. study. Implementation of Operational Research in government can be treated as a case of organizational change or adaptation, implying change in some aspects of attitude at the National Policy level or of activities at the executive level in government.

The process of change falls under the following headings:

(a) *Awareness* : The government machinery is, by tradition and discipline, conservative in its views and wary of change. It is, therefore, necessary to keep up the present trend of running training programmes and seminars on analytical management techniques for government officials ;

(b) *Interest*: Knowledge of the available scientific techniques can create interest in finding their relevance to the practical decision-making problems of government. A cognitive style of management can help here a great deal.

(c) *Evaluation* : This marks a transition from an unfreezing process of mental attitudes to a restructuring one. Evaluation of techniques is greatly helped by proper communications, indication of measurable savings (or improvement in effectiveness), urgency of results, improved information, availability of trained people to implement and availability of detailed implementation schemes.

(d) *Trial* : Small, concrete measures of savings or improvements in effectiveness can go a long way to make the need for implementing scientific techniques in decision-making acceptable to the policy-makers. Field experiments can be conducted in a controlled manner.

(e) *Adoption* : This marks the process of actual assimilation of the new information.

The above need not always be carried through all the stages mentioned. Often, just an awareness of how to gain more confidence in decision-making, by a scientific way of thinking about the problems, is enough of an achievement.

From the O.R. scientists' angle, the above process can be considerably aided by the following procedure :

(a) *Initial appreciation* : All the views, arguments and environmental factors surrounding a plan for analysis must be understood in order to gauge the uncertainties in data, related assumptions and sensitivity of results to these uncertainties.

(b) *Interim discussion* : This is necessary to maintain communication throughout the project, to initiate the policy-makers gradually into the results and also to ensure that the analysis does not depart from the mainstream of relevant argument.

(c) *Method of analysis* : The urgency of government decisions requires that the analytical depth of details and sensitivity analysis have to be dovetailed to the limited time available. It should also be necessary to retain some flexibility in the techniques used for assessing as many courses of action as possible and for identifying the chain of cause and effect leading to a surprising result, if any.

(d) *Final presentation* : Contradictions and inconsistencies revealed by the results need be brought out along with the analysis of results in terms of real factors. Final value-judgement remains the policy-makers' prerogative to whom only a professional view—with supporting evidence—is to be presented.

In order to avoid failure, it is necessary for the Government O.R. scientists to appreciate and allow for the decision-making machinery within the organization they are serving.

Straightforward rational exhortation as a technique of change may fail if it does not take into account the goals of the policy-makers. The following considerations are relevant here :

The relationship between policy-makers and operational analysts

This is a crucially important factor. In general, the participative form of management has been found to work best in practice, in view of the atmosphere of understanding and ease of communications. Burns and Stalker described, for instance, how a rapid application of scientific techniques to operational problems could take place in the TRE during the War on account of an intimate joining of operational needs with technical possibilities in an immediate, personal and informal way.

Group decision-making

Following from (i), this would seem a desirable course to adopt, in which the operational analysts study the problem-areas, include appropriate levels of policy-makers in planning and implementing the change, and improve the policy-makers' competence in evaluating new ideas. One likely consequence of this is that the policy-makers' own anticipation of the results can go up manifold in the process.

Top-management support in implementation

Such support influences positively the implementation of O.R. projects by organizational members of the Government.

It is essential that the reasons given by the operational analysts in support of the proposed changes are sensible, directed at the central issues and not aimed at creating a technocracy shielded from criticism by the intricacies of a specialized knowledge. The reasons cited may be increased effectiveness, reduced costs, or, optimality (or near-optimality) with regard to some other criteria. If there are likely to be "spin off" effects of the change, these needs to be specified also.

Again, it is for the policy-makers to closely question the reasons given by the operational analysts for the recommended adaptation of an analytical technique. Rejection of the idea may be the rational decision for the policy-makers under certain administrative circumstances.

6.4 Application of operational research in defence*

In keeping with tradition of O.R. in the U.K. and the U.S.A., O.R. in the Indian Government started in the Ministry of Defence in 1949. The defence science organization was set up under Dr. D.S. Kothari, which employed Indian scientists trained in Operational Research from the U.K. The O.R. section played an advisory role for the services on such problems as stores purchases, weapon-efficiency assessment and weapon planning. A spurt soon came with the establishment of the O.R. Unit in the Indian Statistical Institute by Prof. P.C. Mahalanobis to apply O.R. in the Indian national planning and survey. By 1957 and, thereafter, defence O.R. Studies under Dr. R.S. Varma and Dr. S.S. Srivastava covered such problems as : (a) reliability of airborne radar sets, electronic tubes and signal equipment ; (b) storage and deterioration of rubber goods used by the services ; (c) training of service personnel at the Infantry School, Mhow, and Air Force training unit, Jamnagar ; and (d) operational problems like diffusion of gas bombs, ballistic projectories, range estimation and combat analysis.

An O.R. conference was organized by DSO in 1954 with Prof. P.M.S. Blackett, adviser to the Ministry of Defence, U.K., as guest who showed considerable interest in the progress of defence O.R. in India. With the formation of

*Comprehensive details can be found in the author's book *Operational Analysis and Indian Defence*, (Concept Pub. Co., Delhi, 1980).

Defence R & D Organization in 1959 a second O.R. conference was held with a technical session on government O.R. Seminars and symposia began to be held at an accelerated pace, always including sessions on O.R. and R & D scientists often taking a leading part.

Despite the availability of good OR talents, there had been little participation in 1954—59 by the army and the other 2 services in the venture by referring services problems for operational analysis. In 1959, Weapons Evaluation Group, later re-named Scientific Evaluation Group (SEG), was created in the new Defence R & D Organization. Its chapter was to carry out "OR studies and cost-effectiveness analysis of defence problems on an inter-services basis". Table 6.1 gives an illustrative idea of the areas of OR study covered.

TABLE 6.1 : Some O.R. studies in Indian defence management applied by government

Service	Field	Nature of study
1	2	3
Army	General Policy	Survival in high altitude ; Low temperature survey of Himalayas ;
	Weapon Systems	Firepowers of 7.62 SA rifle ; Wastage rates of class 'A' stores ; 20 mm Oerlikon gun for air-defence ; Hit probability of Bofors 40 mm. L-70 guns ; Effectiveness of anti-tank weapons ; Effectiveness of RDX/TNT vs. TNT ; Effectiveness of anti-tank missiles ; Fire-pattern and comparison of air-defence gun systems ; Wastage in weapons and ammunitions ;
	Logistic System	Transportation of supplies to Kargil ; Road capacity in an operational area
	Tactics and Strategy	Comparative mobility and firepower between a French Alpine battalion and a standard Indian Infantry battalion ;
	Communication and Control	Radio communication in Jungles ; Satellite communication in

(*Contd.*)

TABLE 6.1—*contd.*

1	2	3
		military defence Service life, replacement and maintenance of electronic equipment ;
	Inventory	Provisioning and procurement of shortlife stores ; Provisioning rates of equipment and optimum economic reserves ; Assessment of interim period of ordnance stores ;
Air Force	Weapon Systems	Efficiency of air-defence system ; Suitability of 35 mm. Oerlikon twin mounting and Bofors 40 mm. L-70 gun for Low-level air-defence ;
	Tactics and Strategy	Aircraft in close support role of the army ;
	Communication and Control	Target detection and range determination by pulsed radar ;
Navy	Weapon Systems	Comparative assessment of effectiveness of 4.5″ shell fuzed with N/97 and DAN-3 fuses ;
	Tactics and Strategy	Optimization of Convoy systems ; Optimum width of harbour entry swept channel at Cochin ;
	Inventory	Disposal decisions on naval stores.

Following are the main fields of work in Government O.R. in India :

(*a*) *Reliability*—as dependability vs. component variability in electronic equipment, in terms of general failure, repair time and waiting time distribution.

(b) *Queuing*—particularly bulk-service discipline, priorities in balking and reneging phenomena.

(c) *Mathematical programming*—including dynamic programming.

(d) *Stochastic duels*—particularly supply of ammunition to combatants range and rate of firing, and single-short kill probabilities.

(e) *Search theory*—different patterns including "variable" and "line abreast" search, and combining stochastic processes with sequencing.

(f) *Network*—critical path scheduling and PERT analysis.

(g) *Inventory control*—particularly in defence industries including procurement lead-time and disposal delays.

6.5 Application of operational research in Post & Telegraph

Indian P&T Department pioneered a number of O.R. applications for solving their operational problems.

'Q' theory was applied to determine the inconsistency and in-built inefficiency of queues formed in front of post office counters. Ratio of arrival time to service time was studied to determine the length of queues, waiting time involved, number of counters, desirability of increasing the service channels and so on.

Another problem studied was the inventory management in the mail motor service department in Delhi in 1978. This study related to classifications of inventory, purchase policy, requirement pattern and forecasting of investment in inventory with reference to requirements, for such items as tubes, tyres and other material. Alongside, mail motor service scheduling was also studied both in Bombay and Delhi. For instance, the pattern of collection of mail from different points in Delhi, their centralization at Delhi GPO and their despatch to the railway station and airport was studied in depth along with the reverse process of collection of mail from the railway station or airport up to their final delivery at different points.

6.6 Application of operational research in health

The Department of Personnel and Administration Reforms carried out an O.R. study of classification and analysis of inventory of medicines with regard to their annual usage and shelf life. The main point in consideration was that finite life of drugs made the latter useless beyond a certain period even though adequately stocked, and such wastages would be undesirable in a poor country. Hence, it was important to establish a relationship between usage and shelf life, at least for the costly drugs with a view to forecasting their inventory level. Another study carried out by CARE related to queues at hospitals with reference to the types and critical nature of specific diseases. The idea was that queues should be classified and counters provided to keep the average periods of waiting within control in relation to critical diseases.

An interesting study was carried out by the ASCI to determine the growth and spread of malaria in the villages of Andhra Pradesh. The study related to epidemiological aspects (to be extended to entomological aspects later on) of malaria as its spread occurred through mosquitoes and patients vectors. The study used Markovian statistics to establish the transition pattern of the disease-spread, knowledge about which could then be used to determine resource planning for fighting the epidemics.

6.7 Application of operational research in Railways

Indian Railways have used operational research intensively and have an O.R. group in the Railway Board, apart from the facility of O.R. training in the Railway Staff Training College at Baroda.

Inventory management programmes have been intensively used by the Railways with particular reference to classification of inventory, purchase policy, total annual investment and strategy for inventory reduction. Reservation system in the railway was studied to improve reservation arrangement at counters and simple colour-schemes were introduced to reduce queue length and make better service available at the counters. Reservation system in the Railways was also studied by the Indian Institute of Management, Ahmedabad, using linear programming project.

A study at Chitranjan Locomotive Factory was carried out to increase the production of electric engines and utilize the capacity optimally for assembly of diesel and electric engines. O.R. studies have continued at Chitranjan through a small group there. Wagon utilization system was also studied in the Railways, based on wagon requirements, in order to provide for better use of wagon capacity for essential commodities.

An interesting study in the Railways was of shuntings and train formation at the marshalling yard of Mughalsarai, initiated by Jagjit Singh. Another interesting study was about the mixing of buses and trains for suburban passenger traffic in Delhi. Starting and ending of bus routes could be so arranged at important nodal points, namely, railway stations, with combined bus-cum-railway ticket, to enable the suburban passengers to undertake travelling, without much botheration.

6.8 Application of operational research in police

Allocation and utilization of police force for police station were studied by the Indian Institute for Public Administration. The study covered determination of strength of a police station and optimal utilization of policemen for different functions. Effort was also made to arrive at some criteria for performance of policemen and to use 'Q' theory for dealing with registration of cases. Another problem studied related to inventory management for such items as police uniform, food stock and spare parts for police equipments. Some work has also been done on patrolling by police parties and determination of route pattern by using dynamic programming.

6.9 Application of operational research in Food Corporation of India

The F.C.I. has been much concerned about the transportation and distribution of food particularly to prevent loss and pilferage during transit and in the warehouses. Determination of level of foodstock, handling of foodgrains and minimum-cost-strategy for transporting food from warehouses to retail points were studied using O.R. techniques. An interesting aspect of the study related to the warehouse where changes were made from "First In Last Out" system of ancient godowns to "First In First Out" system in the modern silos.

6.10 Other applications of operational research in Government

In the non-defence area, one pioneering application of O.R. by the Indian Government was for unloading food-ships at Visakhapatnam in the sixties. The problem concerned the imported foodgrain on a priority basis. As the ships arrived carrying foodgrains, they had to anchor in high seas waiting for berthing facilities at the port. If berths were lacking, the Government had to pay demurrage for the ships kept waiting. At the other end, the ship-owners did not like the idea of indefinite wait and would often leave the port without unloading. If it was simple question of bringing the ships to berths in the port, an obvious solution was to build more berthing facility in the port than was available. But then creation of berthing facility would involve a lot of expenditure and was also a time-consuming affair. What was worse, an excessive creation of berthing facility could leave to an idling of resources and capital lock-up if later on the number of ships dwindled to an insignificant proportion of those coming during the busy period. Clearly it was a complicated question of balancing between the number of ships arriving at any stage and the number of berths to be made available for their clearance. Such a problem required a technical O.R. application of theory of queuing. This problem was talked by a team of scientists from the Council of Scientific and Industrial Research (CSIR), which included Dr. A. Ghoshal and others. Their study led to fruitful insights into the problem and offered some useful solution.

There are heuristic approaches in O.R. which are distinct from the above kind of mathematical analysis and apply little mathematics in trying to solve a problem step by step on a pragmatic basis. One such method is project network analysis which was applied by Brigadier O.P. Narula and others in the case of Deep Water Wharf Project, Port Blair (Andaman Islands). This project was administratively sanctioned in 1967 and allowed for a period of four years for completing all the items of work which included the following :

(a) Land acquisition, development and reclamation ;
(b) Quarrying of construction material ;
(c) Construction of domestic, technical and administrative accommodation for construction staff ;
(d) Construction of wharf, including mooring dolphins ;
(e) Provision of permanent services with other essential facilities ;
(f) Dredging ; and
(g) Road system.

The execution was planned and analysed on a project network. The critical path was identified and drawn on Gantt Charts in order to keep a closer watch on progress. Although this was a simple application of project network, it paid rich dividends in getting the projects completed according to a predetermined schedule.

A third application was of O.R. in the Government relates to formulating an input-output approach for important agricultural and industrial sectors in Bihar. This economic study was entrusted by the Government of Bihar to Dr. Pradhan and others in the A.N. Sinha Institute of Social Study, Patna. It was proposed to extend this model on a mathematical programming framework for which the services of the author were sought. In that event, it would be possible to have a detailed analysis of the economic sectors in Bihar in relation to the availability of resources and other constraints and this will provide an extremely useful insight into regional planning in Bihar.

Another problem-area, which is of tremendous significance to the government, relates to family planning on which scientific analysis was done by Dr. L.H. David and others in the Rural Family Planning Project, Allahabad Agriculture Institute, U.P. They selected some model zones in which statistical sample survey at various periods, continuous vital registration (for births, deaths and migration) and services statistics on the rate of contraceptive acceptance were watched systematically. It was hoped that this information would yield a valuable index of births prevented which can be used to adjudge effectiveness of various Family Planning projects in relation to their cost. They proposed to use population simulation model, developed in North Carolina, U.S.A., to gain some understanding of this most intricate problem. Such a simulation model was again a heuristic approach involving little mathematics and a lot of statistical data.

Other applications of O.R. in the Government have been attempted in shipping, petroleum, airlines, fertilizers and rural development. For instance, the Indian Institute for Public Administration applied goal programming to determine mixing of crudes, keeping in view multiple objectives of self-reliance and cost of procuring petroleum. Another similar study was done for rural development in planning for the mix of local resources and external resources with a given pattern for return on investment and subject to generation of employment, utilization of local resources and marketability of commodities.

6.11 Conclusion

The above is a cross-section of some of the Operational Research application in India in which our Government (either at State or Central level) has shown some interest. It is very likely that there are a large number of applications of O.R. which have not yet been published and are not known to this writer. It can nevertheless be said that a beginning has been made in the right direction and an increasing use of Operational Research to solve real life problems in the Government will yield valuable results. The main dearth here is not of properly trained O.R. scientists nor of problems to which the policy-makers are exposed daily in their decision-making process. Both these are available in plenty. The dearth is of awareness of an analytical approach to problems and interest in solving them in a scientific manner. This is vitally necessary to give a fillip to the process of implementation of O.R. techniques in all fields with which our governments (State and Central) are concerned and for which techniques are already available and so are the talents to use them.

TOWARDS A NATIONAL FRAMEWORK

7

INFORMATION SYSTEM FOR INDUSTRY

7.1 General

The objective of an information system for industry is to store planning and control information relating to industry and to process such information in order to retrieve meaningful indicators regarding performance of industry. Information can be derived felicitously from the extensive historical records existing both in industry and in the Government. The users of the information system are the decision-makers in various production. Ministries and departments in the Central and State Governments (e.g., Departments of Industrial Development and Heavy Industry in the Ministry of Industry and Civil Supplies, Bureau of Public Enterprises, Ministry of Petroleum and Chemicals, Ministry of Agriculture and Irrigation, etc.) and the Planning Commission. Even at present, the decision-makers and planners make an extensive use of the available data in planning and policy formulation for Indian Industry. A centralized and sophisticated data-processing capability is of enormous advantage to the policy-makers for efficient functioning.

An information system for industry, in common with other Management information systems, should consist of: (a) General Historical Records, and (b) Communication Functions.

General historical records

Raw or reduced data and partly processed information can be obtained from the various historical records and transmitted to the general data bank according to the established procedures or on demand. When these data or information are received in the data bank, they are usually further reduced, or combined and processed with other data and information, or stored for future reference. The general historical records may be viewed as a repository of environmental information which may be referred to when necessary or systematically scanned. Such historical records, for instance, exist in the Central Water and Power Commissions for power system and in the Indian National Scientific Documentation Centre for scientific literature.

Communication functions

Output reports in the form of information analysis can be formulated by using the reduced data from the general system and transmitted to the individual operational divisions or sections of the industry as a means of bringing the decision-makers and helping them to coordinate their intelligence and actions. In other words, the general historical records as a repository of formal information can be used by the top management in planning, controlling and coordinating the activities of the industrial organization, for instance, the rapid information analysis report in the organization of the Directorate-General of Technical Development.

To start with, one has to be careful in choosing the communication functions (in the form of output reports) which are to be generated from the general historic records in any industrial system. This is because the representation, content, methods, equipment and indefinite utilization : all pose significant problems to the users and operators of general historical records. Hence, in the national industrial system, it is advisable to first create a data library with bare essentials for generating only the chosen communication functions in the form of selective output reports. Once this is achieved, it should be relatively simple to graft in more sophistications at a later stage after the system is developed more and has offered further insight into the working of communication functions for purposes of planning, controlling and coordination of the industrial organization.

7.2 Methodology

In the Indian situation, the type of complex organization, which is common among large and medium industries, comprises several functional departments, e.g., purchase, stores, production and so on. Since each of these functional departments performs a set of closely related activities, a generic term "environment" is used to denote each functional department. One can then identify the departmental functions to be performed in that environment. The performance of the departmental activities is usually guided by specific objectives. In order that top management can extract from each environment the type of information it needs most for overall coordination and control, it is desirable that the departmental functions are clearly understood in terms of their objectives.

Once the objectives of the organized activities of each environment are clearly spelt out, the interest of the top management can be focussed for understanding and appreciation as to how the objectives are being achieved in practice on a day-to-day basis. The best communication functions for this purpose should comprise a set of *performance indicators* (on a quantitative basis) which will indicate as to how the different functions of the environment are being performed.

Vis-a-vis the performance indicators, it is also necessary to identify *standard norms* for the same activities of the environment which will indicate as to how the different functions of the environment should be performed. If a time-series can be built up for any performance indicator over a sufficiently long period and if this is compared against the standard norms prevailing during the same period, one can judge the performance of a particular function in a clear manner. When this is done for all the major objectives of an environment, certainly an assessment is possible about the health of the entire operating department/division in the particular industrial organization.

7.3 Decision-flow diagram

The methodology, as outlined above, can be represented in the form of a decision-flow diagram (see Fig. 7.1). The main features of this flow diagram are indicated below:

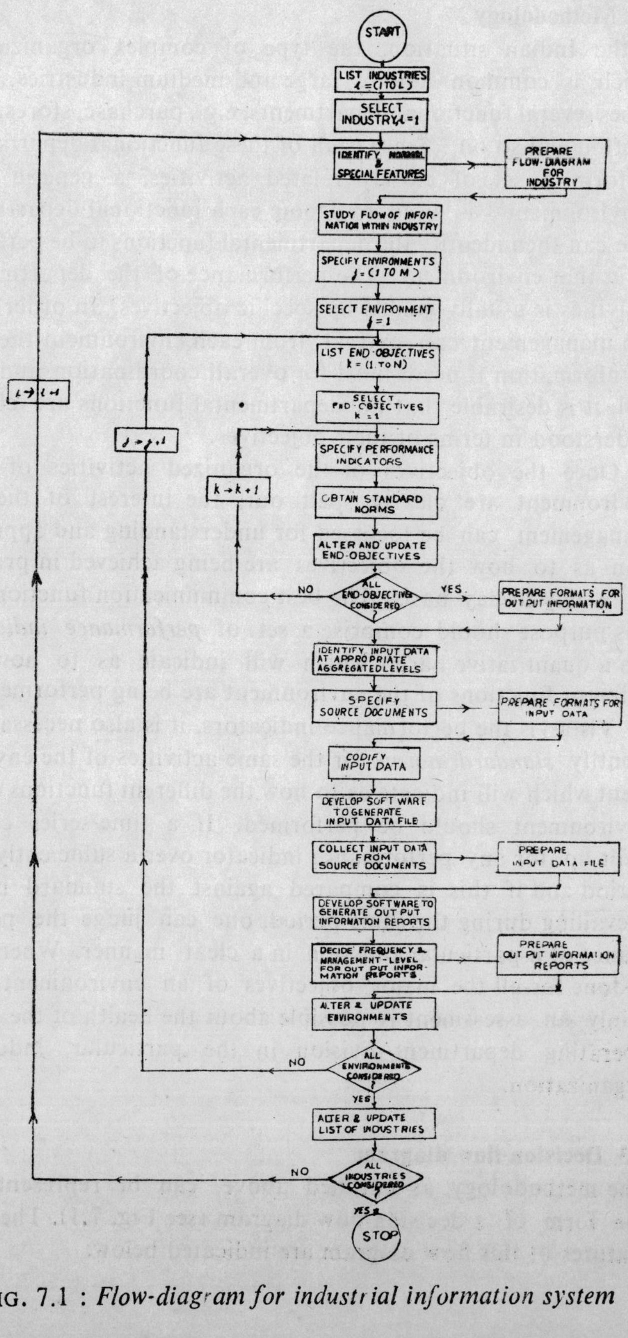

FIG. 7.1 : *Flow-diagram for industrial information system*

(a) Industries are listed and their normal and special features are identified ;

(b) Information flow as within the industry is studied to explain both the general historic process and also the communication functions that need be created ;

(c) Environments (as functional departments/divisions) are selected ;

(d) The objectives for each organized activity in an environment are listed ;

(e) Objective-wise performance indicators are formulated on quantitative basis ;

(f) Objective-wise standard norms are obtained from past knowledge and experience ;

(g) For each environment, objective-wise formats for output reports are prepared, comprising both performance indicators and standard norms ;

(h) Input data are identified at appropriate aggregate levels which will help generate the output reports in the designed proforma ;

(i) Formats are prepared for collection and storage of input data ;

(j) Source documents are specified from which input data are to be collected ;

(k) Computer-based system are designed and developed, and programmes are specified ;

(l) Programmes are coded both for building up and updating the data base and for generating the output information reports ;

(m) At every stage, provision is kept for updating of objectives and environments, etc., so that the information system can remain flexible and cope with figure changes.

7.4 Common aspects

Although industrial organizations vary in their complexity from industry to industry, their development in the past in India has brought out certain common features. Once the common environments relevant to national level planning and control are identified it is possible to bring out some general-purpose indicators for the common environments which can be said to be applicable to a variety of industrial organizations. A tentative list of common environments is given below for illustrative purposes :

1. Planning ; 2. Capacity Creation ; 3. Target Setting ; 4. Industrial Licensing ; 5. Investment ; 6. Import; 7. Production ; 8. Inventory Control ; 9. Export ; 10. Research and Development ; 11. Foreign exchange allocations ; 12. Manpower.

The objectives as well as indicators which have been formulated for the above environments are indicated in Table 7.1.

For each environment, the formats for proposed output reports are indicated (along with their proposed frequency of generation) at Annexure I. This comprises 39 tables, in all, evolved to help in information analysis for all the conceivable common aspects of the industrial organization in India. Obviously, input information has to be collected and stored for generating the output reports shown in Annexure I. These input data have been indicated in the Summary Data File at Annexure II, along with their linkages with individual output items for which they will be needed. Illustrative users are Ministry of Planning, Bureau of Public Enterprises, Ministry of Commerce, Ministry of Industry, the administrative ministry concerned and DGTD.

7.5 Specific aspects

As mentioned above, certain features and problems are peculiar to a specified industrial organization which may not be shared with other industries. While the national information system for industry should take care of all the common aspects of industrial organization, it should also be capable of dealing with these complexities for individual industries because of their importance and relevance in the context of national planning.

Obviously, a national information system is to be gradually developed for individual industries. In order to show the potential of such a development, the following four industries were chosen by the author for developing an integrated project of their information system, covering all aspects : 1. Cement ; 2. Electronics ; 3. Fertilisers ; 4. Power.

TABLE 7.1 : **Common environment, objectives and indicators for industry**

Environment	Objectives	Indicators
(1)	(2)	(3)
1. Planning	To optimize the utilization of existing capacity under the present bottlenecks ; also to remove the bottlenecks to the possible extent.	1. Utilization of capacity ; 2. Bottlenecks ; 3. Achievements in the five year plans ; 4. Supplies to different Government sectors, regionwise ; 5. Order book position ; 6. Gestation period ; 7. Per capita consumption of India and other countries.
2. Capacity creation	To meet indigenous and export demand.	1. Demand forecasts ; 2. Existing production capacity.
3. Target setting	To advise about the increase in capacity to meet the estimated demand economically and to find substitution of imported components.	1. Desirable licensing pattern year by year ; 2. Economic plant size ; 3. Norm of consumption ; 4. Substitution of imported components.
4. Industrial Licensing	Apprising the licensing authority of the facts and figures to help in taking decision about the issuing of licences.	1. Licensing policy ; 2. Existing capacity ; 3. Upcoming capacity ; 4. Production ;

TABLE 7.1—*contd.*

(1)	(2)	(3)
		5. Norm of consumption of raw materials (DGTD) ; 6. Industrial average ; 7. Consumption.
5. Investment	To depict the comparative picture of profitability and the investment structure of the factory, together with their sources of finance.	1. In case of public sector units, proportion of profit to : (a) Total assets ; (b) Production ; (c) Raw materials ; (d) Paid-up capital ; (e) Loans ; (f) Installed capacity ; 2. Proportion of production to raw material and dividend ; 3. Proportion of reserves and dividend to paid-up capital.
6. Import	To apprise the concerned authorities about the facts and figures about collaboration, raw material and capital goods, for taking decision on setting up of an industry with	1. Policy of collaboration ; 2. Norms of export obligation ; 3. Standing of collaboration ; 4. Category of industry ; 5. Norms of C.G. requirement ;

	foreign collaboration.	6. Nature of priority for import assistance in case of raw materials ; 7. Import policy for the entire product ; 8. DGTD norms for raw material consumption and component consumption ; 9. Industry's average consumption of raw materials per unit of production.
7. Production	To study the production trend State-wise and industry-wise, and the reasons (or bottlenecks) for the fall or stagnation in their production.	1. Proportion of production this month out of the total production up to this month ; 2. Comparison with corresponding quarter production of last year. 3. Proportion of this production to that planned for next few months. 4. Production/man-hour ; 5. Down time/man-hour ; 6. Percentage of receipt against planned (i) electricity ; (ii) transport facility ; (iii) fuel ; (iv) raw materials.
8. Inventory Control	To estimate the times at which an industry should get the raw materials; to keep the supply of the finished goods smooth or to estimate the time at which the production should be reduced to avoid stocking difficulty.	1. Critical stock level of raw materials ; 2. Stock level of the finished goods.

TABLE 7.1—*contd.*

(1)	(2)	(3)
9. Exports	To study the self-sufficiency level of the industry.	1. Export/import at constant prices.
10. Research and Development	To study the research and development efforts and achievement in various industries.	1. Amount spent on research and development per unit of production ; 2. Proportion of investment in Research and Development.
11. Foreign Exchange allocation	Estimates of the allocation of foreign exchange for the next 3 years.	1. Actual consumption of foreign exchange in previous years ; 2. Allotment proposal for the current year.
12. Manpower	1. To estimate the manpower requirement region-wise and state-wise in different categories ; 2. To study the availability of personnel of different categories ; 3. To study how effectively the training facilities are utilized.	1. Proportion of No. of persons actually employed to : (a) Capacity ; (b) Annual production ; (c) Standard norm ; (d) Industrial average ; 2. Proportion of No. of trained to untrained personnel.

7.6 Cement industry

Annexure III shows a flow diagram of Portland cement manufacturing process (both wet and dry processes) in order to give an idea of the industry from the receipt of raw materials up to packing and loading for distribution. Cement industry is transport intensive and is dependent on availability of raw material in different Indian States for its development. While India does not depend on foreign technology in cement, there is a continuous evolution from the wet to dry process for increasing the existing productivity. Imports in the case of cement industry are restricted to only the cement machinery and some components and spare parts while manufacture of cement takes place to meet the indigenous demand and exports.

The above features have been incorporated in the information system for cement industry and environment, objectives and indicators are shown in Table 7.2.

For each environment formats for output tables have been designed for cement industry. These are presented in Annexure IV, comprising 9 tables in all. The users would be the Ministry of Planning, Ministry of Industry, and the concerned administrative ministry.

Summary data file for cement industry is shown in Annexure V which also brings out the linkages of the input information with the output indicators.

7.7 Electronics industry

The following main classifications issued by the Electronics Commission are based on alpha numberic system :

0. Components :
   - A. Active Components ;
   - B. Passive Components, except electromechanical ;
   - C. Electromechanical components ;
   - D. Microwave components and hardware ;
1. Mass Electronics :
   - A. Consumer electronics ;
   - B. Mass Communications equipment ;
2. Communications :
   - A. Telecommunications equipment ;
   - B. Radar and Navigational equipment ;

3. Automation :
   A. Computers and related equipment ;
   B. Process control equipment ;
   C. Industrial electronics ;
4. Instrumentation :
   A. Test and measuring instruments ;
   B. Medical electronics equipment ;
   C. Nuclear instruments and equipment.

TABLE 7.2 : Environment, objectives and indicators for cement industry

Environment	Objectives	Indicators
1. Planning	To assess regional availability of limestone	(a) Name of the district where limestone quarries are located ; (b) Production of limestone ; (c) Cement & Steel production countrywise and yearwise.
2. Inventory	To watch the build-up of stock	(i) Storage capacity ; (ii) OB & CB ; (iii) Production ; (iv) Despatches.
3. Transport	To assess the wagon availability	(i) Production ; (ii) Wagon required ; (iii) Wagon allotted.
4. Technology	To determine appropriate technology. To compare norms of consumption of different inputs by various countries.	(i) Rainfall ; (ii) Water availability. (i) R.M. per tonne of production.
5. Distribution	To ensure proper distribution of cement to various regions/sectors.	(i) Quality supplied ; (ii) Quality produced ; (iii) Distribution to regions/sectors.
6. Handling & packing	To ensure economy in handling & packing.	(i) Handling & packing cost/tonne of cement.

The major environments are growth of industries, technology development and export promotion. These environments have been chosen keeping in view the growth orientation of electronics and considerable emphasis that is being laid on developing electronics technology and establishing exports. The flow diagram for the electronics industry is given at Annexure VI to facilitate in forming an idea about the industry.

Environments, objectives and indicators for electronics industry are presented in Table 7.3 which incorporates the features mentioned above.

TABLE 7.3 : **Environment, objectives and indicators for electronics industry**

Environment	Objectives	Indicators
1. Development Planning	(i) to set up industries in different places in the country	(a) District/State where industry is located ; (b) Production of Electronics Equipments : (i) for Defence purpose ; (ii) for Industrial purpose. (iii) for office purpose.
	(ii) to estimate percentage production in organized sector & small-scale sector.	(a) Production in small and organized sectors.
2. Technology Development	(i) to determine appropriate technology	(a) Technology gap ; (b) Expense on R & D ; (c) Cost comparison.
	(ii) to estimate technology performance	(a) Status of technology in development ; (b) Cost of know-how developed.
3. Trade	(i) to identifv exportable items	(a) Export statistics ; (b) per unit value ; (c) Trade agreement.
	(ii) to estimate domestic demand	(a) Export surplus
	(iii) to estimate finance availability	(a) Amount spent till last quarter.

The format for output tables for each environment as designed for the electronics industry are shown at Annexure VII comprising 13 tables in all. The users would be the Ministry of Planning, Ministry of Industry, Department of Electronics and partly Railway Board.

Summary data files have also been devised for electronics industry, which reflect how input informations are to be used to generate the output indicators. This data file is shown at Annexure VIII.

7.8 Fertiliser industry

The following types of fertilisers are used in India :

Name	*Source*
1. Phosphatic	Partly indigenous. Raw material both indigenous and imported.
2. Nitrogenous	Partly indigenous. Raw Material both indigenous and imported.
3. Potash	Fully imported.

For planning purposes, N and P_2O_5 are regarded as nutrients which are obtained from certain basic food stocks. Other than power, coal and phosphoric acid, the raw materials are petroleum products, rock phosphates, sulphur and potash. The production involves extensive chemical process. A flow diagram for the fertilizer industry is given at Annexure IX to show the precise sequence for nitrogenous fertilizer production from raw materials up to distribution.

Environments, objectives and indicators for fertilizer industry are shown in Table 7.4 following a common pattern.

The formats for output reports for the fertilizer industry, which are based on the objectives and indicators as above are given in Annexure X, comprising 8 tables in all. The users would be the Ministry of Planning, Ministry of Industry, Ministry of Agriculture and the concerned administrative ministry.

A summary data, as designed to yield the output reports by using the input information, is shown in Annexure XI.

TABLE 7.4 : **Environment, objectives and indicators for fertiliser industry**

Environment	Objectives	Indicators
1. Planning	1. To assess fertilizer requirement, State-wise	(i) Net cultivated area ; (ii) Irrigated area ; (iii) Annual rainfall.
	2. To assess the gap between targets of consumption and total available capacity, State-wise.	(i) Targets for consumption separately for N, P_2O_5 & K_2O ; (ii) Available capacity in the public sector and private sector separately for N, & P_2O_5.
2. Production control	To ensure the quality of fertilizer material	(i) Moisture content ; (ii) Nutrient content ; (iii) Other specification as given in the fertilizer control order of 1957.
3. Handling & packing	To ensure economy in handling & packing—plant-wise.	(i) Handling & packing cost per tonne of fertilizer material.
4. Distribution	1. To ensure proper distribution of fertilizer material to various States	(i) Quantity supplied to various States ; (ii) Targets of foodgrains production for each State ; (iii) Ratio $= \frac{\text{Qty. supplied}}{\text{foodgrain-targets.}}$
	2. To ensure economy in distribution, State-wise	(i) Quantity distributed during a period ; (ii) Cost of distribution for the period ; (iii) Distribution cost per tonne for the period.
5. Storage	To ensure availability of storage capacity.	(i) No. of warehouses ; (ii) Storage capacity available.

7.9 Power industry

The main environments are generation, transmission and distribution. In India, power is produced from coal, oil, gas, natural steam, water and Uranium-235, comprising thermal, hydel and nuclear power. The main goals of the power industry are as follows :

(a) To deliver power at the cheapest rate at given reliability to specified destinations ;
(b) To optimize plant location ; and
(c) To optimize hydel-thermal-nuclear mix for power.

A flow diagram for power industry is shown in Annexure XII to give a general idea of the generation, transmission and distribution of power in India.

Environments, objectives and indicators for power industry are shown in Table 7.5.

TABLE 7.5 : **Environment, objectives and indicators for power industry**

Energy Unit : KWHr.

Environment	Objectives	Indicators
1	2	3
1. Generation	A. *Hydel* (for each hydrostation)	
	(a) To maximize utilization of available water energy ;	(i) K watt-hour/1000 cusec discharge.
	(b) To meet irrigation needs of the region ;	(i) $\frac{\text{Required-Available}}{\text{Required quantity of water for irrigation.}}$
	(c) To meet the peak demand according to the load pattern ;	(i) $\frac{\text{Energy Supplied}}{\text{Energy Demand on the station.}}$
	(d) To determine an index of plant reliability.	(i) Frequency and duration of down-time for each plant per month.
		(ii) $\frac{\text{Power supplied}}{\text{Power demanded}}$
	B. *Thermal/Diesel/Nuclear* (for each station)	
	(a) To maximize utilization of fuel ;	(i) KWHr./Unit of fuel
		(ii) KWHr./manhour

TABLE 7.5—*contd.*

1	2	3
	(b) To achieve economy of operation for meeting the load ;	in the station
	(c) To meet the full demand ;	(i) $\frac{\text{Energy supplied}}{\text{Energy demand on the station}}$
	(d) To ensure full utilization of the plant (operating plant factor) ;	(i) $\frac{\text{Energy generated}}{\text{Installed capacity}}$ Percentage of capacity utilization
	(e) To determine an index of plant reliability.	(i) Frequency and duration of down time for each plant every month.
2. Transmission	(a) To minimize loss in transmission keeping supply voltage and frequency within specified limits ;	(i) $\frac{\text{Energy Lost}}{\text{Energy Transmitted}}$ (ii) $\frac{\text{Declared Voltage}}{\text{Specified Voltage}}$ (iii) $\frac{\text{Declared frequency}}{\text{Specified frequency}}$
	(b) To reduce installed capacity for meeting specified load by appropriate inter-connection of grids ;	(i) Energy Exchanged (ii) Energy shortage, if any (iii) Surplus energy, if any
	(c) To ensure system reliability.	(i) Frequency and duration of failure.
3. Distribution	(a) To adequately meet the industrial and domestic demand at specified voltages ;	(i) $\frac{\text{Energy supplied}}{\text{energy demand domestic consumers}}$ (ii) $\frac{\text{Energy supplied}}{\text{Energy Demand Industrial consumers}}$
	(b) To ensure adequate growth of power consumption ;	(i) $\frac{\text{No. of electrified villages}}{\text{Total No. of villages (Statewise)}}$ (ii) $\frac{\text{No. of street lights}}{\text{km of macadamized roads (Statewise)}}$

TABLE 7.5 *contd.*

1	2	3
		(iii) No. of domestic connections / Total No. of households (Statewise)
		(iv) Population benefited by electrification / Total population (Statewise)
		(v) No. of electrified tubewells
		(vi) Energy consumed by Industry / Total production of that industry
		(vii) Per capita energy consumption (Statewise)
		(viii) Energy consumed by various sectors.
	(c) To minimize distribution loss ;	(i) Energy Metered / Energy Distributed Statewise
	(d) To ensure economy in energy distribution ;	(i) Total Cost of distribution / Energy distributed Statewise
	(e) To ensure reliable distribution ;	(i) Frequency and duration of down-time in distribution machinery.
	(f) To analyse implications of power rationing (for major sectors).	(i) Loss of production due to power cut (Rs. / quantity) / Total production (Rs./quantity)

The formats for output tables which are based on the objective and indicators as mentioned above are presented in Annexure XIII, comprising 16 tables in all. The users would be Ministry of Planning, Ministry of Industry, Ministry of Steel, Coal and Mines and Ministry of Energy.

A format for the Master Data File, containing input information which are to be used for generating the output tables, is given in Annexure XIV.

7.10 Further developments

As stated in the beginning, the above approach is based on deriving only essential communication functions from the general historical records in order to establish a national information system on a computerized basis. Once the information system is stabilized, there should be scope for integrating different objectives and environments within the same industrial organization, or, at a later stage, among different industrial organizations after establishing the need of such integration.

Another likely area of sophistication should be the scope for developing "complementary" functions among several organizations where output information from one can provide input information to another. Apart from such input-output relationship, it should even be possible to think of "loops" among different organizations where inputs and outputs are made part of an integral whole of the Indian industrial complex.

One aspect at the moment not very well developed is the research and development base. Information linkages can be visualized in future between the established industries on the one hand and the basic and applied research that are going on in the different laboratories in India either under the C.S.I R. or other agencies including Universities. An information system should be capable of making use of knowledge of R & D activities, both on an on-going and on a planned basis, for the purpose of their utilization in industry. Such transfer of technology should be facilitated by an integrated information system on a nation wide basis.

For individual industries, one can visualize more complex communication functions which can be derived from out of the general historical records. These communication functions should eventually form part of various optimization models needed for planning and control in different industrial sectors. The mathematical concepts of two such models, which have already been developed in the power industry and which can be integrated in the national information system for industry, are mentioned below :

(a) *Optimal mix of power plants :* In electrical systems a mix of different types of power plants is bound to be advantageous on account of different operating and cost characteristics of thermal, nuclear and hydel plants. A multi-region, multi-period (20 years from 1975-76) linear programming model has been formulated where the objective has been to meet the national demand for electrical energy over the next 20 years at minimum cost to the nation. The mathematical formulation of the model has been finalized.

(b) *Optimal location of nuclear plant :* The objective is to compare the cost of investment on new transmission lines and the power losses associated with the setting up of a new nuclear plant at one of the few given sites so as to arrive at the optimal site location. The optimization technique for deriving new lines has been finalized.

7.11 Conclusion

To summarize a general methodology has been attempted above for a national information system for industry based on essentially simple communication functions which can be derived by using the general historical records already available. The approach consists in pinpointing the environments, listing the objectives in each environment, developing quantitative performance indicators and then devising formats for output reports which can be generated from input information by using source documents. While the common aspects have been selected and treated together in the Indian context as applicable to more than one industry, there will still be specific aspects which have to be tackled on an industry-to-industry basis. These specific aspects can also be taken care of in a national information system, and an attempt has been made to evolve specific information system, for cement, electronics, fertilizer and power industries. The directions in which the national information system can be further sophisticated have also been indicated, so that as the data bank is developed to cater for our industrial system, more and more benefits can be derived out of the historical data already available. This will need development of appropriate software and also training of suitable manpower, apart from the basic tasks of collection and storage of the relevant data. Once the data bank is established and basic procedures for updating the data are established, such extension should not be a difficult process.

The following further points should be noted:

(a) It is necessary to evolve standard norms for activities in each environment for purposes of knowing how the functions ought to be performed, so that comparisons can be built up in course of time between the norms and the actual performance indicators to understand the state of health in the industry. It is visualized that over a period of time, the norms themselves may change. For this purpose, such experts as in the DGTD scientists and industrialists should help in evolving norms and keeping them updated by constantly comparing the norms with the industrial averages over a period of time. This will have the advantage of also changing the norms, if necessary consequent on changes in technology.

(b) An interesting sidelight from the computer can be the graphical presentation of results, which often are more acceptable to the top level policy-makers, who are hard pressed for time to go through detailed tables. Such graphical presentation can also be obtained manually based on computer outputs.

(c) It is likely that there will be some requests for on-demand reports for the information system from various users, depending upon their special requirements. If the information system is kept updated, both for routine work and for planning and control functions as visualized above, it should not be difficult to generate such on-demand reports as well, on receipt of specific requests from the data bank.

(d) It is anticipated that retrieval time for most of the information should be virtually instantaneous, once software has been developed. On the other hand, if new items of reportage (both of routine nature or of a planning and control type) are added, it might require fresh development of software, which should not take more than a week.

The Information System for industry, at the stage of actual implementation, may face several constraints. The major one may be the likely duplication of efforts from different users which might hamper the actual functioning of the system. It is recommended that various Ministries, Departments, and divisions of the Central as well as State Governments keep operating their individual information systems pertaining to industries under their control for the aspects with which they are concerned. Both collection and processing of data will remain within their purview, while the actual forms used for retrieval of information can be obtained from the present study. A copy of their output reports should invariably be sent to the Ministry or Department, which is administratively concerned with an industry in the long run, so that the latter Ministry or Department can keep a total tally of the output reports on information analysis relating to that industry right from the raw material procurement up to its distribution and control. To give one example, the Ministry of Petroleum and Chemicals is administratively concerned with the fertilizer industry. On the other hand, the DGTD is concerned with the licensing aspects of the fertilizer industry and the STC is concerned with procurement of raw materials for the fertilizer industry. It is suggested here that both STC and DGTD should continue to process the information, as far as their relative aspects of fertilizer industry are concerned, as hitherto, pertaining to the aspects with which they are concerned on the lines suggested in the present study. After processing of information, they should invariably endorse copies of their information analysis to the Ministry of Petroleum and Chemicals. Similarly, the Bureau of Public Enterprises may like to process information on personnel management in public sector undertakings in fertilizer industry and send a copy of their information analysis to the Ministry of Petroleum and Chemicals. It will be for the Ministry of Petroleum and Chemicals to keep a total and comprehensive record of all the information analysis pertaining to fertilizer industry, so that administratively they have the full picture relating to that industry. This will avoid duplication in many respects and will make functioning of the information system smooth in the long run. Furthermore, when data relating to fertilizer industry is required for policy formulation and planning purposes by the Planning Commission and other bodies, the latter can centrally approach the Ministry of Petroleum and Chemicals for all data relating to fertilizer industry.

The other important constraint visualized at this moment is in the collection of relevant data. As has been stated before, there is a wealth of historical records available on most of the industries in India. Once the information system is made operational, ways and means have to be found to streamline the collection and updating of data from the available sources. India has been justifiably well known for its statistical systems and there is no reason to suspect that our Information System on industry will fail for want of relevant statistics.

ANNEXURE I

(Table references as per environments in Table 7.1.0)

TABLE 7.1.1 : **Analysis of capacity utilization among different sectors of industries (for Broad Industrial Categories)**

Environment : Planning
Frequency : Yearly

Year :

State	Proportion of production to installed capacity				Proportion of installed capacity to licensed capacity			
	Public sector undertakings		Larger houses	Others	Public sector undertakings		Larger houses	Others
	Central Govt.	State Govt.			Central Govt.	State Govt.		

TABLE 7.1.2 : **Capacity and production analysis**
(for public sector undertakings under Central Government)

Environment : Planning
Frequency : Yearly

Year :

State	Factory Name & Address	Accounting Unit	Capacity								Production				Installed capacity			
			Licensed		Installed		Installed / Licensed		Upcoming		Last Year		This Year		Last Year		This Year	
			Last Year	This Year	Last Year	This Year	Last Year	This Year	Last Year	This Year	Quantity	Value	Quantity	Value	Quantity	Value	Quantity	Value

TABLE 7.1.3 : Capacity and production analysis (for public sector undertakings under state governments)

Environment : Planning
Frequency : Yearly

Year :

State	Factory Name & Address	Accounting Unit	Capacity								Production				Installed Capacity			
			Licensed		Installed		Inst. × 100 / Licensed		Upcoming		Last Year		This Year		Last Year		This Year	
			Last Year	This Year	Last Year	This Year	Last Year	This Year	Last Year	This Year	Quantity	Value	Quantity	Value	Quantity	Value	Quantity	Value

Table 7.1.4 : Capacity and production analysis (for larger houses)

Environment : Planning
Frequency : Yearly

Year :

State	Factory Name & Address	Accounting Unit	Capacity								Production				Installed Capacity			
			Licensed		Installed		Inst.×100 / Licensed		Upcoming		Last Year		This Year		Last Year		This Year	
			Last Year	This Year	Last Year	This Year	Last Year	This Year	Last Year	This Year	Quantity	Value	Quantity	Value	Quantity	Value	Quantity	Value

TABLE 7.1.5 : **Capacity and production analysis (for sectors other than public sector and larger houses)**

Environment : Planning

Frequency : Yearly

Year :

State	Factory Name & Address	Accounting Unit	Capacity								Production				Installed Capacity			
			Licensed		Installed		Inst. × 100 / Licensed		Upcoming		Last Year		This Year		Last Year		This Year	
			Last Year	This Year	Last Year	This Year	Last Year	This Year	Last Year	This Year	Quantity	Value	Quantity	Value	Quantity	Value	Quantity	Value

TABLE 7.1.6 : **Capacity utilization analysis**

Environment : Planning
Frequency : Six Monthly

Month and Year :

Product	State	Installed Capacity		Production						% change in production over		Capacity utilization		
				Quantity			Ex-factory value							
		Unit A/C	Qty.	Current six months	Corresponding six months of last year	Next six months (planned)	Current six months	Corresponding six months of last year	Next six months (estimated)	Corresponding six months of last year	Corresponding next six months with the current six months	Current six months	Corresponding six months of the last year	Next six months compared to current six months

N.B. : This will be aggregated on the basis of value only.

TABLE 7.1.7 : **Inter-industry bottlenecks analysis**

Environment : Planning *Frequency* : Six monthly *Month and Year* :

Product	State	Capacity	Production		Maintenance	Production	% loss in production due to					
			A/C Unit	Qty. ex-factory value	Frequency and duration of maintenance	Per man hr.	Labour trouble	Machinery break-down	Electricity shortage & other reasons	Shortage R.M.	Shortage of fuel like coal, furnace oil, etc.	Others

TABLE 7.1.8 : **Analysis on targets and achievements in the five-year plans**

Environment : Planning *Frequency* : End of the Plan

Name of Products	Third Plan 1961-66		Fourth Plan 1966-71		Fifth Plan 1971-76		Sixth Plan 1976-82	
	Target	% Achievement	Target	% Achievement	Target	% Achievement	Target	% Achievement

TABLE 7.1.9 : **Analysis on regionwise supplies to various government sectors**

Environment : Planning *Year* :
Frequency : Yearly
Product :

Year	Defence	Railways	Central Water & Power Commission	Communication	Others
West					
Maharashtra					
Gujarat					
Rajasthan					
M.P.					
Goa Daman & Diu					
East					
Assam					
Bihar					
West Bengal					
Orissa					
North					
Punjab					
H.P.					
Delhi					
Chandigarh					
U.P.					
J.K.					
South					
T.N.					
Andhra					
Karnataka					
Kerala					
Pondicherry					
Total Actual Supplies					
Total Targeted requirements					

TABLE 7.1.10 : **Analysis on order-book position of various machinery manufacturers**

Environment : Planning
Frequency : Six Months *Month and Year* :
Product for which the Machinery is required :

Name of the Manufacturer	No. of months for which the manufacturer has order on hand	Average delivery period for the machinery

TABLE 7.1.11 : **Gestation period analysis**

Environment : Planning
Frequency : Yearly *Year* :

Name of Products	Appropriate Technology (nomenclature)	Region	Gestation period (number of years)

TABLE 7.1.12 : **Per capita consumption analysis in India and in other countries**

Environment : Planning
Frequency : Yearly
Name of the product : (only consumer industry)

Year	India	Austria	W. Germany	U.K.	U.S.A.	Japan
1977						
1978						
1979						
1980						
1981						
1982						

TABLE 7.2.1 : **Analysis of capacity creation requirements**

Environment : Capacity creation
Frequency : Annual

Year :
Industry Major Product :
Accounting Unit :

Description of item of Information	1981		1982		1983		1984		1985	
	Public Sector	Private Sector	Public Sector	Private Sector	Public Sector	Private Sector	Public Sector	Private Sector	Public Sector	Private Sector
1. Demand Forecasts										
2. Targeted Production										
3. Existing capacity										
4. Upcoming capacity										
5. Additional capacity to be generated										

TABLE 7.3.1 : Industrial target setting (for the current year and each year of the plan period)

Environment: Target setting *Month and year* :
Frequency : Six monthly *Major Product* :

Sl. No.	Output items
1	2
1A.	Estimated domestic demand
1B.	Estimated export demand
2.	Total demand
3.	Target of production
4.	Capacity required to meet Target of production (item 3)
5.	Total existing installed capacity
6.	Upcoming capacity (year by year)
7.	Targeted Licensed capacity to achieve installed capacity at item 4 above
8.	Total existing Licensed capacity
9.	Desirable licensing pattern year by year to fill the gap between items 7 and 8 above
10.	CG cost for maintenance, replacement and modernization
11.	Total foreign exchange payments for existing capacity to be paid during the current Plan period and for the collaboration envisaged
12.	Foreign exchange outflow (recurring cost) on (a) Raw materials, (b) Components, and (c) Spares
13.	Foreign exchange inflow through exports
14.	Net foreign exchange earnings
	Economic plant size for New Units
15A.	Economic Plant Size
15B.	Investment for item 15A above
15C.	Foreign exchange component of item 15B above

TABLE 7.3.1—*contd.*

1	2
16.	Fixed investment for economic plant size on : (a) Land, (b) Building, and (c) Machinery (imported and indigenous)
17.	Norms of consumption (Rs./Qty. per unit of production) for : (a) Raw materials, (b) Components, and (c) Spares } (imported/indigenous)
18.	Policy of collaboration
19.	Fixed investment year by year (at the beginning)
20.	Foreign Exchange outflow (fixed cost) on C.G. for new units
	Industrial Guidelines
21.	Guidelines for phased programmes regarding : (a) Substitution of imported components/raw materials by indigenous components/raw materials, (b) Capacity build-up, (c) Production build-up, (d) Export build-up, and (e) Process details (for chemical products only)

TABLE 7.3.2 : **Analysis on consumption pattern**

Environment : Target-setting
Frequency : Yearly
Industry : Major product

Year : 1980

Region/ State	A/U	Consumption				Expected consumption		Proportion of State/Regional consumption to All India consumption			
		1979	1980	1981	1982	1983	1984	1981	1982	1983	1984

TABLE 7.4.1 : Industrial licence analysis

Environment : Industrial licensing *Month and Year* :
Frequency : Monthly *Major Product* :

Sl. No.	Output items
1.	Licensing Policy for the product
2.	Existing installed capacity (updated)
3.	Existing licensed capacity (updated)
4A.	Capacity under recommendation but not yet approved (updated)
4B.	Capacity covered under letters of Intent (updated)
5.	Statewise distribution of capacity : (a) licensed, (b) registered, (c) recommended under letters of intent
6.	Statewise production
7.	Policy on export obligation, if any
8.	Statistics for this product for last 3 years under : (a) Import, (b) Export
9.	Data on : (a) World import for the past 3 years (b) Export possibility from India

TABLE 7.5.1 : Inter-industrial units investment analysis (public sector)

Environment : Investment *Frequency* : Yearly *Year* :

Factory	Year of Establishment	Land & Building (value)	Plant & Mechinery (value)	Stocks (value)	Total Assets (value)	Installed Capacity	Production (value)	Profit (value)	Proportion to total assets of			Profit / Production	Profit / Raw Material	Production / Plant & Machinery
									Profit	Production	Installed Capacity			

TABLE 7.5.1.1 : Inter-industry investment analysis report (private sector)

Environment : Investment *Frequency* : Yearly *Year* :

Factory	Year of Establishment	Land & Building (value)	Plant & Machinery (value)	Stocks (value)	Total Assets (value)	Installed Capacity	Production	Proportion to total assets of		Production / Plant & Machinery
								Production	Installed Capacity	

TABLE 7.5.2.1 : Source of investment analysis (public sector)

Environment : Investment *Frequency* : Yearly *Year* :

Factory	Year of establishment	Paid-up Capital			Loans			Total Loans	Installed Capacity (value)	Reserves (value)	Dividends (value)	Profit / Paid-up capital	Profit / Loans	Res rves / Paid-up capital	Dividend / Paid-up capi
		Indian (value)	Foreign (value)	Total (value)	Government	Others	Total								

TABLE 7.5.2.2 : Source of investment analysis (private sector)

Environment : Investment *Frequency* : Yearly *Year* :

Factory	Year of establish-ment	Paid-up capital			Loans (value)	Installed capacity (value)	Reserves (value)	Dividend (value)	Reserves / Paid-up capital (total)	Dividend / Paid-up capital (total)
		Indian (value)	Foreign (value)	Total (value)						

TABLE 7.6.1 : Collaboration analysis

Environment : Import *Month and Year* :
Frequency : Monthly *Major Product* :

Sl. No.	Output items
1.	Current policy on collaboration
2.	Approved terms of past 10 collaborations
3.	Standing of collaborators on the basis of past experience
4.	Norms for export obligations
5.	Statistics for this product for the last three years under : (a) Import (b) Export
6.	Data on : (a) World import for the past 3 years (b) Export possibility from India

TABLE 7.6.2 : Capital goods analysis

Environment : Import *Month and Year* :
Frequency : Monthly *Major Product* :

Sl. No.	Output items
1.	Category of Industry, i.e., Priority, Non-Priority, Export-oriented
2.	Details of the past 5 C.G. applications : (a) Date (b) Capacity (c) CIF value, if any (d) Country of import
3.	Norms for C.G. requirements : (a) Total (b) Imported
4.	Total capacity covered under previous Capital Goods licences

TABLE 7.6.3 : **Raw materials analysis**

Environment : Import *Month and Year* :
Frequency : Monthly

Sl. No.	Output items
1-A.	Nature of priority for import assistance for the end product (Industry)
1-B.	Import Policy for the end product
2.	DGTD norms for (a) raw material consumptions ; and (b) component consumption
3.	Industry's average consumption of raw material per unit of production

TABLE 7.6.4 : **Capital goods utility analysis**

Environment : Import *Frequency* : Six monthly *Month and Year* :

Types of Machine	Name & Address of manufacturer	Year of Installation	Status of Industry	Cost of Installation	Amount spent on Installation at Constant Prices	Technology (nomenclature)	Capacity Achieved	Production Cost	Value of Production at Constant Prices	Export (value)	Major Raw Materials	Other Salient Features

TABLE 7.7.1 : **Analysis of production achievements**

Environment : Production *Frequency* : Monthly *Month and Year* :

Product	Factory Name	Production this month					This month's achievements over this month's planned production	Previous month's achievements over this month's planned production	Man hours worked during this month	Production per man hour	Bottlenecks
		Actual			Planned						
		Accounting Unit	Qty.	Ex-factory value (Rs. '000)	Qty.	Ex-factory value (Rs. '000)					

TABLE 7.7.2 : Inter-unit production analysis

Environment : Production *Frequency* : Six monthly *Product* : *Month and Year* :

State	Factory Name & Address	A/U	Capacity		A/U	Production			The period up to which the factory will be completely occupied based on orders in hand	Raw materials (value Rs. '000)				Exports (Rs. '000)
						Planned for this six months	Produced			Imported		Indigenous		
			Licensed	Installed			Qty.	Ex-factory (value) Rs. '000		Stock	Consumed	Stock	Consumed	

TABLE 7.7.3 : Inter-unit analysis of production bottlenecks

Environment : Production *Frequency* : Half-Yearly *Product* : *Month and Year* :

State	Factory	Transport Facility		Electricity		Fuel		Other Bottle-necks	Raw Materials (value)			
									Imported		Indigenous	
		Required	Received	Required	Received	Requir-ed	Receiv-ed		Applied	Receiv-ed	Applied	Receiv-ed

TABLE 7.7.4 : Analysis of manpower

Environment : Production
Frequency : Six Monthly

Month and Year :

Factory	Workers as defined under the Factory Act	Average No. of persons employed up to June/ December	Total wage/ salaries paid	Reasons for perceptible drop in employment and its likely duration	Installed capacity Qty.	Production Rs.	Production T (3)	Production T (2)
	1. Supervisory							
	2. Clerical							
	3. Skilled							
	4. Semi-skilled							
	5. Unskilled							
	6. Others not if only under Factory Act							
	Total							

TABLE 7.7.5 : **Indicators of production and bottlenecks**

Environment : Production
Frequency : Half-Yearly
Product :

Month and Year :

State	Factory	Production		Six month's production	Six month's installed capacity	Down time	Mandays	Electricity		Transport facility		Fuel		Raw material consumed per unit of production during the six months						Raw material received/required	
		This six months	This six months											Imported (Crucial)			Indigenous Source				
		Corresponding six months of last year	Planned for next six months					Received	Required	Received	Required	Received	Required	RM 1	RM 2	RM 3	RM 1	RM 2	RM 3	Indigenous Source	Imported

TABLE 7.8.1 : **Critical stock level analysis (raw materials)**

Environment : Inventory *Frequency* : Six monthly *Product* : *Month and Year* :

Components or Raw Materials or Spares	A/U	Production	Planned production for the next six months (Qty.)	Raw Material Stock (Qty.)				Material dispatched but not yet received	Material ordered L/C opened	Consumption of raw material per unit of production	Critical stock level limit
				Opening	Expected arrival	Closing	Under consideration				

TABLE 7.8.2 : **Stock-level analysis (finished products)**

Environment : Inventory *Frequency* : Six Monthly *Month and Year* :

Product	A/C unit	Production (Qty.)	Self-consumption, if any	Planned for the next six months (Qty.)	Stock		Demand for next six months	Storing capacity	Delivery time	Stock level to be kept
					Opening	Closing				
Fans	Nos.	80,000	Nil	1,00,000	5,000	10,000	1,00,000	12,000	—	—

TABLE 7.9.1 : **Analysis of self-sufficiency**

Environment : Trade
Frequency : Yearly

Year :

Industry major product	Exports to all countries									Import of all Types for the industry									Export/ Import at Constant Prices		
	Current value (Rs. '000)			Price deflator			Value con- stant prices (Rs. '000)			Current value (Rs. '000)			Price deflator			Value at con- stant prices (Rs. '000)					
Current	1980-81	1981-82	1982-83	1980-81	1981-82	1982-83	1980-81	1981-82	1982-83	1980-81	1981-82	1982-83	1980-81	1981-82	1982-83	1980-81	1981-82	1982-83	1980-81	1981-82	1982-83

N.B. : Current Value=Current value of all raw materials components and spares used for that industry.
Deflator =Average deflator of the different deflators of the above items.

TABLE 7.9.2 : **Trade prospects analysis for 1984-85**

Environment : Trade
Frequency : Yearly

Year :

Product	Country	A/C unit	Percentage of Demand met in Years						Exports made for the past 3 years						Per Unit Value 1980-81	Demand (Estimated in the next year) (Rs. '000) 1984-85	Supply (Estimated in the next year) (Rs. '000) 1983-84	Supply/Demand.
			1981-82		1982-83		1983-84		1981-82		1982-83		1983-84					
			Qty.	Value	Qty.	Value	Qty.	Value	Qty.	Value	Qty.	Value	Qty.	Value				

TABLE 7.10.1 : **Inter-industry research and development promotion analysis**

Environment : Research and Development | *Year* :

Frequency : Yearly

Industry :

Factory	Amount spent on Res. Dev. Activity (Rs. '000)					Cost of Production (Rs. '000)					Total Investment (Rs. '000)					Res. & Dev. percentage of Amount spent on									
																Production					Total Investment				
	1982-83	1981-82	1980-81	1979-80	1978-79	1982-83	1981-82	1980-81	1979-80	1978-79	1982-83	1981-82	1980-81	1979-80	1978-79	1982-83	1981-82	1980-81	1979-80	1978-79	1982-83	1981-82	1980-81	1979-80	1978-79

TABLE 7.11.1 : **Raw material allocation and consumption analysis (name of industry/major product)**

Environment : Foreign Exchange Allocation *Month and Year* :
Frequency : Six-Monthly

Raw Material/ Components/ Spares	Description of Items	Allocation Last Year (value)	CIF Value of Actual Consumption	Production (Product) Last Year				Sources of Import and their Values							
				A/C	Quantity	Industrial Average (Quantity)	DGTD's Norms (Quantity)	1		2		3		4	
								Source	Value	Source	Value	Source	Value	Source	Value

Note : (1) Carriage, Insurance and Freight=CIF.
(2) Directorate General of Technical Development=DGTD.

TABLE 7.11.2 : **Foreign exchange budgeting analysis (major countrywise)**

Environment : Foreign Exchange Allocation *Year* :
Frequency : Yearly

Items	Actual consumption of foreign exchange in previous year							Allotment proposal of foreign exchange for the current year	Estimated/proposed allocation of foreign exchange for the next year	Estimated allocation of foreign exchange for the next 3 years
	Free foreign exchange	GCA*	U.K.	U.S. Aid	Australia	Canada	Other			
Steel										
N F.M. (non-ferrous metal)										
Finished and semi-finished components										
Capital goods										
Total										

*GCA=General Currency Allocation.

TABLE 7.11.3 : **Foreign exchange allocation and production analysis**

Environment: Foreign Exchange Allocation
Frequency : Half-yearly

Month & Year :
Raw Material :

Name of the Industry/Major Product	Annual Production	Foreign Exchange Allocation			
		U.S.A.	U.K.	R.P.A.	I.D.A.

TABLE 7.12.1 : **Analysis of manpower requirement**

Environment : Manpower
Frequency : Yearly
Industry : Major Product

Region/ State	Category of manpower	A/U*	Capacity	Annual pro- duction	Manpower required (No.)			Proportion of No. of persons actually employed to			
					Std. norm	Industrial average	Actually em- ployed	Capacity	Annual production	Std. norm	Industrial average
West											
Maharashtra											
	Unskilled labour										
	Skilled labour cat. 1										
	cat. 2										
	Technical staff cat. 1										
	cat. 2										
	Managerial staff cat. 1										
	cat. 2										
	Administrative staff cat. 1										
	cat. 2										
	Scientists (for R&D) cat. 1										
	cat. 2										

*A/U=Actually utilized.

TABLE 7.12.2 : **Analysis on manpower training**

Environment : Manpower
Frequency : Yearly
Industry : Major Product

Year :

Region/ State	Category of Manpower		No. of persons trained during the years	Total No. of persons trained so far	Proportion of trained to un-trained personnel	Whether easily available or not available
West						
Maharashtra						
	Unskilled labour					
	Skilled labour	cat. 1				
		cat. 2				
	Technical staff	cat. 1				
		cat. 2				
	Managerial staff	cat. 1				
		cat. 2				
	Administrative staff	cat. 1				
		cat. 2				
	Scientists (for R & D)	cat. 1				
		cat. 2				

ANNEXURE II

SUMMARY DATA FILE

Item of Information	Source Agency	Related output tables* (Spl. purpose only)	Remarks
1	2	3	4
1. Factory address and name with district in which located (factory code)	DGTD	7.1, 7.2, 7.3 1.8	
2. Annual licensed capacity (productwise) and licence number/registration number	DGTD/SIA	7.2, 3.1, 1.2, 1.3, 1.4, 1.5	
3. Number of days worked during the month	DGTD(MPR)	7.1	
4. Average daily number of shifts worked during the month	DGTD	7.1	
5. Nature and duration of working of any section over and above the normal shifts	DGTD	7.1	
6. Product manufactured with complete specification	DGTD	All tables	
7. Product code	DGTD		
8. Planned production targets: (a) Monthly (b) Six-monthly	DGTD*	7.1	
9. Production in quantity and ex-factory value in Rs. exclusive of dealers/distributors/agents commission and excise duty	DGTD	7.1, 1.2 to 1.5	
10. Accounting unit of the quantity	DGTD	1.2 to 1.5	

*Prefix 7 to each table and refer to Annexure I.

ANNEX. II—*contd.*

1	2	3	4
11. Cumulative production up to the month in the current calendar year (Preferably in quantity)	To be circulated	1.6	
12. Closing stocks six-monthly : (a) Raw materials (b) Finished products	DGTD	8.1, 8.2	
13. The period for which the factory will remain completely occupied based on orders in hand on 1st day of the next month	DGTD	1.10, 7.3	
14. Raw materials consumed during the month : (a) Imported (b) Indigenous source	DGTD*	7.2	
15. Raw materials required, allotted, received every six months : (a) Imported (b) Indigenous source	DGTD*	7.3	
16. Total manhours worked during the month	To be calculated on the basis of 3,4 & 5	1.7	
17. Manhours lost due to labour trouble, electricity breakdown, machine faults and other	-do-	1.7	
18. Transport facility required, received	DGTD*	7.3	
19. Frequency of maintenance and time lost therein	DGTD*	1.7	
20. Electricity, furnace oil, Coal, Coke required/allotted/received	DGTD*	7.3, 1.7	
21. Exports (six months)	DGTD*	9.1	

1	2	3	4
22. Delivery time, if any, should be reported every six months	DGTD*	8.2	
23. Stocking capacity should be reported every six months	DGTD*	8.2	
24. Time-lag in getting raw-material (every six months)	DGTD*	8.1	
25. Labour statistics together with total wages/salaries of each category (every six months)	DGTD	7.4	
26. Estimated productwise domestic demand (for next six months)	Planning Commission (PPD)/ Dev. Council/ Task force	3.1	
27. Supply (every six months) productwise	(calculated)	9.2	
28. Capital goods imported during the six months	SIA (CG Section)	6.2	
29. Upcoming installed capacity (every six months)	DGTD/SIA (Data unit)	3.1	
30. Land and building acquired or built up to the end of the year	DOS/IL. Forms/Guidelines for industries		
31. Plant and machinery acquired up to the end of the year : (a) Imported (b) Indigenous	DOS/IL Forms/Guidelines for industries		
32. Stocks of raw materials (Imported, Indigenous Source) finished and semi-finished goods and others (yearly)	DOS/IL Forms/Guidelines for industries	5.1.1 5.1.2 5.2.1 5.2.2	
33. Total Assets (yearly)	C.S.O. for public sector/ Deptt. of Co. Affairs		
34. Profit during the year	C.S.O. for public sector/ Deptt. of Co. Affairs		

ANNEX. II—*contd.*

1	2	3	4
35. Name of the manufacturer	DGTD	6.4	
36. Type of machine employed together with its cost, capacity that can be achieved, consumption of power and other salient features	DGTD/SIA	6.4	
37. Appropriate technology	DGTD*	1.11	
38. Gestation period		1.11	
39. Regionwise supply of products to different Govt. sectors such as Defence, Railways, C.W. & P.C., etc.	DGS&D CPWD	1.9	
40. Consumption of product in different countries and their population	UN Statistical Bulletin	1.12	
41. Targets and achievements of Five Year Plans	Planning Commission	3.1, 1.8	
42. Estimated export targets	Export Promotion Council (Ministry of Commerce) E.P. Section/TDA/IIFT/NCAER	3.1	
43. Capacity required to meet target of six months' production	DGTD	3.1	
44. Targeted licensed capacity to achieve installed capacity at item 43	Planning Commission Min. of I.D.	3.1	
45. Desirable licensing pattern year by year to fill the gap between targeted licensed capacity and total existing licensed capacity	Planning Commission/Dev. Council	3.1	
46. C.G costs for maintenance, replacement and modernization	SIA (C.G. Sec.)	3.1	

1	2	3	4
47. Foreign exchange payments for existing capacity to be paid during the current plan period and for the collaboration envisaged	SIA (CIF Sec.)	3.1	
48. Foreign exchange outflow (recurring costs) on : (a) Raw materials (b) Components (c) Spares	C.L.P. Section/ EA's Office	3.1	
49. Economic plant size	To be calculated with the help of DO's	3.1	
50. Investment for item 49 above	-do-	3.1	
51. Foreign exchange component of 50 above	-do-	3.1	
52. Fixed investment for economic plant size on : (a) Land, (b) Building (c) Machinery (Imported and Indigenous)	DO's/IL forms/ Guidelines for industries	3.1	
53. Norms of consumption (Rs./Qty. per unit of production), for : (a) Raw materials (b) Components (Imported/ Indigenous) (c) Spares	Application/ Through DO's from parties	3.1	
54. Policy of collaboration	Collaboration board/SIA/ Guidelines	3.1, 4.2	
55. Fixed investment year by year (at the beginning)	To be calculated (with the help of SIA)	3.1	
56. Foreign exchange outflow (fixed cost) on capital goods for new units	I.L. form/SIA (CG Sec)	3.1	

ANNEX. II—*contd.*

1	2	3	4
57. Substitution of imported components/raw materials	DGTD/Genl. Coordination/ SIA/Red Book	3.1	
58. Substitution of indigenous components/raw materials	DGTD/Genl. Coordination/ SIA/Red Book	3.1	
59. Capacity build-up	DGTD	3.1	
60. Production build-up	DGTD	3.1	
61. Export build-up	DGTD	3.1	
62. Process details (for chemical products only)	DGTD	3.1	
63. Licensing policy for product	SIA (Monitoring Sec.)	4.1	
64. Capacity under recommendation but not yet approved (updated)	DGTD/SIA	4.1	
65. Capacity under letters of intent	SIA (L.O.I.)	4.1	
66. Policy on export obligations	Red Book Vol. II	4.1	
67. World import for the past 3 years	U.N. Bulletin	4.1	
68. Export possibility from India	TDA/IIFT	4.1	
69. Current policy on collaboration	Collaboration board (SIA) (F.C. Section)	6.1	
70. Approved terms of the past 10 collaborations	Collaboration board (SIA) (F.C. Section)	6.1	
71. Standing of collaborators on the basis of past experience	CSIR/NRDC/ Tech. Dev. Sec. of DGTD	6.1	
72. Norms for export obligations	Application for F.C.	6.1	

1	2	3	4
73. Statistics for this product for last three years : (a) Import (b) Export	DGCIS Bulletin	6.1	
74. Data on: (a) World import for the last 3 years (b) Export possibility from India	 U.N. Bulletin IDA/IIFT	6.1	
75. Category of industry, i.e., priority, non-priority, Export-oriented	Red Book/ITC	6.2	
76. Details of the last 5 C.G. Applications : (a) Data (b) Capacity (c) CIF value, if any (d) Country of Import	 C.G. Committee (SIA) DGTD CCI&E CCI&E/EA's Office	6.2	
77. Norm of C.G. requirements : (i) Total (ii) Imported	DGTD	6.2	
78. Total capacity covered under previous C.G. licences	DGTD/C.G. Sec. (SIA)	6.2	
79. Nature and priority for import assistance for the end product (Industry)	Red Book	6.3	
80. Import policy for the end product	Red Book	6.3	
81. D.G.T.D. Norms : (a) Raw Materials consumption, and (b) Component consumption	DGTD	6.3	
82. Industry's average consumption of raw material per unit of production	Party's application for raw material/DGTD	6.3	

ANNEX. II—*contd.*

1	2	3	4
83. Storing capacity		8.2	
84. Export orders in hand	TDA Export Promotion Council industrial units	8.2	
85. Estimated exports	Planning Commission (PPD) M/O Commerce Export Promotion Council (E.A.) TDA/IIFT	3.1	
86. Expected arrivals as on date of application for the period (months for which the import application has been made)	Raw material application ('C' form)	8.1	
87. Raw material to be imported	Raw material application	3.1	
88. Frequency and duration of downtime of each plant	DGTD*	1.7	
89. Appropriate Technology for a product	DGTD*	6.4	
90. Type of machines available to manufacture a particular type of product	DGTD*	6.4	
91. Salient features of that machinery	Firms	6.4	
92. Capacity that can be achieved	Firms	6.4	
93. Cost of the machines	Firms	6.4	
94. Raw materials used together with the quantity and cost	DGTD/Firms	6.4	
95. Estimated production	Firms	6.4	
96. Total cost of installation	Firms	6.4	
97. Consumption of electricity and fuel	Firms	7.3	

1	2	3	4
98. Amount spent on Research and Development over the last 5 years	Firms	10.1	
99. Total income over the last 5 years	Firm/Deptt. of Co. Affairs	10.1	
100. Total investment over the last 5 years	-do-	10.1	
101. Foreign Exchange inflow through exports	E.P. Council (E.P. Sec., Commerce Ministry, Bulletin/DGCIS bulletin)	3.1	
102. Paid-up Capital	C.S.O./Balance-sheets of the companies	5.2.1, 5.2.2	
103. Reserves	C.S.O./Balance-sheets of the companies	5.2.1, 5.2.2	
104. Dividend paid	C.S.O./Balance-sheets of the companies	5.2.1, 5.2.2	
105. Sources of import and their value	EA's Office/ DGTD	11.1	
106. Total investment	DGTD*	10.1	
107. Amount spent on R&D	DGTD*	10.1	
108. Per capita consumption of India and other countries	DGTD/UN Bulletin	1.12	
109. Last year allocation of raw materials	DGTD/EA's Office	11.1	
110. Self-consumption, if any	Firms	8.2	
111. Targeted Production for Public and Private Sectors	DGTD/ Planning Commission	2.1	
112. Deflators :			
(a) for export products	EA's Office	9.1	
(b) for import products			

ANNEX. II—*contd.*

1	2	3	4
113. Additional capacity to be generated in public and private sectors	DGTD/Planning Commission	2.1	
114. Actual consumption of Foreign Exchange in the previous year countrywise on major items capital goods, components and spares	EA's Office	11.2	
115. Allotment proposal for item 114 in the current year	EA's Office	11.2	
116. Estimated/proposed allocation for the next year of item 114	DGTD	11.2	
117. Estimated allocation for the next three years of item 114	DGTD	11.2	
118. Standard norms of manpower required for the industry	Manufacturer of the machinery utilized to produce the goods	12.1	
119. Industrial average of manpower required for the industry	DGTD and DGE & T	12.1	
120. No. of persons actually employed	DGE & T and DGTD	12.1	
121. No. of persons : (i) Trained during the year (ii) Untrained	From the factories	12.2	
122. Availability of the personnel of different categories	DGE & T	12 2	
123. Consumption of the finished product for the last 4 years	NSS	3.2	

*Included in the monthly production return.

ANNEXURE III

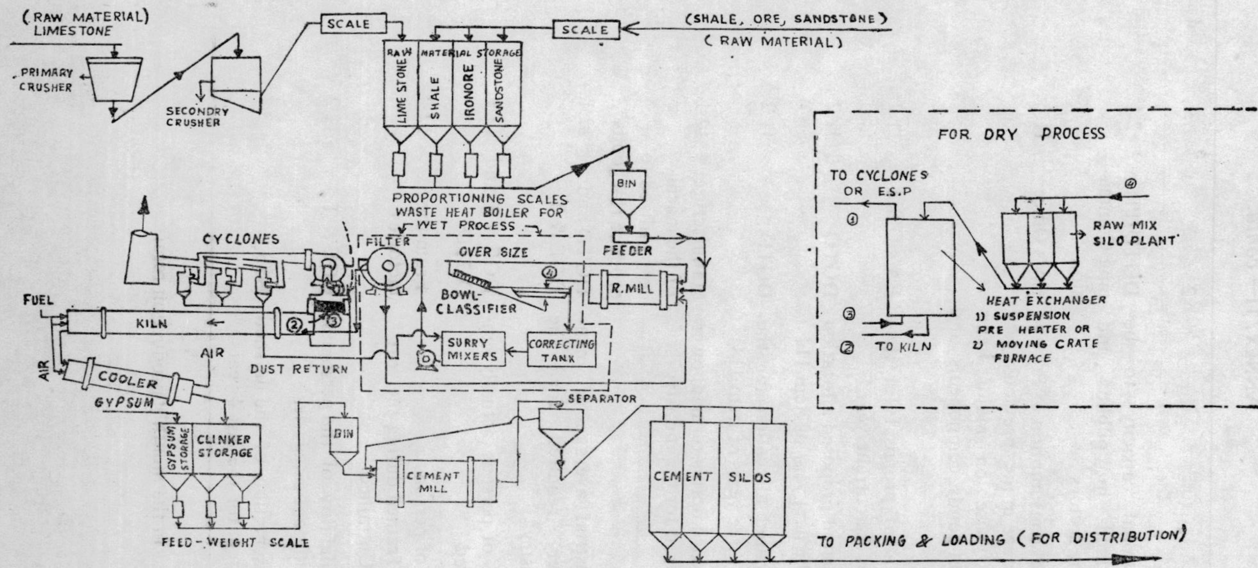

Fig. 7.2 : *Flow diagram of portland cement manufacturing process (wet and dry processes).*

ANNEXURE IV

TABLE 7.1.1 : **Production of limestone (State/districtwise)**

Environment : Planning
Frequency : Quarterly

Industry : Cement
Month and Year :

States/Districts	Production of Limestone (in tonnes)			
	1980	1981	1982	1983

TABLE 7.1.2 : **Production of cement and steel and their production ratio (during the last 5 years)**

Environment : Planning
Frequency : Yearly

Industry : Cement
Year :

Countries	1978			1979			1980			1981			1982		
	Total Cement Production in MT	Total Steel Production in MT	$\frac{\text{Cement}}{\text{Steel}} \times 100$	Total Cement Production in MT	Total Steel Production in MT	$\frac{\text{Cement}}{\text{Steel}} \times 100$	Total Cement Production in MT	Total Steel Production in MT	$\frac{\text{Cement}}{\text{Steel}} \times 100$	Total Cement Production in MT	Total Steel Production in MT	$\frac{\text{Cement}}{\text{Steel}} \times 100$	Total Cement Production in MT	Total Steel Production in MT	$\frac{\text{Cement}}{\text{Steel}} \times 100$
1. U.S.S.R															
2. U.S.A.															
3. Japan															
4. West Germany															
5. U.K.															
6. Italy															
7. France															
8. Spain															
9. India															

TABLE 7.2.1 : Production, storage, despatches and self-consumption analysis

Environment : Inventory *Industry* : Cement
Frequency : Yearly *Year* :

States/Factories	Storage capacity	Production (M.T.)	Despatches	Self-consumption	Closing stock (M.T.)	Wastage in Godown (M.T.)

TABLE 7.3.1 : **Production, wagon-quota indented, received and loaded analysis**

Environment : Transport *Industry* : Cement
Frequency : Half-yearly *Month and Year* :

Regions	Production (M.T.)	Wagon Quota (Nos.)	Wagon indented (Nos.)	Wagon loaded No. Qty. (MT)	Wagon received (Nos.)
East					
1. Assam					
2. Bihar					
3. W. Bengal					
North					
1. U.P.					
2. Punjab					
3. Haryana					
West					
1. Maharashtra					
2. Gujarat					
South					
1. Andhra Pradesh					
2. Tamil Nadu					
3. Karnataka					

TABLE 7.4.1 : **Water availability and requirement analysis**

Environment : Technology *Industry* : Cement
Frequency : Yearly *Year* :

State/ District	Rainfall (mm)	River/canal resources		Cusecs of water required/tonne of production		Year
		Cusecs	Distance (km)	Wet process	Dry process	

TABLE 7.4.2 : **Consumption norms of different inputs by various countries**

Environment : Technology | *Industry* : Cement

Frequency : Annual | *Year* :

Country	Technology		Limestone required/ tonne of production	Coal required/ tonne of production	Gypsum/ tonne of production	Power/ tonne of production	Manpower/ tonne of production	Remarks
	Wet	Dry						
1. U.S.S.R.								
2. U.S.A.								
3. U.K.								
4. W. Germany								
5. Japan								
6. Italy								
7. France								
8. Spain								
9. India								

TABLE 7.4.3 : **Regional distribution of cement analysis**

Environment : Distribution *Industry* : Cement
Frequency : Quarterly *Month and Year* :

Column (Region)	Total Installed capacity	Total production	Despatches from other regions (North)					
			Punjab	Haryana	U.P.	Delhi	J.K.	Etc.
East								
Assam								
South								
Andhra Pradesh								
West								
(i) Maharashtra								
(ii) Gujarat								
North								
Punjab								

TABLE 7.4.4 : **Allocation to regions and sectors as per demand**

Environment : Distribution *Frequency* : Yearly *Industry* : Cement *Year* :

Regions/ Sectors	1981			1982			1983		1984	
							Total		Total	
	Demanded	Supplied	D/S	Demanded	Supplied	D/S	Demand	Supply	Demand	Supply
North										
(i) Punjab										
(ii) Haryana										
South										
(i) Andhra Pradesh										
(ii) Karnataka										
East										
(i) Assam										
(ii) Bihar										
West										
(i) Gujarat										
(ii) Maharashtra										
Defence										
Railways										
Housing										
Agriculture										
Communication										
Industry										

TABLE 7.5.1 : Handling and packing analysis

Environment : Handling and Packing
Frequency : Quarterly

Industry : Cement
Month and Year :

Name of the Factory	January-March			April-June		
	Quantity handled in MT	Cost on handling & packing in Rs.	Cost of handling per tonne of cement	Quantity handled MT	Cost of handling & packing in Rs.	Cost of handling & packing per tonne of cement

ANNEXURE V

SUMMARY DATA FILE FOR CEMENT INDUSTRY
(input-output information matrix)

Item of Information	Source/Agency	Output/ Tables (spl. purpose only)	Re-marks
1	2	3	4
1. Name of district where limestone quarry located	Geological Survey of India/Bureau of Mines	7.1.1	
2. Production of limestone	Geological Survey of India/D.G. Bureau of Mines	7.1.1	
3. Cement and Steel production countrywise	U.N. Statistical Bulletin on Industrial Production	7.1.2	
4. Storage capacity	States Civil Supplies Deptt./factories	7.2.1	
5. OB and CB	Factories	7.3.1	
6. Production	D.G.T.D./Dte. of Industries	7.3.1	
7. Despatches	State Civil Supplies Deptt./factories	7.3.1	
8. Production	Controller of Cement	7.3.1	
9. Wagon required/ allotted	Railways	7.3.1	
10. Rainfall (yearly)	Deptt. of Meteorology	7.4.1	
11. Water availability (river)	River Valley Project/State-Government	7.4.1	
12. R.M. per tonne of production, i.e., norms by various countries	Cement Manufacturers Association/DGTD	7.4.2	
13. Quantity produced/ received	Civil Supplies Deptt./Controller of Cement	7.4.3	
14. Distribution to regions/sectors	Concerned sectors/State civil supplies/Controller of Cement	7.4.4	
15. Handling and Packing cost	Factories	7.5.1	

Note : All Tables refer to Annexure IV.

ANNEXURE VI

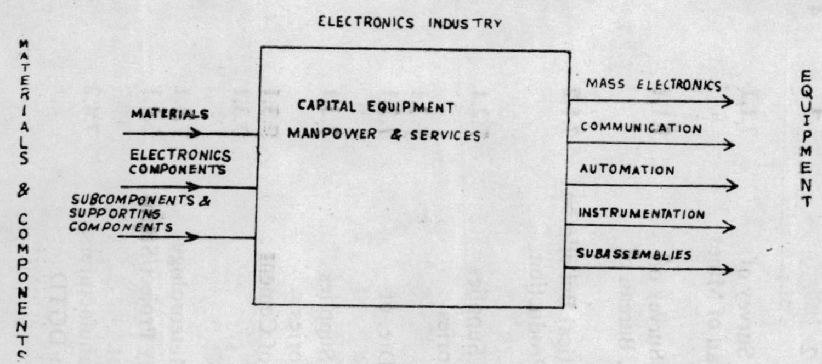

FIG. 7.3 : *Flow diagram for electronics industry (as a multivariate input/output system)*

ANNEXURE VII

TABLE 7.1.1 : **Distribution analysis of production (state-wise)**

Environment : Development Planning
Frequency : Half-Yearly

Industry : Electronics
Month and Year :

State/ Factory	Item	Accounting Unit	Production Jan.-June, 1979		% of total production in the country
			Quantity	Value	

TABLE 7.1.2 : Electronics production-demand analysis (for major user-sectors)

Environment : Development Planning *Frequency* : Yearly *Industry* : Electronics *Year* :

Users	Name of Item	Accounting Unit	Production during—1979		Requirement during—1979	
			Quantity	Value	Required	Supplied
Defence						
Telecommunication						
Atomic Energy						
National Laboratories						
Hospitals						

TABLE 7.1.3 : Analysis on distribution of production (between various sectors)

Environment : Development Planning
Frequency : Half-Yearly
Industry : Electronics
Month and Year :

Item of Production	Accounting Unit	Production Jan.-June—79		Production in Public sector (Jan.-June)		% in value	Production in small-scale sector (Jan.-June)		% in value	Production organized sector (Jan.-June)		% in value
		Qty.	Value	Qty.	Value		Qty.	Value		Qty.	Value	

TABLE 7.2.1 : **Technology import analysis**

Environment : Technology Development
Frequency : Yearly

Industry : Electronics
Year :

Item	Country of origin	Import			Payment for know-how			Annual turnover in value	Know-how payment as % of annual turn-over
		A/C Unit	Quantity	Value	Lumpsum	Royalty	Total		

TABLE 7.2.2 : **R and D expenses analysis**

Environment : Technology Development
Frequency : Yearly

Industry : Electronics
Year :

Product group (Major Product)	R & D expenditure in last year for the industry	Annual turn-over for the industry	R & D expenditure as % of total turnover	Norm for R & D expense	Difference (5–4)
1	2	3	4	5	6

TABLE 7.2.3 : **Cost comparison analysis on import content**

Environment : Technology Development *Frequency* : Yearly *Industry* : Electronics *Year* :

Item	Average cost/ Unit of indigenous product	F.E. content	% of F.E. cost of item	C.I.F. cost of imported equivalent item	Indian cost as % of CIF cost	D.G.T.D. norm

TABLE 7.2.4 : **Cost analysis for indigenous technology development**

Environment : Technology Development *Frequency* : Half-Yearly *Industry* : Electronics *Month and Year* :

Process/ Product	Agency/ Lab.	Work started in	Work completed in	Cost of know-how	Feedback from user

TABLE 7.2.5 : **Analysis of technology performance**

Environment : Technology Development *Frequency* : Half-Yearly *Industry* : Electronics *Month and Year* :

Process/ Product	Agency/ Laboratory	Work started in	Current status	Likely time of completion	If completed whether production started

TABLE 7.3.1 : Export prospect analysis

Environment Division : Trade
Frequency : Yearly

Industry : Electronics
Year :

Item	Accounting unit	Export during the year		Per unit value	Export during last year		Per unit value	% increase or decrease	Corresponding international price	Ratio 8/4	Companies exporting
		Qty.	Value		Qty.	Value					
1	2	3	4	5	6	7	8	9	10	11	12

TABLE 7.3.2 : Export surplus analysis

Environment Division : Trade
Frequency : Yearly

Industry : Electronics
Year :

Item	Licensed capacity	Installed capacity	Accounting unit	Production last year		Estimated production this year		Export surplus
				Quantity	Value	Quantity	Value	

TABLE 7.3.3 : Trade agreements information analysis

Environment : Trade
Frequency : Yearly

Industry : Electronics
Year :

Product Group	Countries with which agreement has been signed	Volume of trade		Import last year		Export last year	
		Quantity with accounting unit	Value	Quantity	Value	Quantity	Value

TABLE 7.3.4 : Finance availability analysis

Environment : Trade
Frequency : Quarterly

Industry : Electronics
Month and Year :

Total finance for Electronics Export Production yearly	Amount spent/committed till the end of last quarter	Amount available for use in next quarter

ANNEXURE VIII

SUMMARY DATA FILE FOR ELECTRONICS INDUSTRY

Item of Information	Source/Agency	Output Table Nos. (special purpose only)	Remarks
1	2	3	4
1. Name of State/district where industry located	Deptt. of Electronics	7.1.1	
2. Production of electronics item	DGTD/Deptt. of Electronics	7.1.2	
3. Demand by users	Deptt. of Electronics	7.1.2	
4. Production in different sectors	DGTD/DCSSI	7.1.3	
5. Technology gap	CSIR/NRDC/Collaboration bond (SIA)	7.2.1	
6. R and D expenses	Concerned Factories/Electronics Deptt./CSIR	7.2.2	
7. Cost comparison	DGTD	7.2.3	
8. Status of technology in development	CSIR	7.2.4	
9. Cost of know-how	-do-	7.2.5	
10. Export statistics	DGCIS Bulletin/Vol. I	7.3.1	
11. Per unit value	-do-	7.3.2	
12. Export surplus	Export Promotion Council/ DGTD	7.3.2	
13. Trade agreement	Ministry of Commerce	7.3.3	
14. Amount spent till last year for export production	Ministry of Commerce/ E.P.C./Ministry of I.D.	7.3.4	

Note : All Tables refer to Annexure VII.

ANNEXURE IX

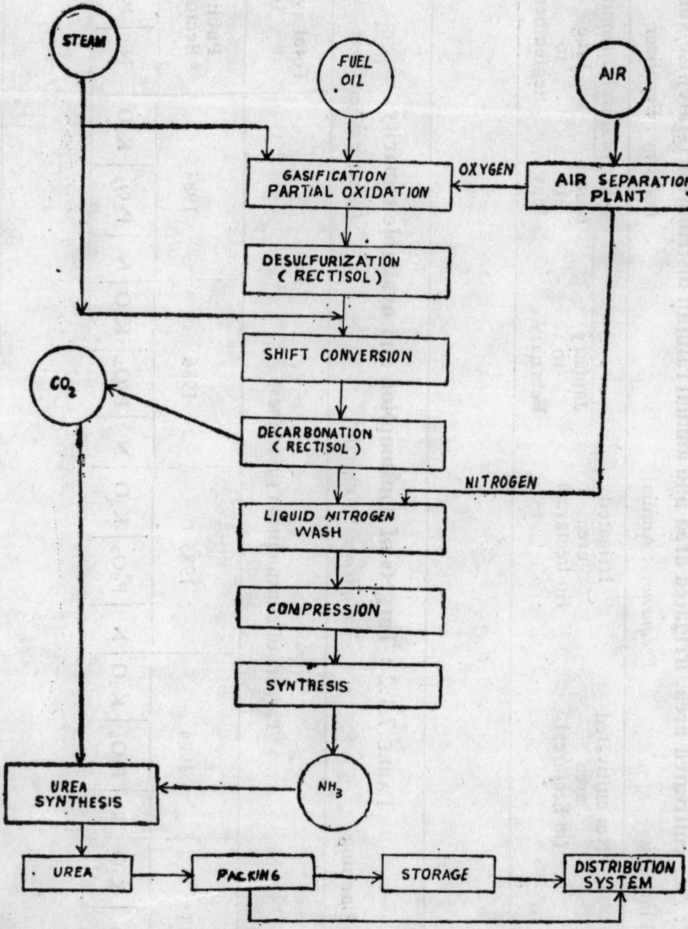

FIG. 7.4 : *Flow diagram for fertilizer industry (using fuel oil partial oxidation process)*

ANNEXURE X

TABLE 7.1.1 : Net cultivated area, irrigated area and annual rainfall distribution (statewise/sub-divisionwise)

Environment : Planning *Frequency* : Annual *Industry* : Fertilizer *Year* :

States/ Sub-division	Net cultivated area (in hectares)	Irrigated area (in hectares)	Annual rainfall in mm			
			January to February	March to May	June to September	October to December

TABLE 7.1.2 : Targets of consumption and available capacity

Environment : Planning *Frequency* : Annual *Industry* : Fertilizer *Year* :

State	Targets of consumption (in tonnes)															Total available capacity (in tonnes)			
	1983			1984			1985			1986			1987			Public Sector		Private Sector	
		P_2O_5	K_2O	N	P_2O_5	K_2O	N	P_2O_5	K_2O	N	P_2O_5	K_2O	N	P_2O_5	K_2O	N	P_2O_5	N	P_2O_5

TABLE 7.2.1 : **Fertilizers quality control analysis**

Environment : Production control
Frequency : Ad hoc

Industry : Fertilizer
Month & Year :

Fertilizer Material	Specification as per control order of 1957		
	Moisture % by weight	Nutrient content	Etc.
1. Superphosphate Triple etc.			

TABLE 7.2.2 : Analysis of nutrient contents of fertilizers

Environment : Production control | *Industry* : Fertilizer
Frequency : Ad hoc | *Month & Year* :

Sl. No.	Materials	Total Nitrogenous	Total Phosphate	Total lime	Total magnesia	Water-soluble potash	Etc.
1.	Nitrogenous Material						
	(i) Ammonia Anhydrous						
	(ii) Ammonium chloride						
	(iii) Ammonium Nitrate						
2.	Phosphorus Materials						
	(i) Basic slag, Bessemer						
	(ii) Dicalcium phosphate						
3.	Potassium Materials						
	(i) Potassium chloride						
	(ii) Potassium sulphate						
4.	Nitrogen phosphorus materials						
	(i) Ammoniated super-phosphate (ordinary)						
	(ii) -do- (Triple or concentrated)						

TABLE 7.3.1 : Handling and packing analysis

Environment : Handling & Packing *Industry* : Fertilizer
Frequency : Monthly *Month and Year* :

Name of the Plant	January			February		
	Quality handled (tonnes)	Handling in packing cost	Handling & packing cost per tonne	Quality handled (tonnes)	Handling & packing cost	Handling & packing cost per tonne

TABLE 7.4.1 : Distribution cost analysis

Environment : Distribution *Industry* : Fertilizer
Frequency : Half-yearly *Month and Year* :

States	Period I			Period II		
	Quantity distribution (tonnes)	Cost of distribution	Distribution cost per tonne	Quantity distributed (tonnes)	Cost of distribution	Distribution cost per tonne

TABLE 7.4.2 : Statewise distribution and foodgrain targets

Environment : Distribution *Frequency* : Annual *Industry* : Fertilizer *Year* :

States	Period I							Period II						
	Foodgrain targets (M. tonnes)	Quantity of fertilizers supplied (M. tonnes)			$\frac{\text{Quantity supplied}}{\text{targets}} \times 100$			Foodgrain targets (M. tonnes)	Quantity of fertilizers supplied (M. tonnes)			$\frac{\text{Quantity supplied}}{\text{targets}} \times 100$		
		N	P_2O_5	K_2O	N	P_2O_5	K_2O		N	P_2O_5	K_2O	N	P_2O_5	K_2O

TABLE 7.5.1 : Warehousing capacity availability analyses

Environment : Storage *Frequency* : Annual *Industry* : Fertilizer *Year* :

State/Union Territory	Number of warehouses		Capacity (tonnes)	
	Central	State	Central	State

ANNEXURE XI

SUMMARY DATA FILE FOR FERTILIZER INDUSTRY

Item of Information	Source/Agency	Related output tables (special purpose only)	Remarks
1	2	3	4
1. Net cultivated area	Ministry of Food and Agriculture, Directorate of Economics and Statistics	7.1.1	
2. Irrigated area	-do-	7.1.1	
3. Annual rainfall	-do-	7.1.1	
4. Targets of consumption for each fertilizer	Ministry of Petroleum and Chemicals	7.1.2	
5. Available capacity separately for public sector and private sector	(i) Ministry of Petroleum and Chemicals (ii) D.G.T.D.	7.1.2	
6. Specification for fertilizers materials	(i) Ministry of Food and Agriculture (ii) Indian Standards Institution	7.2.1	
7. Nutrient contents of various fertilizer materials	Ministry of Food and Agriculture	7.2.2	
8. Handling and packing cost	Fertilizer Plants	7.3.1	
9. Quantity of fertilizer distributed	Central Fertilizer Pool of the Ministry of Food and Agriculture	7.4.1 & 7.4.2	
10. Cost of distribution	-do-	7.4.1	
11. Foodgrain targets	Ministry of Food and Agriculture	7.4.2	
12. No. of warehouses	-do-	7.5.1	
13. Capacity of warehouses	-do-	7.5.1	

Note : All Tables refer to Annexure X.

ANNEXURE XII

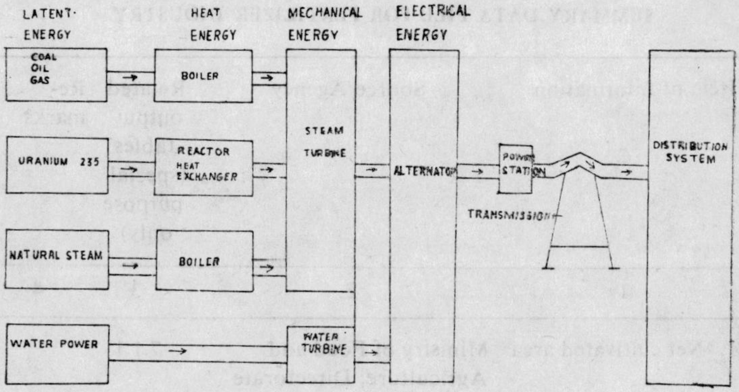

Fig. 7.5 : *Flow diagram for power industry*

ANNEXURE XIII

TABLE 7.1.1 : Analysis on resource utilization

Environment : Power Generation | *Type* : Hydel
Frequency : Monthly | *Plant location* :
Month and Year :

Period	Energy generated in KWHr	Water released in 1000 cusecs	KWHr/ 1000 cusecs	Norm	Variation

TABLE 7.1.2 : Analysis on irrigation needs

Environment : Power Generation | *Type* : Hydel
Frequency : Monthly | *Plant location* :
Month and Year :

Period	Water released in 1000 cusecs	Water as desired for irrigation in 1000 cusecs	Required-Released/ Required

TABLE 7.1.3 : **Analysis on load requirements**

Environment : Power Generation   *Type* : Hydel/Thermal
Frequency : Monthly   *Plant location* :
Month and Year :

Period	Energy generat-ed in KWHr	Power generat-ed in MW	Max. energy demand-ed in KWHr	Power demand-ed in MW	Energy-generat-ed demand	Power-generat-ed demand

TABLE 7.1.4 : **Analysis on plant reliability**

Environment : Power Generation   *Type* : Hydel/Thermal/Nuclear
Frequency : Monthly   *Plant location* :
Month and Year :

Period	Duration of breakdowns in ½ Hr interval	Frequency of breakdown

TABLE 7.1.5 : **Analysis on fuel utilization**

Environment : Power Generation   *Type* : Thermal/Nuclear
Frequency : Monthly   *Plant location* :
Month and Year :

Period	Energy gene-rated in KW Hr	Fuel consumed in tonnes/kg.	KWHr/ tonnes/kg	Norm	Variation

TABLE 7.1.6 : **Analysis on utilization and efficiency**

Environment : Power Generation   *Type* : Thermal/Nuclear
Frequency : Monthly   *Plant location* :
Month and Year :

Period	Energy generated in KW Hr.	Energy gene-rated if the plant were to operate at full capacity	Ratio	Man Hrs spent in plant	KWHr/ man Hr.	Norm

TABLE 7.2.1 : Analysis of transmission loss

Environment : Power Transmission *Month & Year* :
Frequency : Monthly *Region* :

Region	Period	Energy fed to the system in KWHr.	Energy metered as users end in KW Hr.	Loss in %	Norm

TABLE 7.2.2 : Analysis of capacity utilization

Environment : Power Transmission *Month & Year* :
Frequency : Monthly *Region* :

Region	Period	Energy fed to other grids in KWHr.	Energy generated in KW Hr.	Energy obtained from other grid in KW Hr.	Shortage (surplus) as % of energy generated

TABLE 7.2.3 : Analysis of system reliability

Environment : Power Transmission *Month & Year* :
Frequency : Monthly

Region	Period	Duration of breakdowns in ½ hr. intervals	Frequency of breakdown

TABLE 7.3.1 : Analysis of distribution

Environment : Distribution *Month & Year* :
Frequency : Monthly

State	Period	Energy fed to State in KWHr.	Energy metered in KWHr.	Loss as % of Energy fed	Norm

TABLE 7.3.2 : **Analysis of shortfalls/industrial production due to short supply of power**

Environment : Distribution *Month & Year* :
Frequency : Monthly

State	Period	Energy fed to State in KWHr.	Energy demand in KWHr.	% shortage (if any)	Anticipated production loss in major sectors due to shortage

TABLE 7.3.3 : **Analysis of system reliability**

Environment : Distribution *Month & Year* :
Frequency : Monthly

State	Period	Duration of Breakdowns in ½ hr. Intervals	Frequency of Breakdown

TABLE 7.3.4 : **Analysis of electrification effort**

Environment : Distribution
Frequency : Yearly

State	Period	Total No. of villages electrified	Total No. of villages in the State	% of villages electrified	Corresponding figure for last year	Target for this year

TABLE 7.3.5 : **Analysis of benefit to population**

Environment : Distribution *Year* :
Frequency : Yearly

State	Period	Total energy consumed in KW Hr.	Total population benefited by electrification	Total population of State	Per capita consumption of Electricity	% population benefiting

TABLE 7.3.6 : **Analysis impact on agriculture**

Environment : Distribution *Year* :
Frequency : Yearly

State	Period	No. of tubewells electrified	Total no. of tube-wells in State	% of tubewells electrified		
				This year	Target	Last year

TABLE 7.3.7 : **Analysis of energy consumption sectorwise**

Environment : Distribution *Month & Year* :
Frequency : Yearly

State	Period	Total energy consump-tion in KW Hr.	Major sectors	Energy consump-tion in KW Hr in that sector	Output in qty.	Energy con-sumption per unit	Sector consump-tion as % of total energy

ANNEXURE XIV

SUMMARY DATA FILE FOR POWER INDUSTRY

Data Input	Source	Related out-put table
1	2	3
1. Daily discharge of water	State Electricity Board	7.1.1
2. Daily energy generation	,,	7.1.1, 7.1.3, 7.1.5, 7.1.6
3. Daily water demanded for irrigation from the station	State Irrigation Department	7.1.2
4. Energy generated and obtained by the grid to meet the load	State Electricity Board	7.2.2
5. Duration of all breakdowns during the month	,,	7.2.3
6. Quantity of fuel at the station at the end of period	,,	7.1.5

ANNEX. XIV—*contd.*

1	2	3
7. Quantity of fuel at the station at the end of period	State Electricity Board	7.1.5
8. Daily man hours spent in the station	,,	7.1.6
9. Rated capacity of the plant	,,	7.1.6
10. Daily Energy fed to the system from every station in the region	,,	7.2.1
11. Energy which has been metered every month in the region	,,	7.2.1
12. Energy consumed by the region	,,	7.2.2
13. Energy shortage if any in the region	,,	7.2.2
14. Duration of breakdowns due to transmission failures in the region	,,	7.2.3
15. Daily energy demand by domestic users	,,	7.3.5
16. Daily energy demand by industrial users	,,	7.3.7
17. No. of villages electrified in the State	,,	7.3.4
18. Total No. of villages in the State	State Agriculture Dept/CWPC	7.3.4
19. Population benefited by electrification in the State	State Electricity Board	7.3.5
20. State population	Census Department	7.3.5
21. No. of tubewells electrified in the State	State Electricity Board	7.3.6
22. No. of tubewells in the State	State Agriculture Deptt.	7.3.6
23. Total energy consumption in the State	State Electricity Board	7.3.7
24. Energy metered	State Electricity Board	7.3.1
25. Energy fed to the State	State Electricity Board	7.3.1
26. Duration of breakdowns due to distribution failures in the State	State Electricity Board	7.3.3

8

INFORMATION SYSTEM FOR SOCIAL SCIENCES

8.1 Background

The objective of a social science information system is to store, process and disseminate planning and control information on social sciences on a selective basis. The system is designed to acquire organized data in a processed form, subject to the criteria of urgency, broad basis and inter-disciplinary nature, and diffuse such information to national planners, policy-makers and research scientists in need of it. The information is meant to include basic census and detailed socio-economic data.

The following problems peculiar to the Indian situation have been noted by the Indian Council of Social Sciences Research (ICSSR) :

(a) Shortage of trained manpower;

(b) Limited access to data produced by major data-producing agencies due to non-availability of the specified data format in which data can be easily utilized by social scientists ; and

(c) Limited access to computing and software facilities for social science data processing.

Keeping in view the above problems, the ICSSR initiated a programme of data archives, with a view to improving the quality of social sciences research in India. The following objectives have been stipulated for this programme :

(a) To acquire, organize and manage data sets relating to social science research ;
(b) To acquire and develop computer programmes, so as to facilitate computer processing of social science data, and help in the task of managing and transforming data sets ;
(c) To organize training courses in the application of computer in social science research ;
(d) To act as a *liaison* between official data-producing agencies and social scientists in order to incorporate the research interests of social scientists in data gathering and tabulating efforts of these agencies ;
(e) To provide consultancy services to those social scientists who may require such assistance in computer processing of data ; and
(f) To establish collaborative relations with social science data archives abroad.

8.2 General methodology

The national information system for social sciences, in consonance with other management information systems, should comprise :

(a) General Historical Records, i.e. acquisition, classification and maintenance of data and its analysis ;
(b) Communication of relevant results to the decision-makers.

8.3 General historical records

A large number of research objects are either completed or are under active progress, as financed by the ICSSR. An inventory of such studies is available, but it appears that no systematic evaluation has been done to assess the following from the above research projects :

(a) Types of variables on which data have been collected or utilized in the research projects ;
(b) Listing of the above variables in order of sequence for centralized data needs ; and

(c) Codification and storage of the data through appropriate card designs.

The general historical records can be used to generate the following types of information :

(a) Primary Information, and
(b) Secondary Information.

As regards original information, the same are obtainable from the following sources :

(a) Research Projects which have been funded by the ICSSR after being sponsored by various social science institutions ;
(b) Research Projects which fall in priority programmes and are directly sponsored by the ICSSR ; and
(c) Research Projects which are carried out in different social science centres recognized by the ICSSR and other academic institutions and organizations.

The information, which was originally meant for use for certain other objectives and which can be used also for social science research, is termed secondary information. The sources for such information are :

(a) Registrar-General of India (responsible for Census data) :
Literacy ; Religion ; Sex ; Migration ; Occupation Structure ; Industry Classification ; Residential Status ; Mother Tongue.
(b) National Sample Survey Organization :
(30 rounds of survey) :
Household Composition—urban/rural ; Consumer Expenditure ; Income/Expenditure and Indebtedness ; Capital Formation ; Transport Facilities ; Land Litigation ; Land Holdings ; Small-Scale Industries and Handicrafts ; Livestock Holding.

(c) Reserve Bank of India :

Rural credit survey ; cost benefit studies relating to, tubewells in Punjab ; field study to assess benefits from construction of wells and pump sets ; banking facilities ; determination of norms ; assessment of repaying capacity and valuation of hypotheses.

(d) Commissioner of Scheduled Castes and Scheduled Tribes :

Representation in services ; Educational Development ; Eradication of Untouchability, Protective Legislation ; Allotment of land to landless labour.

(e) Directorate of Economics and Statistics, Ministry of Agriculture :

Cultivation—cost of principal crops ; agro-economic research coordination ; crop-estimation surveys ; *ad hoc* agricultural and livestock census (under the aegis of F.A.O.) ; market intelligence on arrivals, sales, prices, etc ; assessment and evaluation of Intensive Agricultural District Programme (IADP).

Apart from the above organizations, some foreign scholars working in India and some Indian scholars working abroad under the aegis of foreign institutions and organizations do social science research, although the objectives may be laid down by the foreign institutions.

There has been a proposal from the ICSSR to centrally collect and store social science information as derived from the above general historical records (both primary and secondary). For this purpose, an assessment has been made of the likely number of data cards from the different institutions which will be stored. Also, some of the organizations such as Reserve Bank have been requested by the ICSSR to "freeze" their existing records and documents containing social science information, so that later on, these could be used for preparing central data archives. An important point, however, is that at this moment the assessment is far from complete as to what will constitute the data that will go into the central data archives. Above all, in the absence of a records-selection process in gathering and storing information, it may be difficult to visualize completely computerized data archives.

Perhaps an electro-mechanical or even cardex system may be called for if volumes of raw data are decided to be kept in any central data archives at a future date.

8.4 Communication functions

Communication functions are the quantitative measures for deriving processed information from the raw data in as systematic and condensed a manner as possible and their distribution, when relevant, to the decision-makers. With this aim in view, the general historical records can be taken as an inventory for raw data from which formal information can be derived for use by the following :

(a) Decision-makers in the different central Ministries, Departments and Divisions, and various Directorates in the Central and State Governments ;

(b) The Planning Commission for purposes of multilevel and perspective planning activities ; and

(c) Social science researchers who are looking for guidance and assistance from a centralized data-gathering and processing system available centrally to all research scientists in the country.

Besides the above categories of users, processed information from the central data bank can also be made available to the regional Social Science Centres as a feed-back process, first, to apprise them of the trends and patterns of research that have emerged with an all-India character, and, secondly, even to furnish them with an information base which will be of special interest to them in the form of analysis of both temporal and spatial character.

As is well known, no clear-cut approach exists by which information indicators can be derived for the above users from the mass of social science data. Also, the prevalent feeling in India is that most of the social science data collected have to be rigorously screened for their reliability and homogeneity before deducing any general inferences from this data. Moreover, the sample size is to be checked for its efficiency in ascribing confidence in the results derived. Finally, the environments in which studies are carried out have to be critically checked before drawing general conclusions. In other words, any general information indicator must have built-in safeguards for applying corrections for sample-size, sample-reliability, sample-homogeneity and sample-environment.

With the above limitations in view, it is useful in the Indian situation to have a look at the regional research studies done in various social science centres to find out as to whether such a study contains any information from among the various factors studied, which would be of some interest to the users categorized above. In other words, the relevance for central needs is an acid test which is to be applied before data can be processed for deriving aggregated information measures for users of the centralized data bank. Once this test is applied sample information indicators can be derived from the relevant factors by applying such measures as percentage frequencies, relative distributions, etc. Beyond this stage, it should also be possible to aggregate some of these sample information indicators into one or more compound indicators to increase their relevance for central needs.

It will be desirable to store both simple and compound information indicators in a centralized data bank so that meaningful communication functions can be derived out of them for the potential users, as outlined above. In the matter of their future use, one has to start from the proposed research project (which can also include the planning exercise) and to segregate factors proposed to be investigated. Then, there has to be an exercise to identify either simple or compound information indicators from the storage data files which can be related to the proposed factors for investigation. Once this relationship is established, there should be no difficulty in retrieving only the relevant information indicators and make them available for use. Due caution, however, is needed to note down the specific scope of the proposed study inclusive of its size of samples, its environmental limitations, and both reliability and homogeneity of the samples. The aggregated information indicator is to be suitably modified at this stage to make any statistical sense in its specific applications.

8.5 Decision-flow diagram

The general methodology as explained above can be represented in the form of decision-flow diagrams. The main features of the flow diagram for information storage are the following :

(a) Social Science Centres are listed and the current social science projects identified ;
(b) The sample-size, the sample-reliability, the sample-homogeneity and the sample-environment are noted to take into account the limitations of the research project ;
(c) Factors investigated are selected one by one to adjudge their relevance for Central Information needs ;
(d) If any of the factors are adjudged so relevant simple information indicators are derived from individual factors in the form of percentage frequencies, etc ;
(e) Compound information indicators, whenever feasible, are derived from a combination of multiple factors to increase their relevance for central information needs ;
(f) Corrections are applied to the information indicators for the limitations mentioned at (b) above ;
(g) Forms are prepared for storing the above information indicators in the data "files" ; and
(h) Software (in the form of programming) is developed to actually storing relevant indicators in the storage data files.

The main features of the flow diagram for information retrieval are the following:

(a) The proposed social science projects (inclusive of planning and decision-making exercises) are listed ;
(b) The limitations such as sample-size, sample-homogeneity, sample-reliability and sample-environment are noted in the proposed project ;
(c) The major factors proposed for investigation are identified and examined in respect of their relationship centralized information already stored ;
(d) If some information in the centralized data files are found to be also related, the information is retrieved ;
(e) The retrieved information of an aggregated nature is

then clarified for the specific limitations for the proposed study ;

(f) Retrieved information is presented as data sets to their potential users.

8.6 Illustrative studies

Eventually a national information system for social sciences is to be gradually developed to gather, store and retrieve processed information. Assuming that a systematic machinery can be evolved to achieve this, it should be possible to build up a centralized data bank from both the primary and the secondary data. The secondary type of information can be easily collected from their parent organizations and stored with minimal processing in the centralized data file. On the other hand, it will require comprehensive efforts to gather and store processed information from the primary information available in the social science projects available in published and unpublished forms in various research centres in the country.

In order to provide illustrations as to how the latter process can be achieved, a brief exercise was undertaken for identifying simple information indicators and deriving compound information indicators from a few selected social science research projects from the following social science centres :

(1) The Centre for Study of Developing Societies, Delhi ;
(2) The Tata Institute of Social Sciences, Bombay ;
(3) The University of Bombay, Department of Economics, Bombay ; and
(4) The Gokhale Institute of Politics and Economics, Pune.

The yardstick for selecting the above Centres was the volume of studies undertaken. The criteria for selection of the social science projects in each Centre were the following :

(a) Were the projects of national importance already or were they capable of being pooled together for such purposes?
(b) Were the projects of inter-disciplinary nature?
(c) Were they sufficiently urgent in today's context?

Based on the above criteria, the following projects were selected for study from the above four different institutions :

(a) *The Centre for Study of Developing Societies, Delhi :*

General Elections in India—1967, 1969 (Mid-term Elections), and 1971.

(b) *The Tata Institute of Social Sciences, Bombay :*

(i) sociology of Education ;
(ii) study of Scheduled Caste and Scheduled Tribe Students at Schools and Colleges ;
(iii) family Composition Studies ;
(iv) professional Social Workers in India—Employment Position and Functions ;
(v) village profile.

(c) *The University of Bombay, Department of Economics, Bombay :*

(i) evaluation of Land Reforms ;
(ii) urban Labour Market in a Developed Economy (with reference to Bombay) ;
(iii) analysis of Trade Policies in India ;
(iv) linkages and Industrialization in the ECAFE countries ;
(v) exports from India under the General Scheme of Preference ;
(vi) inter-Regional Planning Model for Trade Cooperation in ECAFE countries ;
(vii) economics of Scale in the Indian Manufacturing Industry ;
(viii) capacity utilization in Indian Industry ;
(ix) effects of Public Expenditure with special reference to Education and Health ;
(x) evaluation of Indian Fiscal System.

(d) *The Gokhale Institute of Politics and Economics, Pune :*

(i) construction of an Input-Output Table for India, 1963 ;
(ii) land Resources in relation to Population in India ;
(iii) compilation of Forest Resources in a State (with reference to Maharashtra) ;

(iv) income, Saving and Investment in a District (with reference to Ahmadnagar) ;

(v) evaluation of Small Farms, Development Agencies (SFDA) in a district (with reference to Mysore) ;

(vi) socio-Economic Studies of the Scheduled Castes in a State Rural Area (with reference to Maharashtra) ;

(vii) crash Scheme for Rural Employment and Evaluation of Programmes in a District (with reference to Satara) ;

(viii) impact of Assistance under PL-480 on Indian Economy ;

(ix) youth Policy in a State (with reference to Maharashtra) ;

(x) progress of Literacy in Villages in a State (with reference to Maharashtra) ;

(xi) exploitation of Forests through Forest Labour Co-operatives.

As will be evident from the above, most of the research projects selected were of national importance. In a few cases, the projects were such that although they pertained to a region, they were capable of being usefully extended for a nation-wide study. Also, the projects covered such diverse disciplines as sociology, politics, psychology, economics, education, commerce, forestry and labour relations. Lastly, most of the studies could be interpreted as sufficiently urgent in today's socio-economic context.

8.7 Analysis of studies

The results of the exercise on the illustrative studies are presented in Table 8.1 (for the Centre for Study of Development Societies, Delhi), Tables 8.2 to 8.6 (for the Tata Institute of Social Sciences, Bombay), Tables 8.7 to 8.16 (for the University of Bombay, Department of Economics, Bombay) and Tables 8.17 to 8.27 (for the Gokhale Institute of Poli ics and Economics, Pune).

The standard design used in presenting the above analysis has the following features :

(a) Names of the study centres and the selected research projects ;

(b) The sample period and the sampling pattern (the universe of the sample, the nature of sampling, etc.) ;

(c) The listing of the compound information indicators (as derived from multiple factors) ;
(d) Simple information indicators (as derived from single factors) ;
(e) Quantitative measures that can be used to derive the above information indicators.

From the analysis, it will be seen that most quantitative measures of the information indicators are of the nature of percentage frequencies. Very often, simple averages can be worked out from these percentage frequencies. In other cases where data are more reliable, both trend analysis and regression pattern can be used. Before storing the indicators in the computerized data files, it is possible to perform tests of reliability and homogeneity on the indicators.

8.8 Standardization of social indicators

Work on standardizing social indicators has been under progress for some time and it is useful to take note of this situation for their eventual use in the computerized information system for social sciences. The United Nations Research Institute for Social Development, Geneva, carried out in June 1968, a review of the recent and current studies conducted on evolving indicators. These were related to social and demographic aspects (health and demographic, nutrition, education, housing and communications) and economic aspects (transport and services, agriculture, industry, trade and general), growth rates aspects and topological aspects. Table 8.5 presents a summary of these indicators.

Attempts are being made to develop social indicators pertaining to various aspects of Indian national life for some time. These relate to the demographic aspect, social structure aspect, political development aspect, economic life aspect, education and progress aspect, wealth aspect, public order and safety aspect, science and technological aspect, environmental aspect, cultural and literary aspect, and social welfare aspect. The work on the last aspect, for instance, is in progress at the Tata Institute of Social Sciences, Bombay, and a tentative formulation of the social indicators at that Institute is given at Table 8.6.

Once the various working groups for the social indicators relating to the above aspects finalize their formulations, it will be worthwhile to apply these indicators for gathering, processing, storing and retrieving information on social science on a fairly uniform basis.

8.9 Conclusion

To summarize, a General Methodology has been attempted above for national information system on social science based on simple communications functions which can be derived by using the general historical records already available. For this purpose, a distinction has been made between regional information contained in various sponsored and financed research projects carried out at social science centres, and secondary information which is obtainable from such establishments and organizations as the Registrar-General, Reserve Bank of India, etc., which essentially exist to meet other national needs than pure social science research. Concentrating on the original information, the approach consists in pinpointing specific research projects, selecting the factors investigated, finding out their relevance for central needs and deriving information indicators in simple as well as aggregated form from these factors. The approach also visualizes corrections for sample size, sample homogeneity, sample reliability and sample environment. Once data sets are computerized and stored as data files in the centralized data bank, it will be possible to retrieve relevant information for future social science projects to be used by planners, policy-makers and researchers. When information is retrieved for their potential use, some qualifications have to be applied to bring the information indicators down to the level of the specific areas of investigation, after taking into account the sample size, sample reliability, sample homogeneity and sample environment for the latter.

As stated earlier, it is to be emphasized that it is not visualized to collect the entire raw data pertaining to the social science research carried out in the country to be stored in the centralized data bank. This is due to the limitations in the computer storage at the centre and also due to the fact that there need not be any central data bank to serve as repository of social science data which are not needed for a national purpose. On the other hand, there can still exist central archives for social science which can store raw data in a mechanical or electro-mechanical form. Secondary data organizations in the form of regional social science centres can still exist to process and store scattered data on social science research which are of great regional interest.

Once the central data bank takes a concrete form, it should be possible to establish relationships among different information of indicators in the form of statistical associations and correlations, relating to the time distribution and space distribution of social science data. In fact, once these relationships and linkages begin to be established, it will be tremendously useful for policy-making and further national investigation of socio-economic factors of an all-India nature.

It is to be expected that the social science indicators for which the approach has been evolved above afford varied criteria for planning and decision-making. There should be a state when computer utilities even at the regional social science centres can be linked on national basis by time—sharing and multi-programming so that processing of the existing data into useful information is possible. These will offer help to the regional social sciences centres with limited computer facilities available at present where large input-output matrices, simulation problems and mathematical programming models with many variables cannot be tackled. Using the central data bank facilities in association with an inter-linked computer utility at various regions, both extensive and intensive social science research studies can be undertaken in future. This will be a direct benefit arising out of the centralized information system of social science.

The above approach does not deal with the input and output organizations for handling the documents before computer processing and after the outputs are received from the computer. The approach does not touch upon the question of the efforts needed for data collection from the regional social science centres which have to be organized well to make the information system a success. Also this approach does not cover such questions as evolving nation-wide social science records (such as "population register") which are not feasible at present for lack of comprehensive data collection and updating facilities.

The following further points should be noted :

(a) The compound information indicators should be evolved only after careful consideration and through a suitable body of experts. Sufficient caution is necessary in this regard, since there is no clear-cut unanimous procedure to evolve such aggregated indicators. Often simple indicators should be more relied upon.

(b) The statistical tests on sample size, sample reliability, sample homogeneity and sample environment should be devised by drawing upon the experience and knowledge of social science research scholars with quantitative background.

(c) The information indicators/storage in the Central Bank data have an identification of the institution from which originated and also the experts or research scholars who originated them, in view of the fact that in social science, there is often more reliance on acknowledged experts than on others.

(d) Before storage of the indicators, the same should be subjected to a rigorous process of selection and screening by experts from the organization which would be expected to use the data bank. Great care need to be exercised to ensure selectivity at this stage.

(e) The information indicators should be reviewed from time to time to decide the time period for which they are to be stored. This review should be done from the viewpoint of necessity for storage as well as frequency of usage.

TABLE 8.1

Centre : Centre for Study of Developing Societies, Delhi.
Study Area : Study of the General Elections in India.
Study Period : 1967, 1969 (Mid-Term Election), 1971 Elections.
Sample Coverage : A total of 7,000 persons covered in villages all over India in 3 studies.
Model : Questionnaires personally administered.

Compound Information Indicators	Simple Information Indicators	Quantitative Measures
1. Political awareness of rural public	Identity of (a) The candidates for the election & their political party (b) The winning candidate for assembly & Parliament (c) The Chief Minister's name (d) The Chief Minister's party (e) The Prime Minister's name (f) The Prime Minister's party	Percentage & ratio distributions
2. Orientation to democratic norms	Views on (a) Necessity of party elections (b) Responsiveness of democratic structure to people's needs (c) Technique of choice of leaders (d) Political efficiency (e) Value of vote (f) Government efficiency in the event of no-party system (g) Awareness & interest in national affairs (h) Party loyalties and strength of attachment (i) Voting behaviour (j) Reasons for specific voting behaviour (k) Media exposure (l) Campaign participation & involvement (m) Radical orientation (leftist/rightist)	—do—
3. Attitude towards modernization	(a) Awareness of family planning needs (b) Adoption of improved agriculture practices (c) Class consciousness and resistance (d) Problem perception	—do—

TABLE 8.2

Centre : Tara Institute of Social Sciences, Bombay.
Study Area : Sociology of Education.
Study Period : 1964-66
Sample Coverage : 8 States of India, 2,300, students, teachers, parents, head masters covered
Mode : Personal interviews

Compound Information Indicators	Simple Information Indicators	Quantitative Measures
1. Social background of respondent groups	Classification in terms of (a) Age (b) Sex (c) Educational status (d) Urban/rural heritage (e) SC/ST (f) Parental education (g) Parental occupation (h) Language spoken, etc.	Relative frequencies, percentage ratios & comparisons in States
2. Attitudes & Aspirations	(a) Expectations of teachers regarding students (b) Students regarding teachers (c) Teachers, students and parents regarding educational systems, etc. (d) Occupational aspirations of students (e) Job satisfaction of teachers, etc.	—do—
3. Social values	Values on relation to (a) Secularism (b) Achievement Orientation (c) Acceptance of citizenship responsibilities (d) Activity approach to life (e) Optimism, etc.	—do—
4. Equality in educational opportunity	As related to (a) SC/ST groups (b) Student/teacher ratio, etc.	—do—

TABLE 8.3

Centre : Tata Institute of Social Sciences, Bombay.
Study Area : Study of Schedule Caste/Schedule Tribe students.
Study Period : 1973 to date
Sample Coverage : 17 States in India (average 400 interviews in each State.)
Mode : Standardized questionnaire, personally administered in all States.

Compound Information Indicators	Simple Information Indicators	Quantitative Measure
1. Social background and composition of respondents	Classification of students in terms of (a) Age (b) Sex (c) Religion (d) Parental education (e) Parental occupation (f) Economic standard of living	Frequency distribution, percentage ratios, comparison in States
2. Academic life of respondents	Information about (a) Choice of a particular discipline (b) Study habits (c) Time devoted to domestic work (d) Facilities for studies (e) Academic performance & gaps (f) Need for special coaching (g) Comprehension of teachers (h) Occupational aspirations (i) Extra-curricular activities, etc.	—do—
3. Social life and outlook of respondents	In relation to (a) Composition of friendship (b) People they admire (c) Experience of discrimination (d) Outlook on marriage (e) Authority of parents (f) Exposure to mass media (g) Politicization	Frequency distribution, percentage ratios, comparison in States
4. Outlook on status and facilities for SC/ST (by both male and female students and comparative)	Views on the adequacy of (a) Reservation in education institution (b) Scholarships for education (c) Hostel accommodation (d) Allocations in jobs in Government (e) Job position in private sector (f) Overall government programme for SC/ST, etc.	—do—

TABLE 8.4

Centre : Tata Institute of Social Sciences, Bombay.
Study Area : Family Compositions in Rural and Urban India.
Study Period : 1954-58
Sample Coverage : 34 City surveys and a large number of rural surveys all over India.
Mode: Personal interview

Compound Information Indicators	Simple Information Indicators	Quantitative Measures
1. Family size	No. of persons per family	Relative frequencies, percentage ratios, cross-section studies
2. Family's sociological typology	Information about (a) Family structure (joint, etc.) (b) Age, sex, marital status of every family member (c) Relation to head of the family (d) Relation and caste of family (e) Educational qualifications of head of the family (f) Occupational status of head of the family, etc.	—do—
3. Family's economic typology	Information related to (a) Worker/Non-worker ratio (b) Permanent dependency (c) Temporary dependency (d) Dependency per earner (e) Income per family (f) Family budget and indebtedness, etc.	—do—

TABLE 8.5

Centre : Tata Institute of Social Sciences, Bombay.
Study Area : Professional social workers in India.
Study Period : 1969-72
Sample Covered : Large number of social workers all over India.
Mode : Personal interview

Compound Information Indicators	Simple Information Indicators	Quantitative Measures
1. Employment History	Information in relation to (a) Number of jobs held (b) Setting in which employed (c) Expectations per job in terms of salaries	Relative frequencies, percentage ratios, etc.
2. Service & Working conditions (Composite index of 29 variables)	Information related to (a) Salaries (b) Allowances (c) Working hours (d) Fringe benefits (e) Professional/Clerical assistance, etc.	—do—
3. Functions	(a) Job details (b) Whether using specialized skills	—do—
4. Views on profession	(a) Employees view on need for training (b) Image of fellow professional workers (c) Employers' views on social workers	—do—

TABLE 8.6

Centre : Tata Institute of Social Sciences, Bombay.
Study Area : Village profile of India.
Study Period : 1962-69
Sample Covered : More than 200 villages covered in all States. 100 per cent coverage for each village
Mode: Personal interviews

Compound Information Indicators	Simple Information Indicators	Quantitative Measures
1. Geographical/ Physical features	Salient (a) Physical features (b) Residential pattern, etc. (c) Average rainfall	Comparative and aggregate ratios & frequency
2. People	In relation to (a) Caste (b) Occupation (c) Houses, etc.	—do—
3. Economy	In relation to (a) Land holding (b) Land utilization (c) Workers/Non-workers ratio (d) Animal husbandry (e) Village crops	—do—
4. Facilities	In relation to (a) Electrification (b) Drinking water schemes (c) Sanitation facilities (d) Irrigation schemes (e) Cooperative store (f) Roads (g) Roadways and Railways connections, etc.	—do—

TABLE 8.7

Centre : Department of Economics, University of Bombay.
Study Area : Evaluation of Land Reforms
Study Period : 1957-1965
Sample Coverage : 48 villages in Gujarat and Maharashtra. 100 per cent coverage of villages.
Mode : Structured interviews.

Compound Information Indicators	Simple Information Indicators	Quantitative Measures
1. Concentration ratio of land holding/ownership	(a) Area of land owned/family (b) No. of fields & plots (c) Profile of landlord in terms of income, caste, education, etc. (d) Investment made on the land	Absolute measures & ratios
2. Land operation	(a) Owner & farmer relationship (b) Irrigation & other facilities (c) Profile of farmer in terms of income, caste, education, etc. (d) Productivity of land	—do—
3. Land tenancy	(a) Size and extent of tenancy (b) Ratio of unrecorded tenancy to total tenancy (c) Incidence of tenancy laws	—do—
4. Land transfer	(a) Pattern of purchases (b) Size of transfer (c) Profile of buyer (d) Profile of sellers	—do—

TABLE 8.8

Centre : Department of Economics, University of Bombay.
Study Area : Urban Labour market in a developing economy.
Study Period : 1974 to date
Sample Coverage: 6,000 factory worker and casual labourers in Bombay region.
Mode : Personal interview.

Compound Information Indicators	Simple Information Indicators	Quantitative Measures
1	2	3
1. Socio-economic profile of labourer	In terms of (a) Age (b) Sex (c) Place of origin (d) Education (e) Training (f) Language spoken (g) Occupation	Absolute figures, percentage & ratios
2. Inter-generation mobility	(a) Family's occupation (b) Father's occupation (c) Father's education (d) Reasons for changing from family occupation	—do—
3. Migration from rural to urban area	Information about (a) Age at migration (b) Reason for migration (c) Type of migration (Ind/family) (d) Per capita income in the native place and the source (e) Wage rate at native place (f) Channel of information about the job (g) Waiting period before getting the job (h) Cost of waiting (i) Permanent/Temporary migration	—do—

TABLE 8.8—*contd.*

1	2	3
4. Mobility	For every job (a) Salary drawn (b) Occupation (c) Size of establishment (d) Reasons for changing (e) Extent of work availability	Absolute figures, percentage and ratios
5. Family living	(a) Age & relation of family members (b) Status of members in terms of workers, students, etc. (c) No. of dependants in village and money remitted (d) Type of housing (e) Cost of housing (f) Family expenses—extent of indebtedness (g) Sources of loans and rates of interest	Absolute measures & ratios
6. Family Planning	(a) Age at marriage (b) Age of wife at marriage (c) Age at first child (d) Number of kids (e) Whether using contraceptives	—do—

TABLE 8.9

Centre : Department of Economics, University of Bombay.
Study Area : Analysis of Trade Policies in India.
Study Period : 1960-1971 to date
Sample Coverage : Published data of customs and other sources on imports, exports, etc., for 77 sectors.

Compound Information Indicators	Simple Information Indicators	Quantitative Measures
1	2	3
1. Structure of imports and exports (time series)	Growth and structural patterns in (a) Exports (b) Imports for various commodities	Absolute measures, ratios

TABLE 8.9—*contd.*

1	2	3
2. Relation between trade policies and trade flows	(a) Export demand as function of policies (b) Exports supply as function of policies (c) Price elasticity of domestic supply of exportable items (d) Elasticity of export with respect to each component of policies like incentives (e) Estimation of implicit exchange rates (shadow price) for various commodities	Absolute measures, ratios
3. Import flow matrix	(a) Import flow vectors for various commodities (end use classification) (b) Imports by major companies (c) Financial ratios of companies and linkage to imports	—do—
4. Price effects of trade policies	For selected commodities the effect of following factors on variation in international and domestic price (a) Tariff (b) Excise duty (c) Premium on industrial licences (d) Premium due to other factors like monopoly, etc.	—do—
5. Technological change and export performance	For 20 selected groups of products, determination of: (a) Elasticity of substitution (b) Returns to scale (c) Efficiency parameter (d) Relationship between production characteristics & export performance	—do—

TABLE 8.10

Centre : Department of Economics, University of Bombay.
Study Area : Linkages and Industrialization.
Study Period : 1960-71
Sample Coverage : Published data of I/O tables for 60 industries for India, Korea, Ceylon, Philippines & Indonesia

Compound Information Indicators	Simple Information Indicators	Quantitative Measures
1. Measurement of backward and forward linkages	Determination of direct & total linkages	Absolute measures for various industries
2. Relationship between linkages and other characteristics	Relationships with: (a) Capital productivity (b) Capital intensity (c) Value added/output ratio (d) Labour productivity	—do—
3. Effect of Government policies on linkages	Effect of: (a) Import controls (b) Industrial licences (c) Protection	—do—

TABLE 8.11

Centre : Department of Economics, University of Bombay.
Study Area : Exports of India under General Schemes of Preferences
Study Period : 1971-72
Sample Coverage : Published documents for all commodities

Compound Information Indicators	Simple Information Indicators	Quantitative Measures
1	2	3
1. Relation between GSP concessions and export performance	(a) Tariff reduction and effect on exports (b) Comparison of growth rates of GSP with non-GSP exports	Absolute measures, ratios and correlation figures
2. Effect of UK entry in EEC on Indian exports	(a) Elasticity of substitution between exports to UK and other EEC countries	—do—

TABLE 8.11—*contd.*

1	2	3
	(b) Projection of effects of UK's entry on Indian exports for various commodities	
3. Consistency between government's policies and G.S.P. concessions	(a) Government's policies as relevant to GSP concessions (b) Effective rate of protections compared with GSP concessions	Absolute measures, ratios and correlation figures

TABLE 8.12

Centre : Department of Economics, University of Bombay.
Study Area : Economics of scale in the Indian manufacturing industries.
Study Period : 1960-74
Sample Coverage : 300 manufacturing units belonging to 25 industries covered.
Mode : Published data and field investigations.

Compound Information Indicators	Simple Information Indicators	Quantitative Measures
1. Factors contributing to economics of scale	For various industries, contribution of: (a) Technological factors (b) Managerial factors (c) Financial factors (d) Marketing factors to reductions in cost	Absolute measure, percentages & ratios
2. Long-term average cost functions	(a) For various manufacturing units relationship between cost functions with size of the unit (material cost, labour cost, overheads, capital cost, etc.) (b) Aggregation of cost elements for average industry costs as a function of size	—do—

TABLE 8.13

Centre : Department of Economics, University of Bombay.
Study Area : Capacity utilization in Indian industries.
Study Period : 1946-67
Sample Coverage : Monthly statistics of 300 products in selected industries.
Mode : Published data.

Compound Information Indicators	Simple Information Indicators	Quantitative Measures
1. Degree of capacity utilization	For each industry: (a) No. of manufacturing units (b) Installed and utilized capacity	Ratios and absolute measures
2. Trend in capacity utilization	For each industry: (a) The trend in capacity (time series)	—do—

TABLE 8.14

Centre : Department of Economics, University of Bombay.
Study Area : Effects of public expenditure (with special reference to Education and Health).
Study Period : 1950-67 data
Sample Coverage : Published data on public expenditure

Compound Information Indicators	Simple Information Indicators	Quantitative Measures
1. Measurement of "education level"	Information on: (a) Enrolment (b) Teachers/students ratio (c) Expenditure on education (d) Training of teachers	Absolute measures, percentage & ratios
2. Measurement of "health level"	Information on: (a) Doctor/population ratio (b) Number of hospitals (c) Number of beds (d) Infant mortality (e) Epidemic frequencies	—do—
3. Measurement of capital formation in education and health	Information on: (a) Direct cost of education (b) Direct cost of health (c) Private expenditure on education (d) Private expenditure on health	—do—

TABLE 8.15

Centre : Department of Economics, University of Bombay.
Study Area : Evaluation of Indian Fiscal system.
Study Period : 1950-70
Sample Coverage : Published government statistics on expenditure.

Compound Information Indicators	Simple Information Indicators	Quantitative Measures
1. Sources of finance for planning (trend analysis)	Information on: (a) Tax earnings (b) Surplus from public undertakings (c) Public borrowings (d) Foreign loans/aids (e) Budgetary savings (f) Deficit financing	Absolute values, ratios & percentages
2. Important of various tax measures (trend Malaysia)	Cross-section and time series analysis of components of tax measures like: (a) Income tax (b) Corporate tax (c) Commodity tax (d) Sales tax, etc.	—do—
3. Role of deficit financing	Relationship of: (a) Price levels and deficit financing (b) Price level and public borrowing (c) Price level and taxation (d) Sectoral growth and taxation	—do—

TABLE 8.16

Centre : Department of Economics, University of Bombay.
Study Area : Inter-regional planning model for trade cooperation in ECAFE countries.
Study Period : Trade during 1962-68
Sample Coverage : Trade between ECAFE region countries (26 sectors).
Mode : Published data.

Compound Information Indicators	Simple Information Indicators	Quantitative Measures
1. Trade co-efficients between various countries	Based on trade flows, the trade co-efficients between various countries (time series data)	Absolute value, ratios, etc.
2. Consistency of trade flows and extrapolation	Extrapolation of past trends to predict future trade between countries	—do—
3. Implication for trade policies	Implications of trade cooperation on: (a) Tariff (b) Subsidies	—do—

TABLE 8.17

Centre : Gokhale Institute of Politics & Economics, Pune.
Study Area : Construction of an Input-Output table for India, 1963.
Study Period : 1967
Data Coverage : 1963 (240 Sectors)
Mode : Published Census data

Compound Information Indicators (for multiple factors)	Simple Information Indicators (for single factors)	Quantitative Measures
1. Commodity-wise Inter-Industry-use (for 2000 commodities)	Quantity and value (Matrix) of commodities being utilized in different industries	Ratios
2. Purchase-producer price differences (commodity-wise)	Margins of trade ; margins of transport; margins of taxes ; combined margins (Matrix)	—do—
3. Total demand on industries for a unit of final demand	Material Input-costs (for industries) backward & forward linkages	Aggregated measures
4. "Vin Neumann Growth Level" for Indian Economy	Input-output matrix	Maximum rate of growth
5. Capital co-efficient Matrix for Indian Economy (30 sectors) (Balance-sheet data from R.B.I.)	Purchase prices of equipment ; Trade value of equipment ; output by equipment	Ratios
6. "Cost Ratios" for cottage Industries	Marginal inputs, wages, value added	—do—

TABLE 8.18

Centre : Gokhale Institute of Politics & Economics, Pune.
Study Area : Land Resources in relation to population in India.
Study Period : 1970-71
Data Coverage : 1961
Mode : Published records

Compound Information Indicators (for multiple factors)	Simple Information Indicators (for single factors)	Quantitative Measures
1. Land utilization & cropping pattern	Land acreage (under different crops), land for different non-crop usages	Multiple regression analysis (with computer)
2. Population pattern (at district level)	Total population inter-relationship between population and land	Multiple regression

TABLE 8.19

Centre : Gokhale Institute of Politics & Economics, Pune.
Study Area : Compilation of Forest Resources in a State (with reference to Maharashtra).
Study Period : 1968-74
Data Coverage : 1960 to 1970
Mode : Published & unpublished records of Forest Departments (different types of sampling procedures).

Compound Information Indicators (for multiple factors)	Simple Information Indicators (for single factors)	Quantitative Measures
1. Tree-enumeration data	Girth-wise and Species-wise	Percentage frequencies summaries

TABLE 8.20

Centre : Gokhale Institute of Politics & Economics, Pune.
Study Area : Income, savings and investment in a district (with reference to Ahmednagar).
Study Period : 1972
Data Coverage : 1969
Mode : Sample survey of 700 cultivators in 10 villages, random sampling for 5 stratified groups.

Compound Information Indicators (for multiple factors)	Simple Information Indicators (for single factors)	Quantitative Measures
1. Asset structure in a firm	Hand-stock ; implements ; residential houses ; durable consumer goods (excluding holding of gold and ornaments)	Percentage frequency
2. Asset formation in a firm	Investment in land ; outright purchase of equipment ; outright purchase of livestock ; purchase of other consumer durable goods ; depletion in the year	Simple average regression
3. Saving-income relationship	Change in the assets (in a given year) change in the liabilities (in the same year) ; estimates of savings (as a difference) ; relationship of savings & income	Regression (for marginal propensity to save)

TABLE 8.21

Centre : Gokhale Institute of Politics & Economics, Pune.
Study Area : Concurrent Evaluation of Small Farmers Development Agencies (SFDA) in a district (with reference to Mysore).
Study Period : 1972 and 1973. 50,000 small farmers in the whole district, 148 small farmers in 7 villages.
Mode : Sample surveys, stratified sampling (on the bases of beneficiaries)

Compound Information Indicators (for multiple factors)	Simple Information Indicators (for single factors)	Quantitative Measures
1. Impact of different Schemes on the agricultural development of small farmers' holdings	Implement in land base reflected in (a) the area under irrigation, (b) changes in the cropping pattern, (c) increase in productivity of different crops ; improvement in the quality of livestock resulting in higher milk-yield ; introduction of new variety of seeds ; higher meat-content of the animal	Percentage frequency
2. Impact on asset-formation	Credit given to small farmers for various schemes ; different types of productive assets (e.g. irrigation wells, new breeds of cows & sheep), electric pump sets	—do—
3. Impact on employment	Employment in terms of days worked (male/female, adult/not-adult) relationship of employment and asset-formation ; relationship of employment and improved land-base	—do—
4. Impact on Income	Value of different agricultural products and by-products (at current and constant prices), change in income levels	—do—
5. Organizational aspect of SFDA & its working and role of cooperatives, and other institutional factors in SFDA Scheme	Structure of administrative hierarchy ; extension service procedure for credit distribution to small farmers	—do—

TABLE 8.22

Centre : Gokhale Institute of Politics & Economics, Pune.
Study Area : Socio-Economic Study of the Scheduled Castes in State rural area (with reference to Maharashtra).
Study Period : 1970-73
Data Coverage : 1970 (206 Villages/8 Districts of Maharashtra covered).
Mode : Sample survey, random sampling.

Compound Information Indicators (for multiple factors)	Simple Information Indicators (for single factors)	Quantitative Measures
1. Economic conditions of Scheduled Castes	Income from different sources ; land-holdings ; livestock holding, if any ; indebtedness	Percentage frequency
2. Social relationship between Scheduled Castes and Caste Hindus	Whether inter-marriages ; whether dining together ; whether mixing in social functions ; whether taking water from common wells ; own evaluation & scaling of non-scheduled castes	—do—
3. Impact of modernization on Seheduled Castes	Use of improved seeds ; loan facility given by co-operatives ; whether taken to improved locality ; whether irrigated land owned or not, use of modern implements ; use of fertilizers	—do—
4. Conversion to Buddhism	Benefits/hardships before conversion; same after conversion ; mental change in the converts ; relationship between the converts and caste Hindus ; access to temples, schools, shops and other public places (facilitated/non-facilitated)	—do—

TABLE 8.23

Centre : Gokhale Institute of Politics & Economics, Pune.
Study Area : Crash Scheme for rural employment & evaluation of programme in a district (with reference to Satara).

Study Period : 1971-72
Data Coverage : 1971-72
Mode : Complete enumeration of 2 road-building schemes published records.

Compound Information Indicators (for multiple factors)	Simple Information Indicators (for single factors)	Quantitative Measures
1. Employment profile	Knowledge regarding the scheme ; waiting period for the job ; migration of labour ; quantum of wages received ; complaints about low wages ; duration of their job in the scheme ; nature of work	Percentage frequency
2. Composition of the employees	Sex distribution (unequal ?) ; No. of same family's members having job in the scheme	—do—
3. Socio-economic background of the families	Land details—production & value ; livestock production ; expenditure ; income from different sources ; investment in the year ; sale of assets during the year ; indebtedness ; need of credits	—do—

TABLE 8.24

Centre : Gokhale Institute of Politics & Economics, Pune.
Study Area : Impact of Assistance under PL-480 on Indian Economy.
Study Period : 1962
Data Coverage : 1956-62
Mode : Government records

Compound Information Indicators (for multiple factors)	Simple Information Indicators (for single factors)	Quantitative Measures
1. Change in price structure in the selected commodities (e.g. wheat, cotton)	Wholesale prices of commodities relating to d fferent imports—under the assistance ; consumption needs related to imports	Regression analysis & elasticities
2. Assistance profile	Period of assistance ; terms of assistance ; any special features	—do—

TABLE 8.25

Centre : Gokhale Institute of Politics & Economics, Pune.
Study Area : Youth Policy in a State (with reference to Maharashtra).
Study Period : 1972
Data Coverage : 1972
Mode : Attitude survey (760 Responses).

Compound Information Indicators (for multiple factors)	Simple Information Indicators (for single factors)	Quantitative Measures
1. Identification of youth problems	Types of youth problems ; categories of youths ; (political/social/family/education/personals)	Percentage frequency
2. Youth development & proposals	Frustration among youth ; new institutions for development, additional facilities in existing institutions, different information devices for youth; education services; employment services	—do—
3. Active cooperation of youth in nation-building activities	Attitudes regarding destructive activities of the youth ; suggestions for constructive activities (e.g. stopping wastage of food, stopping dowries, stopping black-marketing) ; participation in political parties ; participation in schools & colleges management	—do—
4. Evaluation of leadership and efforts to build leadership and cooperation	Special efforts by teachers and by youth organizations for building leadership ; training needed for teachers themselves (group study) ; cooperation between different youth organizations ; agreements/disagreements ; lines of action ; methods of coordination	—do—
5. Financial structure of different Youth organizations	Grants given ; degree of self-sufficiency ; extent of burden on society ; methods to raise funds ; possibility of youth tax ; granting codes for different organizations (sincerity of purpose, relative-importance)	—do—

TABLE 8.26

Centre : Gokhale Institute of Politics & Economics, Pune.
Study Area : Progress of Literacy in villages in a State (with reference to Maharashtra).
Study Period : 1968
Data Coverage : 1947-63 (67 villages in different period-spans and linked with Census data).

Compound Information Indicators (for multiple factors)	Simple Information Indicators (for single factors)	Quantitative Measures
1. Literacy profile	Education level attained ; age ; sex ; caste ; occupation ; income	Percentage frequency
2. Relationship between literacy and other socio-econ mic factors	Relationship between literacy among different castes ; whether change in literacy percentages within the same caste over the years	—do—

TABLE 8.27

Centre : Gokhale Institute of Politics & Economics, Pune.
Study Area : Exploitation of Forests through forest labour cooperatives.
Study Period : 1974
Data Coverage : 1968-69. 2 Districts—entire area.
Mode : Sample survey of labourers ; selective sampling on performance basis.

Compound Information Indicators (for multiple factors)	Simple Information Indicators (for single factors)	Quantitative Measures
1. Cost & Returns through exploitation by cooperatives	Administrative costs ; costs for felling trees ; return through auctions	Percentage frequency
2. Employment opportunities to tribes	Pattern of labour contractorship ; pattern of wage payments ; prevalence of malpractices ; continuity of employment to tribes ; dependence on contractual jobs	—do—
3. Impact of society on the welfare of the tribes	Special activities for tribal labour ; educational facilities ; road building ; other welfare activities undertaken by the Zilla Parishad for tribes	—do—

TABLE 8.28 : **Summary of social science indicators**

(Numbers)

Topic	Developmental	Structural
A. Social & Demographic Indicators :		
(i) Health and Demographic	6	11
(ii) Nutrition	3	1
(iii) Education	8	2
(iv) Housing	3	—
(v) Communication	5	—
B. Economic Indicators		
(i) Transport and Services	5	3
(ii) Agriculture	1	1
(iii) Industry	3	3
(iv) Trade	2	9
(v) General	3	6
C. Typological Indicators		
Miscellaneous	3	—

TABLE 8.29 : **Illustrative list of Indian indicators of social welfare**

(i) percentage of 3 to 6 years old children receiving pre-school instructions.
(ii) percentage of 3 to 6 years old children with good nutritional level.
(iii) percentage of out-of-school adolescents aged 15-19 years who have education and/or training for a special skill.
(iv) percentage of persons aged 60 years and more whose health needs are not met.
(v) incidence of the physical handicaps.
(vi) incidence of the mental handicaps.
(vii) incidence of mental illness ; and
(viii) percentage of youth aged 20-24 years whose preparation is inadequate for the adult social votes.

9

INFORMATION SYSTEM FOR SCIENCE AND TECHNOLOGY

9.1 Background

The Pearson (1968) report recommended that 5 per cent of the total aid transferred in the world should be devoted to the specific area of the transfer of scientific and technical information whose sheer volume warrants that documentation centres produce abstracts on behalf of a large group. Apart from the U.N. advisory committee for science and technology considering this proposal for implementation, the OECD—in association with the European Economic Community—has been studying the issue of automatic information processing in the European area.

In order that technological information and experience can be made available on a very wide range of matters, Hawthorne (1970) recommended the services of national institutions which can be exemplified as follows :

(a) Technical bodies, e.g., productivity councils, management associations, centres of economic research, expert panels attached to government ministries and departments, etc. ;

(b) Educational bodies, e.g., universities, institutes of science and technology, etc. ;

(c) Documentation units, e.g., centralized documentation centres and those attached to various R & D laboratories ;

(d) Associated research units, e.g., those associated with financial organizations like reserve banks, etc.

The National Committee on Science and Technology (1973) recognized that the primary object of our information policy was to provide research workers, scientists, engineers, technicians, managers and more generally, all who had some part to play in scientific activity with access to information they needed and this as economically as possible. Accepting that the Governments in developing countries had a major responsibility for providing information services, the NCST considered that information policy was a major component of policy for science and technology. Just as science policy was to be a major component of policy for science and technology, information policy was to assure that the world's specialized and professional knowledge was fully and properly used in guiding a social evolution.

Since science information dissemination processes were essentially to enrich information resources and to optimize the latter's utilization by all those who needed information, the NCST laid down the following objectives for a national information system :

(a) Provision of a national information service on science and technology relevant to present and future needs of users ;
(b) Optimum utilization of existing information services, and development of new ones ;
(c) Promotion of national and international cooperation on information exchange ;
(d) Development of facilities for training, education and R & D in information services.

Building up of adequate computer facilities for information handling was made part of national science information policy.

Taking into account the above, the NCST recommended development of a national information system on science and technology (NISSAT), with the nucleus of information facilities available in the laboratories of government scientific agencies, and those of public and private sector industries, and functioning in several tiers, as follows :

(1) The present and proposed national centres (NCs) of information in science and technology, medicine, agriculture, defence science, nuclear science, patents, standards, small industries, social sciences, etc., would constitute the top level of organization. They would be mission-oriented centres maintaining computer-based data banks which would store data relevant to the activities and development of specified sectors. They would also organize information dissemination services, including data retrieval, based upon their own data-storage and utilizing information services available on magnetic tapes.

(2) The regional centres (RCs) of information would constitute the second level in various parts of the country. The RCs would not be subject-oriented and would cover all branches of science and technology (including agriculture and medicine) at major centres of scientific and technological activity, in order to meet the information demands of the region.

(3) The branch centres (BCs) of information would be subject-oriented to provide national service at the third level of organization. They would assist in analysis, design and implementation of information systems on scientific, technical and economic data, and build up computer-based data banks in cooperation with the NCs, after assuring national and international compatibility and utilizing specialized information services available on magnetic tapes. The BCs would be developed, to start with, in major industrial disciplines, such as metallurgy, chemical, leather and food technologies, aeronautics, electronics, mechanical engineering, petrochemicals, pharmaceuticals, oceanography, and so on.

(4) The local information units (LIUs) would form part of individual R & D establishments and serve specific user-needs, at the lowest level of organization. LIUs would be the ultimate recipient of information from NCs and BCs, and would provide scientific, technical and economic information needed by their parent institutions.

Information, in machine-readable form, is increasingly available in the West, particularly through network concepts, such as UNISIST (world science information system) programme of UNESCO. Further, computer-based indexing and abstracting services on magnetic tapes are freely available, such as CA for chemistry, COMPENDEX for engineering, INSPEC for physics, MEDLAR for medicine and agriculture, and so on. It is visualized that NISSAT would participate in the world-wide cooperative management of science information and would also acquire tape services from abroad for storage, evaluation and synthesis at computers of the NCs, passing only selective information to the BCs and lower down.

9.2 Technology data bank

Users in industrial and technological fields need selected data of practical importance. Their requirement of information is as follows :

(a) digested, for direct assimilation ;
(b) analysed in detail, for application to specific problems ;
(c) relevant portions culled out from source documents and promptly served, for timely use.

Raw data or merely bibliographic citation of pertinent literature are unlikely to satisfy discerning users. Hence the need of a suitably designed technology data bank, with primarily aggregated information for use by those at high levels concerned with planning, coordination, execution and monitoring of technology development in India. An example is decision-making for foreign technical collaboration where industrial planners would naturally be interested in the state-of-the-art of technology in Indian laboratories and manufacturing units. DST, as a modal agency for technology development in the country, would be a major user of this bank and also an important provider of data into the system.

The data bank structure can be outlined in the following sequence :

(1) Division of the industrial and technological fields into specific sectors (as per 24 sectors identified in the

Science & Technology Plan), then into areas and finally into specific projects which could be either product or process development ;

(2) Identification of the needs and priorities in technology development based on the country's national planning and investment policies (technology needs and priorities) ;

(3) Enlisting of the various technological alternatives for specific projects (technology forecasting) ;

(4) Monitoring of foreign technologies that are appropriate for Indian conditions (technology monitoring) ;

(5) Selection of Indian technologies that are suitable for nurturing and potential application (technology assessment) ;

(6) Identification of technology gaps and agencies, development of which could be undertaken and funding assistance for the development work (technology planning) ;

(7) Establishing of mechanism for efficient transfer of knowhow (technology transfer) ; and

(8) Keeping track of utilization of knowhow in practice (technology utilization).

It may be noted that the same technology has often applications in different fields and can be in various stages of development for each field. Although, to this extent, some overlapping exists, fairly independent information systems can be structured around sub-data bases as follows :

s_1 : sub-data base on technology needs and priorities ;

s_2 : sub-data base on technology forecasting and monitoring ;

s_3 : sub-data base on technology assessment and planning ; and

s_4 : sub-data base on technology transfer and utilization.

Each sub-data base can be on a low-cost mini-computer under the control of the organization which is the natural focus for the collection, storage and processing of the specified system.

Since information relating to development of product/process for a particular technology area would be culled in a precise, quantitative form and since the format and description of such information are expected to follow a similar pattern, it would be desirable to use the concept of *qualified keyword index* for information retrieval. For example, in order to obtain the information regarding item w of product (or process) development z for technology area y of sector x, the user can state his query by using the key-word :

$$1.\ x.\ y.\ z.\ w,$$

the item w being qualified by the product (or process) z, technology area y, the sector x and sub-data base 1.

In order to retrieve information details of a particular item w for all the products (or processes) developed for a particular technology area y of sector x from the sub-data base 1, we may use the key-word :

$$1.\ x.\ y.\ w$$

This concept can be extended to all the items, all the products (or processes), all the technology areas and all the sectors. The method basically aims at retrieving the specified information as efficiently as possible. When a query is made, the key-word has to be checked for correctness, the required information retrieved using the sub-data base's thesaurus and a standard output generated.

In order to promote exchange of ideas and provide feedback among the different sub-data bases, the latter may be conceived of as fully interactive within an overall technology information system, as shown in Figure 9.1.

A well-planned computer network can then be developed by inter-connecting the mini-computers with the four sub-data bases. The latter can be, in the beginning, a distributed data base on off-line basis and made on-line with phased integration. The "ring" computer network may later on be made "star" network by hooking to a giant host computer, perhaps at the National Informatics Centre.

The broad design of the technology data bank is indicated in the following sections for each sub-data base.

9.3 Sub-data base on technology needs and priorities

This sub-data base relates to technology demand and aims to

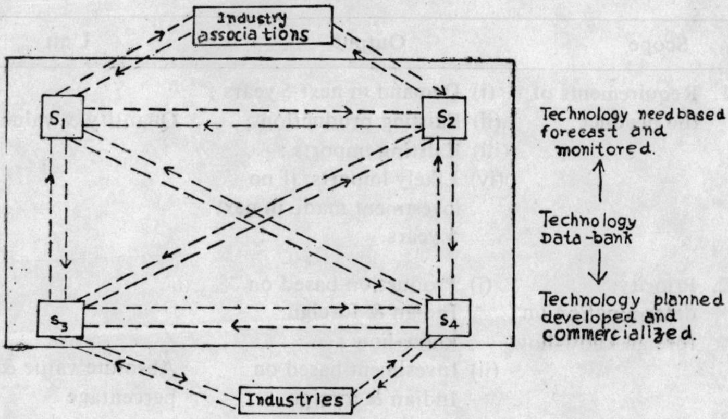

FIG. 9.1 : *Technology information system*

establish priorities for product/process development, after scanning for their needs each sector and all its technology areas. The design of the sub-data base is indicated in Figure 9.2.

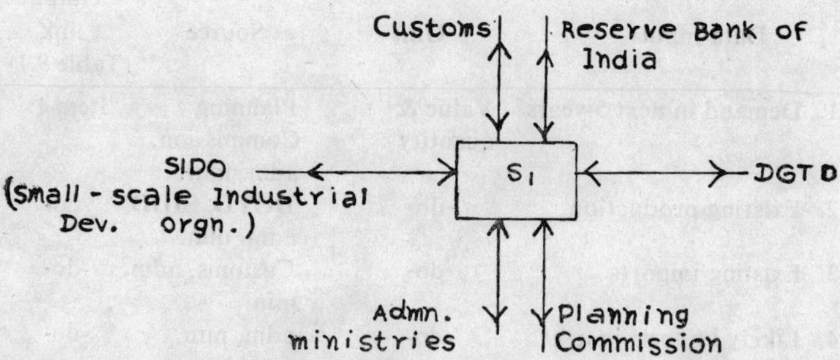

Possible location at DGTD or Planning Commission

FIG. 9.2 : *Sub-data base on technology needs and priorities*

The useful output information for each product (or process) for the sub-data base is given as in Table 9.1. Corresponding input details are furnished in Table 9.2.

TABLE 9.1 : **Useful outputs (product-wise)**

Scope	Output	Unit
1. Requirements of the product	(i) Demand in next 5 years ; (ii) Existing production ; (iii) Existing imports ; (iv) Likely imports, if no investment made in next 5 years.	Quantity & value
2. Priority determination on foreign know-how	(i) Production based on Indian & foreign know-how ; (ii) Investment based on Indian & foreign know-how ; (iii) Foreign exchange-outflow for royalties, know-how fees, etc., out of total production.	Absolute value & percentage

TABLE 9.2 : **Input details (product-wise)**

Data input	Unit	Source	Output link (Table 9.1)
1. Demand in next 5 years	Value & quantity	Planning Commission, adm. min.	Item 1
2. Existing production	-do-	DGTD, SIDO, adm. min.	-do-
3. Existing imports	-do-	Customs, adm. min.	-do-
4. Likely imports in next 5 years, if no investment made for technology development	-do-	adm. min.	-do-
5. Annual production based on Indian & foreign know-how	Absolute value & percentage	DGTD, SIDO, adm. min.	Item 2
6. Annual investment based on Indian & foreign know-how	-do-	DGTD, SIDO, adm. min.	-do-
7. Foreign exchange outflow for royalties, know-how fees, etc.	-do-	RBI	-do-

9.4 Sub-data base on technology forecasting and monitoring

This sub-data base relates to technology supply and aims to determine various technology alternatives (including those in commercial operations as well as those under development) from both Indian and foreign environment for their use in appropriate projects. The design of the sub-data base is given in Figure 9.3.

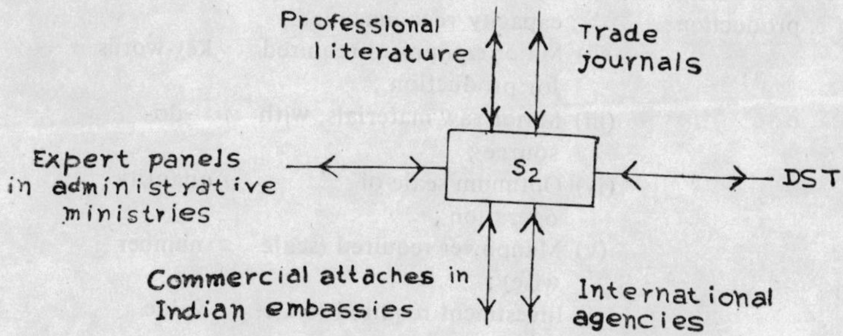

(possible location at DST)

FIG. 9.3 : *Sub-data base on technology forecasting and monitoring*

The useful output information for each product (or process) from the sub-data base is obtained as in Table 9.3. Corresponding input details are indicated in Table 9.4.

TABLE 9.3 : **Useful outputs (product-wise)**

Scope	Output	Unit
1	2	3
(A) *For each foreign and Indian technology (already commercialized) :*		
1. Status of commercial usage	(i) Technical details ;	Key-words, ratio,
	(ii) Critical specifications like yield, efficiency, etc. ;	Quantity
	(iii) Year of first commercial production ;	number
	(iv) Likely year of obsolescence ;	-do-
	(v) Whether proprietary in nature ;	yes/no
	(vi) Where in use in India.	key-words
2. Economics of development	(i) Likely cost of know-how, if to be imported, with source ;	value, key-words

TADLE 9.3—*contd.*

1	2	3
	(ii) Terms of know-how, if to be imported ;	key-words
	(iii) Likely cost of indigenous development, with foreign exchange content.	value
3. Economics of production	(i) Optimum production capacity recommended ;	quantity
	(ii) Major equipment required for production ;	key-words
	(iii) Major raw materials, with source ;	-do-
	(iv) Optimum scale of operation ;	quantity
	(v) Manpower required (scale-wise) ;	number
	(vi) Investment required (scale-wise) ;	value
	(vii) Cost of final product (scalewise).	-do-
(B) *For each foreign and Indian technology (under development)* :		
4. Status of development	(i) Technical details ;	key-words
	(ii) Status of development, with critical specifications ;	-do-
	(iii) Places where being developed ;	-do-
	(iv) Technology it would replace or improve ;	key-words
	(v) Likely year of commercial production.	number
5. Economics of development	(i) Likely cost of know-how, when developed ;	value
	(ii) Economic advantages of know-how ;	value, ratio
	(iii) Special raw materials required for later production ;	key-words
	(iv) Special equipment required for production.	-do-
(C) *For each foreign and Indian technology (futuristic)* :		
6. Status of anticipation	(i) Likely technical details ;	key-words
	(ii) Likely places for development ;	-do-
	(iii) Status of anticipation (stage, etc.) ;	-do-
	(iv) Likely impact.	-do-

TABLE 9.4 : **Input details (product-wise)**

Data input	Unit	Source	Output link (Table 9.3)
(A) *For technologies already commercialized :*			
1. Technical details	key-words	DST and other sources as in Figure 9.3	Item 1
2. Critical specifications	-do-	-do-	-do-
3. Years of first commercial production and obsolescence	number	-do-	-do-
4. Whether developed in India or abroad, where and by whom	-do-	-do-	-do-
5. Cost of indigenous development, with foreign exchange content	value	-do-	Item 2
6. Cost and terms of know-how, if imported	value, key-words	-do-	-do-
7. Major equipment and raw materials required for production	key-words	-do-	Item 3
8. Optimum scale of operation	quantity	-do-	-do-
9. Investment and manpower required (scale-wise)	quantity & number	-do-	-do-
10. Cost of final product	value	-do-	-do-
(B, C) *For technologies under development and futuristic:*			
11. Technical details	key-words	-do-	Item 4, 6
12. Critical specifications	-do-	-do-	Item 4
13. Places where being developed and status of development	-do-	-do-	Item 4, 6
14. Likely year of commercialization	number	-do-	Item 4
15. Likely cost of know-how	value	-do-	Item 5
16. Special raw materials and equipment required	key-words	-do-	-do-
17. Likely impact	-do-	-do-	Item 6

9.5 Sub-data base on technology assessment and planning

This sub-data base relates to technology gaps and developmental efforts to fill these gaps. Having identified the technology options which are appropriate for Indian conditions, it aims to initiate development work through suitable agencies and with proper financial support. The design of the sub-data base is presented in Figure 9.4.

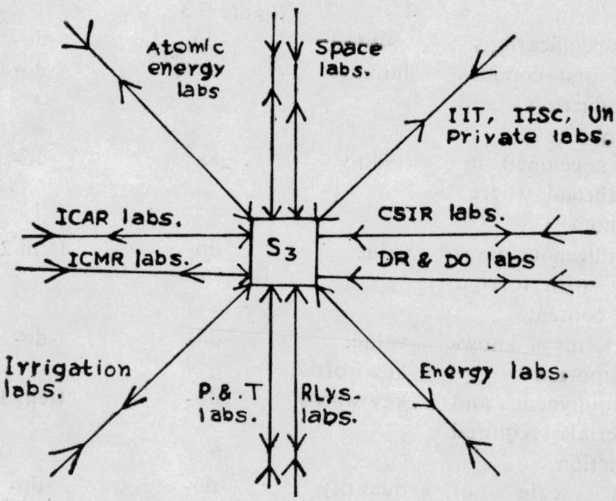

(possible location at CSIR, ICAR, etc., headquarters, on a mini-computer network)

FIG. 9.4 : *Sub-data base on technology assessment and planning*

It is important to visualize here not just one mini-computer for each of ICAR, ICMR, CSIR, etc., headquarters, but all these mini-computers linked in a network and hooked to a central processor for selective information storage and processing. For this purpose, we can conceive of a component of s_3 at CSIR headquarters, as presented in Figure 9.5,—based on an information management scheme recommended by the author to DG, SIR at the latter's behest in 1976. This assumes slightly reorganized responsibilities for specific information from different divisions, laboratories and other units under CSIR.

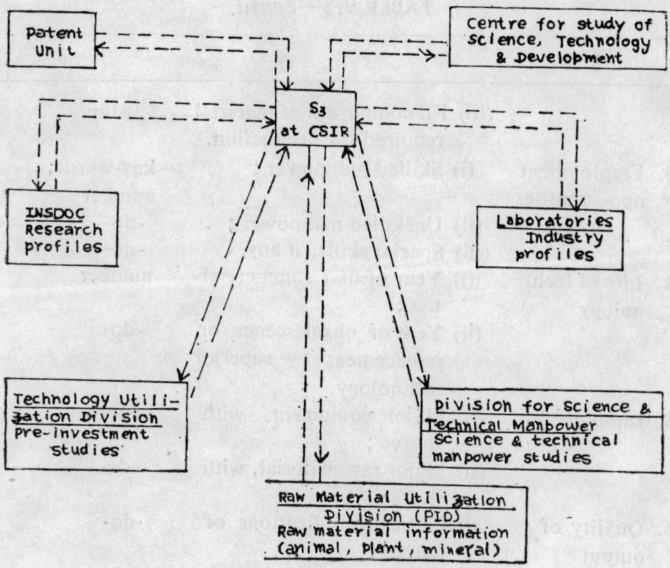

FIG. 9.5 : *S_3 sub-data base at CSIR headquarters*

The useful output information for each product (or process) from the sub-data base is as indicated in Table 9.5. Corresponding input details are shown in Table 9.6.

TABLE 9.5 : **Useful outputs (product-wise)**

Scope	Output	Units
1	2	3
(A) *For assessment of each technology* :		
1. Cost comparison	(i) Cost of know-how, with source ;	value, key-words
	(ii) Terms of know-how;	key-words
	(iii) Cost of indigenous development ;	value
	(iv) Investment required for production ;	-do-
	(v) Cost of final product ;	-do-
2. Foreign exchange (FE) implication	(i) FE component of indigenous development ;	-do-
	(ii) FE component of investment required for production ;	-do-

TABLE 9.5—*contd.*

1	2	3
	(iii) FE component of material required for production.	value
3. Employment opportunities	(i) Skilled manpower ;	key-words, number
	(ii) Unskilled manpower ;	-do-
	(iii) Special skills, if any.	-do-
4. Life of technology	(i) Year of first commercial use ;	number
	(ii) Year of obsolescence or replacement by superior technology.	-do-
5. Input needs	(i) Major equipment, with source ;	key-words
	(ii) Major raw material, with source.	-do-
6. Quality of output	(i) Critical specifications of output ;	-do-
	(ii) Yield, efficiency, etc.	quantity
7. Environmental impact	(i) Locational constraint ;	key-words
	(ii) Pollution effect.	quantity
(B) *For planning of each technology* :		
8. Technology status of Indian production facilities (firm-wise)	(i) Investment based on foreign & Indian technology ;	value
	(ii) Production based on foreign and Indian technology.	quantity
9. Status of on-going development work	(i) Type of institution (national lab., university, public sector lab., private lab., etc.) ;	key-words
	(ii) Technical details ;	key-words
	(iii) Year of commencement ;	number
	(iv) Status of development ;	key-words
	(v) Likely year of completion ;	number
	(vi) Cost incurred, with FE component ;	value
	(vii) Likely total cost of development.	-do-

TABLE 9.5—*contd.*

1	2	3
10. Development expertise (institution-wise)	(i) Type of institution ;	key-words
	(ii) Past achievements ;	-do-
	(iii) Technical manpower employed, with categories ;	number, key-words
	(iv) Equipment facilities ;	key-words
	(v) Production facilities.	-do-
11. Status of completed development work (institution-wise)	(i) Type of institution ;	key-words
	(ii) Starting & completion time ;	number
	(iii) Critical specifications ;	key-words
	(iv) Cost of know-how ;	value
	(v) Terms of know-how ;	key-words
	(vi) Investment required, with FE component ;	value
	(vii) Major equipment required ;	key-words
	(viii) Major raw material required.	-do-
12. Identification of agencies for development	(i) Name & type of institution with development expertise ;	key-words
	(ii) Equipment facilities ;	-do-
	(iii) Technical manpower employed, for specific categories.	key-words, number
(C) *For development of each technology* :		
13. Justification of development	(i) R & D input, with FE component ;	value
	(ii) Extent of import substitution, in 5 years ;	-do-
	(iii) Value of expected production, in 5 years ;	-do-
	(iv) Employment potential during development phase, with categories ;	number, key-words
	(v) Employment potential during production phase, with categories.	-do-
14. Evaluation of proposals (for development assistance)	(i) Name & type of institution ;	key-words
	(ii) Salient features of proposal ;	-do-

TABLE 9.5—*contd.*

1	2	3
	(iii) Development cost, with FE component ;	value
	(iv) Likely time of project completion ;	number
	(v) Equipment facilities ;	key-words
	(vi) Technical manpower, for specific categories ;	-do-
	(vii) Distinctive advantages.	-do-
15. Monitoring of progress (for development assistance)	(i) Name & type of institution ;	key-words
	(ii) Status of development versus original target ;	ratios
	(iii) Likely completion time versus original target ;	-do-
	(iv) Expenditure incurred versus original budget ;	-do-
	(v) Likely total cost versus original estimate.	-do-

TABLE 9.6 : **Input details (product-wise)**

Data input	Unit	Source	Output link (Table 9.5 items)
1	2	3	4
(A) *For technology assessment :*			
1. Cost and terms of know-how	value, key-words	Various laboratories, DGTD and adm. mini.	1 11
2. Critical specifications and yield, specifications	key-words quantity	-do-	1 6
3. Years of first commercial use and obsolescence	number	-do-	4
4. Cost of indigenous development, with FE component	value	-do-	1 2
5. Investment and manpower required (scale-wise), with FE component	value, number	-do-	1 2 3
6. Equipment and raw material required, with FE component	key-words, value	-do-	5
7. Locational constraints and pollution effect	key-words, quantity	-do-	7

TABLE 9.6—*contd.*

1	2	3	4
(B) *For technology planning :*			
8. Firm-wise investment, based on Indian and foreign know-how.	value	various laboratories, DGTD and adm. ministries	8
9. Firm-wise production, based on Indian and foreign know-how	quantity	-do-	8
10. Institution-wise name and type ; years of commencement and actual/likely completion ; present status of development ; amounts spent and likely total cost ; technical manpower and equipment facilities.	key-words, value, quantity	-do-	9, 10, 11, 12
(C) *For technology development :*			
11. Institution-wise project scope and completion time ; equipment and manpower, R&D input with the FE component ; import substitution and production in next 5 years ; employment potential in development and production phases ;	-do-	Proposing agency, DST, adm. ministries	13, 14
12. Proposal-wise scope and present development status ; targets and budgets originally estimated ; expenditure incurred and likely total cost ; present progress and likely completion time.	-do-	-do-	15

9.6 Sub-data base on technology transfer and utilization

This sub-data base relates to the end use of technology and aims to transfer a developed technology to industry for its proper use. The design of the sub-data base is given in Figure 9.6.

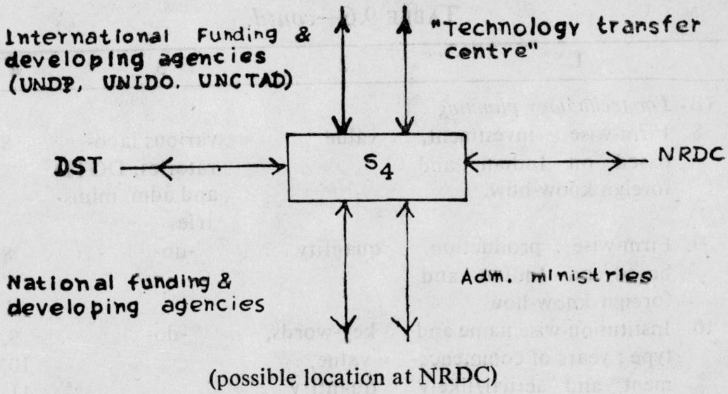

FIG. 9.6 : *Sub-data base on technology transfer and utilization*

Functions of a "technology transfer centre" (Ramachandran, 1978) are assumed to be (i) identifying technical needs ; (ii) obtaining need-based information on alternative sources of technology ; (iii) assistance in evaluation and selection of technologies ; (iv) assistance in unpackaging of imported technology ; (v) negotiation for favourable terms for imported technology ; (vi) assistance in absorption and adaptation of foreign technology ; and (vii) promoting of the diffusion of technology already assimilated, indigenous or foreign.

The useful output information for each product (or process) from the sub-data base is as shown in Table 9.7. Corresponding input details are presented in Table 9.8.

TABLE 9.7 : **Useful outputs (product-wise)**

Scope	Output	Unit
1	2	3
1. Status of the developed technology	(i) Name and type of institution developing technology ;	key-word
	(ii) Technical details of the know-how ;	-do-
	(iii) Current status vis-a-vis other technologies abroad ;	key-words, ratio
	(iv) Current status vis-a-vis other technologies in India ;	-do-
	(v) Likely time of obsolescence.	numbe r

TABLE 9.7—*contd.*

1	2	3
2. Cost and terms of the know-how	(i) Name and type of institution developing technology ;	key-words
	(ii) Cost and terms of the know-how ;	value, key-words
	(iii) Cost and terms of comparable foreign know-how ;	-do-
	(iv) Cost of final product based on the know-how ;	value
	(v) Cost of final product based on comparable foreign know-how, with FE component ;	-do-
	(vi) Investment required for the know-how, with FE component ;	-do-
	(vii) Investment required for comparable foreign know-how, with FE component.	-do-
3. Input needs	(i) Name and type of institution developing technology ;	key-words
	(ii) Major equipment ;	-do-
	(iii) Major equipment for comparable foreign know-how ;	-do-
	(iv) Major raw materials ;	-do-
	(v) Major raw materials for comparable foreign know-how.	-do-
4. Know-how performance	(i) Name and type of institution developing technology ;	key-words
	(ii) Year of the know-how transfer ;	number
	(iii) Cost of the know-how ;	value
	(iv) Name and type of agency buying the know-how ;	key-words
	(v) Production generated ;	value
	(vi) Feedback from the buying agency.	key-words, number

TABLE 9.8 : **Input details (product-wise)**

Data input	Unit	Source	Output link (Table 9.7 items)
1	2	3	4
1. *Know-how details* :			
(i) Name and type of institution developing technology ; (ii) Scope of the project; (iii) Status of the know-how vis-a-vis comparable foreign know-how ; (iv) Economic life of technology.	key-words, value, ratio	funding & developing agencies, NRDC	1, 2, 3, 4
2. *Know-how transfer* :			
(i) Cost and terms of know-how ; (ii) Investment required, with FE component ; (iii) Equipment and raw material required, with FE component ; (iv) Information and assistance given with know-how.	key-words, value	-do-	2, 3
3. *Comparable foreign know-how details* :			
(i) Sources of know-how ; (ii) Cost and terms of know-how ; (iii) Investment required, with FE component ; (iv) Equipment and raw material required, with FE component ; (v) Information and assistance given with know-how.	key-words, value, number	-do-	1, 3
4. *Know-how monitoring* :			
(i) Name and type of agency buying the know-how ;	key-words, value, quantity	NRDC, adm. ministries	4

TABLE 9.8—*contd.*

1	2	3	4
(ii) Name and type of institution developing the know-how ;	key-words, value, quantity	NRDC, adm. ministries	4
(iii) Cost and terms of know-how transfer ;			
(iv) Time of transfer ;			
(v) Value of production generated ;			
(vi) Feedback from the buying agency.			

9.7 Compilation of information

Primary information coming from technical literature, professional journals, laboratories, universities, etc., need considerable "working" before they can be fed in the technology data bank. This involves identification of key-words in the information, their classification and codification, and construction of thesaurus. Such "taxonomy" of information needs to be done by technically competent persons who, fortunately, are available in India.

A step towards compilation of the following information has been taken by Indian National Scientific Documentation Centre (INSDOC), which would be relevant for technology data bank :

(a) *R&D institutions* : An updated directory plans to cover more than 2,000 R&D institutions (including their names, objectives, areas of specialization, facilities available for industries, publications, etc.) for both public and private sectors ;

(b) *Current R&D project*: Publications covering more than 2,000 current research projects in CSIR laboratories and 10,000 research projects in universities are available which include information on name and scope of project, name and type of institution undertaking development, name and category of scientists involved, time of commencement and likely completion of project and status of development. On-going research projects in the country should be above 40,000 involving nearly 60,000 scientists ;

(c) *Current scientific literature* : Abstracts published in a monthly abstract journal cover around 20,000 in the form of scientific work done, patents and standards.

INSDOC apart from many other agencies like individual divisions and laboratories of CSIR, DST, Electronics Commission, Planning Commission, etc., compile information on specialized subjects which may be of selective interest for technology data bank.

9.8. Interfaces of information

Suitably compiled information in technology data bank, with facilities for updating and maintenance, sorting and merging of data, and generation of useful output reports would go a long way in properly planning and managing Indian technology environment. It is equally essential that the different sub-data bases, illustrated earlier, provide suitable interfaces to each other as was envisaged in Figure 9.1.

The scheme, outlined above, is capable of having the following interfaces in technology data bank :

(i) Interface between technology forecast and technology in the "pipeline" (finished and in laboratories) ;

(ii) Detailed appraisal on forecast and forthcoming technologies ;

(iii) Summarized reports on industry's need of current and future technologies ;

(iv) Interface between technology in the pipeline and technology implemented ;

(v) Interface between technology commercialized and technology in the pipeline ;

(vi) Interface between technology forecast and technology commercialized ;

(vii) Interface between technology forecast and technology implemented ;

(viii) Interface between technology commercialized and technology implemented ;

(ix) Detailed appraisal on commercial and productive technologies ; and

(x) Summarized reports on commercial and productive technologies.

9.9 Conclusion

Most new technologies emerge from physical concepts into technologies at a finite rate (Rohatgi, 1979). It is not merely possible, but also highly desirable, to identify the majority of probable future technologies by a careful monitoring of new ideas at an early stage, and follow them through the logical process of assessment, planning and development to the ultimate goal of wide industrial use. Technology data bank can serve in this framework to give management a powerful capability to become aware of useful technology opportunities before they have been commercialized and to plan progress towards a target in all the important sectors.

REFERENCES

Pearson, Lester B., *Partner in Development* : *Report of the Commission on International Development*, Pall Mall Press, London, 1968.

Rohatgi, P.V. *et al.*, *Technology Forecasting*, Tata-McGraw Hill, New Delhi, 1979.

(iv) Detailed appraisal on commercial and productive technologies ; and

(v) Summarized reports on commercial and productive technologies.

7.9 Conclusion

Most new technologies emerge from physical concepts into technologies at a finite rate (Rohatgi, 1979). It is not merely possible, but also highly desirable, to identify the majority of probable future technologies by a careful monitoring of new ideas at an early stage, and follow them through the logical process of assessment, planning and development to the ultimate goal of wide industrial use. Technology data bank can serve in this framework to give management a powerful capability to become aware of useful technology opportunities before they have been commercialized and to plan progress towards a target in all the important sectors.

REFERENCES

Pearson, Lester B., Partners in Development: Report of the Commission on International Development, Pall Mall Press, London, 1969.

Rohatgi, P.K., et al., Technology Forecasting, Tata-McGraw-Hill, New Delhi, 1979.

COMPUTER FOR CONTROL INFORMATION

10

COMPUTER AND INFORMATION MANAGEMENT CONCEPT

10.1 General

In this 1500th birth anniversary year of Aryabhata, confinement of rational thinking to laboratories and lecturehouses has elicited wry comments from the *cognoscenti*. Mrs. Indira Gandhi on this occasion cited an observation by Alberuni saying that our scientists "are by nature niggardly in communicating that which they know and they take the greatest possible care to withhold it from men of another caste among their own people".

In the new-fangled world of information science, do these still ring as prophetic words? Is there a mis-placed sense of self-reliance which refuses to accept information as a national resource needing exploitation for the betterment of the entire country? Or, do we scientists realise that compartmentalisation fetters growth and dwarfs all initiative?

This chapter seeks to examine the above issues, in the context of the available information power and computer technology *vis-a-vis* our informational scene and the management thinking. It explores the interfaces and interrelationships among these factors, and attempts to visualise the premises which are needed for a cohesive informational growth. It tries to obtain an integrated framework for information management which can give rise to synergistic benefits through a proper information planning.

10.2 Computers and management—the Indian scene

Just as atomic fission and fusion have placed in our hands a physical power so much greater than what we ever wielded before, the information power offered by the digital computer—although less visible, less audible and less tangible—has introduced into our lives something essentially new and extremely potent. Perhaps the full realisation of the informational revolution has only started now with the widespread distribution of the power of information processing, when an organisation often asks not for a large computer but for only console-sockets or micro-computers in offices, shops, laboratories and vehicles. On the minus side, the typical tight sequencing and microscopic logical bonds within the informational granite of programs of routines of instructions limit the effectiveness of the informational power mainly to large and repetitious pre-plannable applications and render it unresponsive to subtle guidance or precise control by men. This is notwithstanding the recent developments for transforming arguments into functions in ways that have approximately the same stimulus-response characteristic as good human thinking, judgment, problem-solving and decision-making—in the domain of artificial intelligence.

While the above is the essence of the computer culture prevalent in the West today, the scene is perhaps quite different in India. From a modest beginning in 1961 of first installation of a business computer by a U.S. oil firm, today the number of computers are around 800, out of which more than half are located in industrial units with a concentration in the technologically advanced industries like engineering, chemicals and electronics. Earlier, most of these computers have been second generation models, due to the then policy of restricting imports and the supply constraint being imposed on the computer manufacturing facilities in the country. While the Electronics Corporation of India Limited (ECIL) started to manufacture scientific and business computers, the under-supply situation in the computer field was all too evident due to import of computers only on a limited scale for academic institutions, industrial firms and defence departments.

Indications, of late, are that the government will encourage the production and use of computers to applications which will promote economic growth. A number of third-generation and fourth-generation computers have been cleared for industrial firms and public sector undertakings. Planning has been made already to set up regional computer centres in the various metropolitan centres of the country—with large computer systems and program support with the bias for applications in the management decision-making area. The National Centre for Software Development and Computing Techniques (NCSDCT) has come up in Bombay and the National Informatics Centre (NIC) in Delhi is active in such diverse areas as archival information management finance, and financial resources information, social and economic information, trade and media information, agricultural and water information, natural resources information, industry information, construction and tansport information, energy information, demography information, and education and manpower information. These centres were funded under the United Nations Development Project (UNDP) and make available computer facility to various government departments, semi-government organisations and small-scale industry who cannot afford machines of their own. Out of the government aided Regional Computer Centres at Culcutta and Chandigarh, 200 organisations and 1000 industrial users utilise the facility at Calcutta alone for scientific, R&D, education and commercial data processing.

It is admittedly true that the Indian industry has not played its due role in the computer scene, regardless of the Government's role. There is a genuine fear that use of computers would lead to displacement of clerical labour in a labour-rich economy like India's. This fear is somewhat justified by many of the current computer applications to routine accounting tasks which are of a labour-saving nature. Other applications, such as increase in efficiency, better allocation of resources and improvement in the customer's service, have not always been properly emphasized. This is primarily because the prevailing business and industrial culture has, until recently, not been very productivity-conscious, added to a tacit acceptance of simple technology, low wages, shoddy and wasteful production, and a certain lack of consideration for the consumer. In the face of glorious exceptions like the Tata House and others, industry has often found it inexpedient to put in the extra effort required to get more out of the resources due to the availability of both sheltered market and ever-increasing labour force.

The management style in both government and private sectors have only recently shifted to what is emphasized as "professional management". The public sector, with the largest segment of the country's industrial economy, has been recruiting its managers largely from out of the Government civil services. In the private sector, although there are some professionally managed enterprises mostly as subsidiaries of the multinational firms, there are large segments of family-owned enterprises who have grown in size, technology, complexity and product range, and are only now beginning to professionalize their management. The same is yet to be true for many other firms in the private and small-scale sector. It is also only recently that demand for trained managers has started exceeding supply from the 86 or so institutions in India offering both MBAs, and short-term executive development programmes in general management and functional areas. Their efforts in the area of management training are now supplemented by AIMA, NPC, Operational Research Society of India, Computer Society of India and Institution of Engineers, among a few others, who are interested in improving managerial techniques. Under these circumstances of overall shortage of "professional management", it is hardly surprising that the clamour for computer usage from the management rank and file is yet to be made felt.

10.3 Current and proposed linkages

A 1973 study sponsored by UNIDO estimated that India would need 500 computers by 1978, at the least, of which around 50 should be large systems. Under a presidential notification issued in August 1975, the department of electronics was made responsible for "all matters concerning computer-based information, technology and processing—including hardware and software, standardization of procedures and matter relevant to international bodies such as the IFIP, IBI, ICC". In keeping with this directive, the NIC has established linkages with 50 government departments and semi-government organizations by 1982. These details have been indicated in section 1.3 of Chapter 1.

From the research and development angle, the National Information System for Science and Technology (NISSAT) under the Department of Science and Technology has visualized 40-50 centres in the country to become documentation outposts with foreign funds and documentation equipment. Selective Dissemination of Information (SDI) on a computerized basis was initiated by the INSDOC. Their on-line data transmission project, conducted with satellite aid in collaboration with Frascati computers of European Space Agency, proved an unqualified success in 1977-78.

Within the framework of the NIC and NISSAT, the management aspects of Government data-centres have not yet emerged very clearly. Information systems in the Government have been described as "fuzzy systems" by some, due to the common lack of explicit goals and system boundaries. While the above description may not be untrue in many contexts, the data-base for planning and control purposes in the Government cannot often be precise and accurate, due to their shear extensiveness in a political, social and economic set-up. Within these limitations, studies are being made to evolve an improved structure for information management within many organizations. The author was associated with a project in the DGTD where a computerized information system has already made some progress and is currently being extended to comprehensive production analysis (see "Data Bank on Industrial Planning", *Economic Times*, December 13, 1975). The author was also associated with a study for the CSIR, where some suggestions have been given for a cohesive system for information management with linkages properly established among different headquarters units and divisions, and national laboratories. An attempt in this direction, for science and technology data-linkages within the CSIR, has been indicated in Chapter 9.

It is interesting to explore the potential of a link-up among such organizations as the CSIR and DGTD mentioned above, placed in the wider context of the Planning Commission, NRDC and other Government organizations at the one end, and industries and their associations at the other. Such a conceptual link-up for technology data-bank interfaces is explained in Chapter 9. In as much as the building blocks of information already exist, it is highly desirable that along with a development of individual data-banks, such interfaces are simultaneously developed so that they can easily connect with NISSAT and NIC without any conflict.

Linkages between Government systems and the private industrial sector have also been visualized in Chapter 9. Some of these linkages can be of a specific kind, too. One such instance is the utilization aspect of each licence issued to an industrial sector in respect of values of orders placed, amount for which letters of credit are opened, values of shipments received and total payments made : all of which need a specific linkage between the data-bank of an industrial unit and the information system in the Government to effectively cope with such statistical information.

The information management in the business and industrial sector is normally more well defined than in the Government installation to the extent of coverage, system-goals, information flows, and operational control. The same, however, is not true for policy review and expansion of the planning base for such information systems. It is again imperative that linkages are conceived and established so as to make the best use of the given information situation in the country. Efforts are on—and should be strengthened—to allow computers to communicate among themselves in order to share a common information base and knowledge of systems work done for very similar applications. The Tata Consultancy Service (TCS), for instance, had placed a small computer with the ACC to carry out minor jobs locally and transfer major jobs to the Burroughs B-6748 computer at the TCS centre.

10.4 Interfaces and interrelationships—a qualitative framework

As seen from the above, computers have been with us for a decade and a half, with a gathering of momentum in the past few years; and the scene is already beset with problems. The first problem is one of change—where to instal a computer when none existed before, if this is a cost-effective step. This is the most difficult choice to be made when one has to be careful about the selection criteria speed, accuracy, capability and mechanization potential, to name only a few with regard to such objectives and goals as better documentation, reduction in arrears, input schedules, timely information for management control, and quick response to change. Thereafter, there is a need to assess the physical workload of different tasks handled, and to evaluate a few alternative systems—ranging from a computer to a manual one (with electronic calculators)—which could perform the specified tasks in order to serve the objectives defined. In a study for Indian ordnance factories, the author used quantitative merit-rating through the Delphi method to adjudge systems' effectiveness *vis-a-vis* systems costs, so as to determine the most preferred system. This, of course, had to be accompanied by a wide-ranging analysis to check the systems sensitivity with regard to all the parameters, so that there was confidence in the predicted results.

Beyond the choice of computer, if at all, lies the choice of the configuration for the system. This again is a dodgy problem. In batch-type applications, experience appears to indicate that "throughput" (defined as the number of computer operations per unit time) increases more than proportionately with computer cost (Grosch's Law), so that large computer systems are economical. On the other hand, the economics of multi mini-computers *versus* large time-shared multi-processing computers depends upon the specific utilization of specific installations. The question is nevertheless worth examining, since mini-computers and micro-computers are becoming cheaper and more powerful, while the same is also true for the new multi-processing computers and their systems software. In any case, the inexpensive mini-computers permit intelligent automation of all kinds of data-gathering operations and generate convenient displays for human operators, whether on laboratory desks or wheeled cars, in large or small factories, in ships or satellites.

The next question of choice is the physical interfacing of digital computers among themselves, with or without the real-world sensor apparatus. Distributed processing network has been recommended for the breaking up of problem sources and solving them locally instead of bringing them to a central location, which can support process control applications as well. For Government organizations, academic bodies and health organizations, the idea to let each data centre handle only one type of application and remain functionally specialized is a sound one. The problems of telecommunication links, and compatibility in file designs and programme parameters among geographically dispersed "mini" data-centres (with or without link-up with a large system, as need be) have to be solved in designing industrial and non-industrial distributed networks.

Two other choices—qualitatively different from the above—relate to choices of time and manpower. Regarding time, the choice is that of an individual organization but relative to the overall information management scene. Chances are ten to one that if such choices are not exercised soon enough within an overall informational scheme, it may become too late. As regards manpower, this point has been touched upon before, except to emphasize that our graduates have often "pure" intellectual background and should be given an orientation for experimental investigation rather than formal analysis.

The hardest choice of all is that of interdependence and co-existence among different computer systems in the national context. Organizations may have similar goals and objectives and may be so placed in business and industry as to be competitive with each other. Even then, there is a case for sharing information activities and reduce individual costs for developing separate systems on identical lines. Where organizations are dissimilar, one can often discern linkages, if not actual complimentary relationships. It is again necessary to identify these linkages and relationships.

Above all, the choice of interdependence and co-existence should lead to not merely reduction of costs but also sharing of benefits in a manner in which there is a better allocation of scarce resources, optimal utilization of available manpower and an avoidance of overlapping designs to the extent possible, within a properly perceived and planned informational perspective. Such perspectives have already started emerging on a national scale and our information planning for the entire country.

10.5 Interfaces and interrelationships—an overview

Various organizations in India needing computerized or non-computerized information systems fall into the categories of Government departments, semi-government organizations, academic institutions, health organizations and public and private industrial sectors. If their interfaces and interrelationships are to be harmonious in a situation of adequate information planning, the following conditions have to be fulfilled :

(a) Goals and objectives (illustrated before) of these organizations should be defined as far as their informational activities are concerned ;

(b) Needs for an appropriate information system should be properly identified in terms of output reports (with specified frequencies, levels, aggregation and formats) and input data (with specified sources, agency, frequencies and formats) for batch-mode applications ; in addition, such factors as time to reach the EDP, response-time for EDP to any transaction and time to relay results back to persons or processes for use should be considered for real-time applications ;

(c) Suitable EDP or non-EDP capabilities should be planned and installed after determining the effectiveness of each available or proposed capability which could perform the specified tasks with regard to the evaluating criteria (illustrated before) ;

(d) The EDP or non-EDP capabilities as installations should be efficiently run and their maintenance should be fully taken care of either with in-house maintenance capability or through contracts with original hardware vendors or through the new Computer Maintenance Corporation of India.

The above expectations are not unreasonable, as potential to realize them on ground does exist in India and much has already been achieved in Indian organizations, as seen before. Variable characteristics associated with each EDP or non-EDP facility are frequency of service, volume of service, level of service, aggregation of service, reliability of service and spin-off benefits derived out of service. In concrete terms the benefits from such service can be : decrease in management planning cycles, increase in turnover, better use of the organization's capabilities, provision of information when and where required, timeliness of despatches, improved customer service and, in general, better efficiency. Saving in manpower is not mentioned here in the light of our labour-intensive economy and in view of the fact that EDP or non-EDP capabilities properly planned often need better methods of data-capture and data-cleaning, thus needing some extra manpower.

If we consider any two organizations, A and B, having EDP (or non-EDP) capabilities, each may adopt any of the two strategies : share information or not share information. The need and relevance of such strategies come in sharp focus if A and B are active in the same or related fields of operation, and may even compete with each other for market-share. We may then use any common non-zero-sum two-person game (prisoner's dilemma or "chicken") and formulate generally a pay-off matrix as shown on page 263, where the entries in the matrix indicate the order of preferences of the two players. The absolute value of the payoffs are not relevant in the application of the theory of games.

Game theory suggests that A and B should play strategy (2,2) because it is an equilibrium point, but this is not intuitively satisfying. On the other hand, the strategy (1,1) is intuitively satisfying, but does not appear to provide stability. In order to resolve this dilemma, there has to be conscious working towards the strategy (1,1) where cooperation and interdependence become the order of the day so that there is mutual gain of a satisfying nature. Hence the need of information planning, where communication is found to contribute towards a higher probability of reaching stability in a game-theoretic sense and reaching it sooner.

Considering again the two organizations A and B, we may conceive of the following :

A=(the set of information activities in A) ;
B=(the set of information activities in B) ;
$A\bar{B}$=(the set of information activities which are in A but not in B).

A \ B	1. Share information	2. Not share information
1. Share information	(3, 3) Both benefit and achieve cost reduction	(0, 4) B benefits and achieves cost reduction—advantage to B
2. Not share information	(4, 0) A benefits and achieves cost reduction—advantage to A	(0, 0) Status quo

$\bar{A}B$=(the set of information activities which are not in A but in B).

AB=(the set of information activities common to A and B).

We may also define a measure C on the set A as C(A) which denotes the investment needed and bornc by EDP (or non-EDP) capabilities for handling the set of information activities A.

If now the system consists of two organizations working *independently*, we have the following relationships :

C(A)=investment borne by organization A
$=C(A\bar{B}+C_{indep.}(AB)$;

C(B)=investment borne by organization B
$=C(\bar{A}B)+C_{indep.}(AB)$;

Then the total investment borne by the system
$=C(A\bar{B})\ C(\bar{A}B)+2C_{indep.}(AB)$.

On the other hand, if the system consists of two organizations working on a cooperative basis for handling the *common* information activities, it can be shown that the total investment borne by the system is $C(A\bar{B})+C(\bar{A}B)+C$ joint (AB). Therefore, the difference in investment borne by the two systems is $2C_{indep.}$ (AB) *less* C joint (AB). As long as this difference-value is positive which is commonly likely to be the case, the second system is more economical.

In general, for a system of n organizations with EDP (or non-EDP) capability, total investment borne by the system is

$$C=\sum_{i}^{1,n} C_i$$

where C_i is the investment borne by organization i.
Similarly,

$$S=\Sigma S_i$$

and $$O=\Sigma O_i$$

where S,O are the total services available from these capabilities and the total operational (including maintenance) cost of these capabilities. Then, benefit B as return on the investment for the system as a whole is :

$$B=\frac{\Sigma S_i-\Sigma O_i}{\Sigma C_i}=\frac{S-O}{C}$$

Out of the above parameters, quantification of S is the most difficult one, but has been attempted successfully by the author in an industrial context.

The simple summations as above are valid if the investments are unrelated to or if there is no interaction among the EDP capabilities. On the other hand, advantages of scale can be obtained by integrated information planning among the organizations of the system so that the same total service S may be derived by pooling the operational and maintenance facilities for the separate organizations. The total investment C under integrated information planning can similarly be lower than the simple sum of respective investments. If C^1, S^1, O^1, B^1 denote the respective quantities in an environment of integrated information planning for the system then we get from the above,

$$S^1=S,\ O^1<0 \text{ and } C^1<C;$$

consequently, $B^1>B$

Again, for a given level of investment, organizations of the system can suitably share all relevant information where such sharing takes the shape of an open (or closed, if there are no other contiguous systems to share information with) and dynamic input-output model. This arrangement can usually realize the advantages of higher total service and/or lower operational costs than competing independent organizations. In this case,

$$S^1=S,\ O^1<0 \text{ and } C^1=C;$$

consequently, $B^1>B$.

10.6 Conclusion

The synergistic benefits of such joint efforts are clearly far-reaching. Organizations of a commercial system, which jointly take care to select their EDP facilities and information-flow of shared communication so as to optimize the mutual benefit have great flexibility in choosing their competitive stance. With increased efficiency and other all-round benefits, they can gain a larger market-share with better service or even lower price in a commercial environment.

For organizations of an academic or health system a larger investment can be made in research and development on software as well as hardware than is possible by similar but disjointed systems elsewhere. For business and industry, total benefits can be maximized and growth capital attracted to the firms, even after remaining fully competitive with firms whose information management has not gone for such careful planning.

As a relative newcomer in the field of information sciences, Indian national scene has very advantageous green-field conditions and is poised for a propitious take-off. A little initial integrated planning can take it very far indeed. Absence of it will make for the most resounding crash in the field of information management from which it will be hard to recover. The choice is entirely ours.

11

COMPUTER CONTROL FOR SOCIO-ECONOMIC INFORMATION

11.1 General

If one charts out the growth of computers in India in the current decade, one is faced with a phenomenal growth-rate in terms of computing power. While the number of computers in use in this country is over 400 today (against more than 20,000 in the USA), the computing power has increased almost eight-fold, treating 1971 as a base. In other words, there is a compound growth-rate of nearly 56 per cent every year on the available computing power which allows this power to double itself every year and a quarter.

Such advent in computing power has made it possible today to solve feedback control problems in regulating real-life phenomena, many of which had remained in the realms of theoretical studies so far. The computational aspects of most control problems are fairly complicated and cannot make use of optimization techniques without a powerful digital processor. The availability of both cheap and highly efficient computing power today makes possible the following:

(a) Application of almost any control algorithms (i.e., pre-determined logical instructions and rules for calculation) to real-life processes ;

(b) Simulation of any environment in the analysis, design and synthesis of control system as a feed-back process.

Use of digital computers as a tool of control system has been familiar for some time to solve theoretical and applied research problems in science and engineering. The speed, accuracy and logical capability of a computer has already had a revolutionary impact on the system design for *automatic* control. With the introduction of high performance of today's micro-computers and the considerable size reduction due to high-packing density in "chips," new concepts have come in the engineering design of feed-back control systems. The main advantages reaped have been in (i) more flexible control, (ii) improved product quality, and (iii) more efficient operation by implementing optimal policies.

It is high time we considered systematically how the insight gained in the above scientific and engineering activities could be applied to socio-economic phenomena by using computers to control environmental processes through a *non-automatic* monitoring and control system design. In this study, first a few engineering applications are considered and then suitable lessons are drawn to suggest computer-aided control and monitoring systems for management of socio-economic processes.

All physical and managerial activities can essentially be viewed to comprise the following functions :

(a) *Data-collection* : for all relevant and meaningful data pertaining to the process and their timely communication ;
(b) *Processing* : of information for setting up decision rules and commands needed for control ;
(c) *Control* : of the process according to the decision rules and commands so that the process is performed in the desired manner.

It will be immediately apparent that only if data collection is relevant, accurate and available on time, processing of information—howsoever fast—will have a meaning. Again, the control function will depend how swiftly the process can or would react depending, in turn, on the type of activity being controlled.

The above may be illustrated with a few engineering applications in India where data from environment are collected manually or through sensors; processing is done on digital computer in an on-line or off-line mode; and on-line or off-line control of environment is achieved with a varying response-time.

11.2 Industrial process control

This usually takes place for automatic control of industrial processes where a high degree of instrumentation is possible. Data are collected on-line for the industrial process through automated sensors, and also from direct access files by a dedicated compiler or micro-processor. Appropriate control programs and the sets of control variables needed are built into the memory of the computer. Optimization algorithms provide the bases for adjustment of the control variables to bring the industrial process up to a desired optimal performance.

For instance, an IBM-1800 computer is used for controlling every LD operation in the "heat" of the steel-making shop No. 1 at the Bokaro Steel Plant. The process control function is carried out round the clock by the thermo-chemical model which uses the criteria of temperature of the steel at the completion of the blowing of oxygen and the end-point carbon, for successful end-results. The model runs through the following stages :

(i) initial charge calculation based on quality and quantity of steel for every "heat" ;

(ii) calculation of blow requirements (including bath additions) ;

(iii) corrective action in case the blow did not result in desired specifications of steel ;

(iv) calculation of ladle additives, e.g., ferro-manganese or ferro-silicon ;

(v) self-correction based on the results of the present "heat" to make adjustments in the marginal drift in the values of coefficients.

The last feature actually ensures that any deviation in the values of the coefficients is taken care of by an adaptive feed-back loop.

The important parameter in the above kind of application is the "response time" of the process control, since the computer has to control its environment by receiving data processing them and by returning the results sufficiently quickly to affect the environment at that time. The response time of often less than 5 seconds is needed, which justifies the real-time computer use. The algorithms for controlling the process are usually well defined, thus making it possible to calculate the "worst case" response time in order to assess the risk margin with some precision. If the computer is not *dedicated* to the process, it must be capable of handling multiple interrupts, as the transaction needing a fast response time has to break into programs doing less immediate work. Files or data bases become significant only where tables or data sets have to be maintained in the computer memory, usually in the case of optimal control calculations.

11.3 Missile flight control

The control policy here requires dynamic compensations even in large signal conditions to ensure optimal performance level. Design requirements of a computer-based missile "auto-pilot" are the following :

(a) Uniform manoeuvrability (fast response even with large guidance command) for all signal conditions ;
(b) Uniform stability even with major disturbances ;
(c) Uniform manoeuvrability for varying flight conditions (with respect to aerodynamic and environmental variations) ;
(d) Simplicity in design.

For instance, at the Hyderabad Defence Research and Development Laboratory, detailed systems analysis with a performance criterion has been carried out to achieve the above design objectives and a suitable design algorithms has been arrived at. A micro-computer, based on INTEL 8080 micro-processor, has been built which implements the control algorithm based on on-line data, adopts a suitable control policy for dynamic compensations depending on the environmental conditions and generates finally the analog signal to the actuator servo in order to control the missile trajectory.

The benefits in the above process are elimination of human

manipulation by logic being firmly wired, implementation of optimal control algorithms through a micro-processor, and realization of the objective with minimum resources.

11.4 Thyristorized shear control

This is yet another application of on-line process control in steel industry. The system consists of the following :

(i) Automated sensors for measurement of the length of a semi-rolled red-hot billet while in motion ;

(ii) Thyristor control system for regulating the speed of 1.2 MW flying shear motor ; and

(iii) Computer programs and necessary interface for cutting billet lengths to minimize the end-crops.

The shearing operations in a one million tonne billet mill at the Bhilai Steel Plant are controlled using a TDC-312 computer. The on-line control system measures the length of the semi-rolled products and estimates the length of the final rolled products. It then determines the optimum billet length to produce a minimum end-crop. Finally, it generates and supplies the desired signal value to the thyristor control unit in order to regulate the flying shear speed for obtaining the desired billet length.

The complete system, developed at a total cost of Rs. 10.5 lakhs (without the computer cost) is expected to save Rs. one crore every year through decrease in end-crop lengths.

11.5 Machine tool control

Here the control program is implemented through off-line data processing by a digital computer, to achieve the following benefits :

(i) machining of components of great complexity with tolerance condition and repeatability ;

(ii) flexibility and economy in the production of simple and complex parts.

The above benefits relate to increased efficiency and better service, and are hardly linked with saving of manpower.

The functions of the numerically controlled machine are as follows :

(a) The product to be machined is dimensionally defined in an engineering drawing, along with material type, surface finish and tolerances ;

(b) The complete description of all motions and machine-functions required to fabricate the part is manually specified in the program and the off-line data-processing on the computer creates the *control paper tape* with detailed instructions ;

(c) The machine is loaded with the job and the proper cutter. The control paper tape is now read on-line, and the feed-back control system executes the command by guiding the cutter in the pre-determined path.

It is to be noted that the entire job can be undertaken by on-line, real-time computer which can generate the necessary cutting instructions after executing the part program instructions and the results can be communicated on-line to the numerically-controlled machine so that the material is moved accordingly.

Benefits in the above control process are assured quality of performance on a repetitive basis, elimination of operator errors and feasibility of all operations being done at a lesser skill level once the basic programs are properly written.

11.6 Other illustrations

A few more examples of computer-based control systems are as follows :

(i) *On-line process control systems* (data through sensors, on-line data-processing, on-line feed-back control, short response time) :

(a) India's largest computer-based control system for monitoring the fast breeder test-reactor at the atomic power plant at Kalpakkam near Madras ;

(b) Computer-based control system with telemetry-interface operational at the Sriharikota Rocket

Launching Facility for data acquisition and analysis;

(c) Computer-based data-logging and control system under installation at Gujarat State Fertilizer Company at Baroda.

(*N.B.* : The fabrication and supply of the TDC computer systems for the above three process-control applications are by ECIL, Hyderabad.)

(ii) *On-line management control systems* (data through manual terminals, on-line data-processing, off-line feed-back for operator guidance, medium response time) :

(a) Computer-based production-data logging and control system for production planning and scheduling, linked with order processing at the one end and with sales invoicing at the other, particularly for the Slabbing Mills, Hot and Cold Rolling Mills, and Merchant Mills operations ;

(b) Computer-based materials-data logging and control system providing corrective, follow-up and review action, facilitating control of inventory-levels, triggering automatic purchase-orders, cutting out excessive lead-times and generating "alerts" for undue delay in supplies, low-stock or over-stock items, etc. ;

(c) Computer-based raw-materials data-logging and control system—maintaining a complete map of all raw-material stacks and silos, and using statistical models to decide the blend and composition of raw material going to Sinter Plant and Blast Furnace operations.

(*N.B.* : Supply of Burroughs computer system for the above three applications is planned at Bokaro Steel (on its way to be the biggest steel plant in India), where these operator-guidance applications on the large central computer are planned to be linked with the small dedicated computer for process-control applications.)

(iii) *Off-line management planning systems* (manual data, off-line data-processing, off-line feed-back of control information for planning, long response time) :

(a) Computer-based maintenance planning and repair-shops scheduling system ;

(b) Computer-based structural design planning, research and development-support system ;

(c) Computer-based manpower planning system—to cover areas like recruitment, growth planning, training, technical refresher courses, management development programmes, trade conversion training and welfare facilities.

(*N.B.* : The above three applications are also planned on the Burroughs computer in a batch mode at the Bokaro Steel Plant.)

On generalizing from the above instances of engineering applications of control processes, we observe that the operations in the above areas are dynamic in nature and considerations for ensuring optimum and efficient control are widely varying in nature. If any computer-based control system can be presented as in Fig. 11.1, it becomes immediately obvious that *the crux of effective control is the ability to respond in a meaningful time-frame, keeping in view the large volume of data, likely delay in communication, complexities of analysis and needs of follow-up on the corrective decision.*

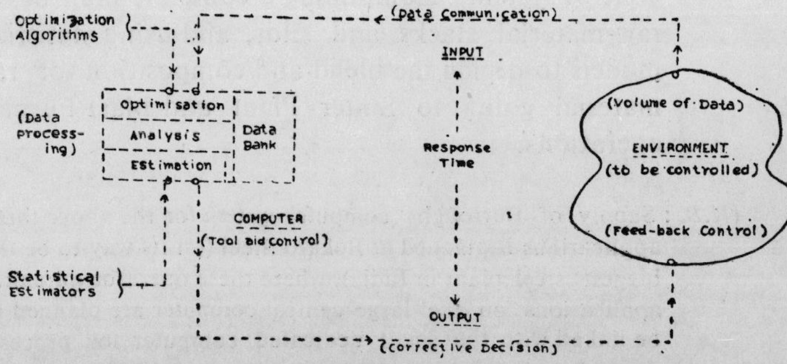

FIG. 11.1: *Computer-based control system*

We can now draw the lesson from the engineering applications that if we want to use computers for giving effective aid to managerial control of the wider socio-economic phenomena, then the following requirements have to be fully met :

1. Effective and reliable means of collecting a large volume of data at different levels and control points in the socio-economic area ;
2. Effective and reliable means of communication of data so that necessary information could be received in time for decision-making processes ;
3. Facility for storing a large volume of data, so that the current status is always reflected in the decision-making process, and facility for rapid evaluation of the information-flow by means of well-tested decision models (of both O.R. and statistical kind) so that alternative strategies could be worked out in time :
4. Effective and reliable means of implementation of the preferred decision-strategies for achieving control in the socio-economic area with proviso to monitor any deviations which have to be sensed quickly and evaluated again, to change—if necessary—the decision-making process.

The above may now be illustrated with a few socio-economic applications.

11.7 Transportation management

Experience at the integrated steel plant indicates that the rolling stock of wagons and locomotives operate over a large network within and around the plant—bringing in raw material of diverse kind ; being formed into homogeneous trains at the inward exchange and marshalling yards ; unloading the contents at ore/coal tipplers ; loading with finished material at various shipping points with the finishing mills ; being collected and formed into trains again at the marshalling and outward exchange yards ; being despatched to widely different destinations. At Bokaro Steel at 1.7 million-tonne ingot-level, there are about 800 incoming and 800 outgoing wagons daily and 2,000 additional wagons in the plant, i.e. about 3,500 wagons to be tracked, located and moved daily by the traffic management. At Tata Steel at two-million-tonne ingot-level, about 10 million tonnes of material are handled annually in wagons through 4 marshalling yards, over a total track-length of about 400 km within the plant alone. Manual planning and control for such a large number of wagons and locomotives over the track network is difficult and contributes to the exccssive demurrage of about Rs. 1.8 crores per year charged by the Railways at each of these steel plants.

Computer-based traffic-data logging and control systems are contemplated now, with terminals at all key traffic control points and connected with a major computer installation for data collection and for ensuring information on up-to-date status of the traffic movements. Operating personnel are planned to report via *terminals* events and actions, e.g. arrival of a rake, loading of a wagon, breakdown of a locomotive, and so on. *On-line* traffic data files are to be maintained current by the computer and suitable decision algorithms (developed for decisions at control points) are to ensure requisite prompt decisions with regard to traffic movement and control. The computer is also to be programed to generate "alerts" about undue delays and to provide information on wagon turn-round and loco-utilization schedules. Likely benefits are reduction in wagon detention and consequent savings (10% or more) in demurrage and handling costs, and higher (5% or more) loco utilization.

A logical extension of the above control system is to use dedicated micro-processors for such key traffic control points as inward/outward exchange and marshalling yards where formations of trains are decided manually now involving rakes, loose wagons and locos, and their movements with limited shunting and signalling facilities. Large-scale simulations are known to have been carried out on the latter facilities for such major railway yards as Mughal Sarai and some of the decision algorithms can be adapted, through micro-instructions to the processors, if need be. The necessary data-logging will then yield prompt decision-strategies which can be used for operator guidance.

Integrated steel plants can visualize such micro-processors to be linked to the large computer through magnetic tapes in an off-line mode, or simply using the terminal for data-logging for the information already processed. There could be many other applications in Railway marshalling yards, large material-handling and transhipment points, etc., where micro-processors could be used as above on a stand-alone basis. The resultant benefits to accrue on improved materials movements and traffic control operations are immediately obvious and should pay back, hands down, for the cost of hardware and software to be obtained and utilized.

The merits of the above control process would be improved decision-making on efficient shunting patterns and appropriate train formations within very short response times and after using suitable decision rules. Such recurring benefits and quality performance, error-free operations and need for a lower skill level would follow from the above.

11.8 Agriculture management

Intensive extension efforts—following extremely systematic transfers of farm technology operating from the lowest levels of average and progressive farmers upwards—have, since its start in 1974, almost struck root in India. As advocated by Daniel Benor of the World Bank and as practised in about 10 States today, the efforts are based on recognition of a given time-sequence of operations in agriculture. At every stage from seed-bed preparation, through plant-growth to post-harvest practices, there are critical operations whose *timely* and diligent performance is essential to the ultimate purpose of maximizing yields and income. The "training and visit" rhythm—which can swing from a weekly to a fortnightly, and back to a weekly, cycle to match the requirements of rabi, kharif and inter-crop seasons—is meant to enable the village-level workers to know and transfer the above knowledge to the farmer and to ensure its proper application at the right time. The extension officers, and the assistant and deputy directors of agriculture covering the extension circles and divisions respectively, follow a similar rhythm of "training and visit" reinforced by subject-matter specialists in the disciplines of agronomy, plant protection, extension and training, water management and agricultural implements.

If extension advice is to retain credibility, a systems approach as above must ensure the following :

(i) Prescribed inputs of seeds, fertilizers, pesticide, water, implements and credit are available in time, matching the demand ;

(ii) Regulation of irrigation systems and the energization of pumps dovetail with the extension schedule ;

(iii) "Alerts" are generated on likely shortages or supply difficulties so that a specific-period's extension service can be tailored accordingly ;

(iv) During the first 45 days of crop growth, the nutrient deficiencies, pests and management problems found in the standing crop are identified and corrected as soon as possible.

Since the approach does not depend on favourable factors like good soil or irrigation, it has to maximize the opportunity in any set of circumstances—by calling for an optimal pattern and package for every crop in arid or rain-fed zones. Further, corrective practices or options have to be adopted in case the rains are delayed or interrupted, or floods threaten.

Installation of a mini-computer for the extension division could precisely help in the above situation for operator-guidance by carrying a data base of prescribed inputs of seeds, etc., for a wide spectrum of demands ; logging data on irrigational releases and pump-set operations ; generating periodic "alerts" or deficits, etc. In addition, it could maintain many optimization algorithms for promptly analysing and deciding on techniques of seed-bed preparation ; choice of crops and rotation ; seed treatment (e.g. sowing of pre-germinated seeds) ; differential spacing to alter the plant geometry (to ensure the optimal plant population, say, 20,000 plants per acre of maize) ; timing and modes of water and fertilizer application ; and inter-cropping—at set stages or as refinements.

If found successful, there is no reason why similar computer-based data-logging and control systems cannot be applied within the extension division for (1) cash-crops, (2) horticulture, (3) animal husbandry, and (4) mixed farming, with equal advantage and with very little extra cost except for manual collection of data through the same pattern of field visits. The merits, to win and build the farmer's (especially marginal and small ones) confidence and to ensure a virtually guaranteed improvement through fuller utilization of family, labour and given resources in any situation, are obvious.

11.9 Water management

Planning and management of water resources depend on voluminous and inter-linked information on the hydrological phenomena ; catchment-area particulars, e.g. soil, area, slopes, etc. ; river-basin particulars ; storage-tanks ; irrigation and power-projects ; cropping pattern and power-generation needs in the region ; flood-control aspect ; and so on. The last-mentioned feature comprises different kinds of structural measures (constructed to reduce flood damage by restricting movement of flood-water in the flood plain), viz. reservoir and retarding structures to store peak flows of flood ; channel improvements to increase its carrying capacity for eventual irrigation purposes ; levees to keep water away from highly developed areas ; and by-passes and flood-ways to divert flood-flows from the main channel and carry them around large villages and townships.

Complexity of the above parameters has, in the West, made imperative the use of computer which models complex run-off ; forecasts the hydrological phenomenon ; evolves optimal operational policies for reservoirs ; and uses advanced operational research techniques and computer simulations. One such instance occurs in the Colorado river system, starting from Sheista dam at 5,700 feet, followed by Boulder dam and other dams below, with lower reaches nearly 3,000 feet below Grand Canyon. Data are logged, among others, by automatic flow-gauge recorders installed in small canals with 30-40 cusecs of flow and computers help to control run-off and to close automatically the minor canals during lean seasons.

In India and other developing countries, the situation is beset by lack of authentic and accurate data for fairly long periods. Focusing attention on flood-control, setting up of good operating rules (or even guidelines) for reservoirs mainly designed for flood-control purposes can be a good starting point. Setting up of operating procedures for a multipurpose reservoir, or a group of reservoirs inter-connected as a system, can lead to objectives which are conflicting in nature. The objective of pure flood-control is to store least possible water in the reservoir, whereas power-generation requires a minimum head (to match the discharge capacity of the turbines) and irrigation requires large storage of water (to ensure maximum possible releases through the irrigation canal). Under such conditions, optimal operation of reservoir would require use of operational research and forecasting techniques involving the stochastic process.

The Nagarjuna Sagar reservoir is one of the largest multi-purpose reservoirs in India, with its canals among the longest in the world. Its full storage capacity is 400 thousand million cubic-feet (TMC), with a one-foot height of the dam providing a flood of 1, 2 or 4 TMC between the levels 520 and 590 feet. Fifteen flood-gates (60 feet by 40 feet) can obtain a total release of 18 lakh cusecs at the rate of 1.8 TMC per second. The Administrative Staff College initiated for the Department of Irrigation and Power, Andhra Pradesh, a study for computer-based operation guidance system to economize water resource; operations at the Nagarjuna Sagar reservoir, ensuring that peak-flood at Vijayawada (at the downstream) was within the safe limits of about 10 lakh cusecs and taking into account the following factors:

(i) weather forecasts for various zones in the catchment area;
(ii) the run-off observed at specified higher gauging stations;
(iii) the flood-absorbing capacity of the upper reservoirs;
(iv) the probable flood expected from the catchment below the Nagarjuna Sagar at any specified time;
(v) the full reservoir level or any specified lower level, varying between the lowest at the beginning of monsoon and the highest in November;
(vi) water demand at various periods for irrigation and power generation, and the economic benefits arising from the water release for these purposes.

Using past several years' data, the operator-guidance system would comprise a flow-forecasting model and an optimization model (with reservoir continuity, capacity, power plant and irrigation constraints) in order to lay down an operating policy of the reservoir for the next one year. The water release would be indicated for a sub-operating period of a week or a fortnight (which can be split equally over each day for operational convenience), with provision for a minor manual correction to modify the releases based on past performance. Figure 11.2 illustrates the above operator-guidance system.

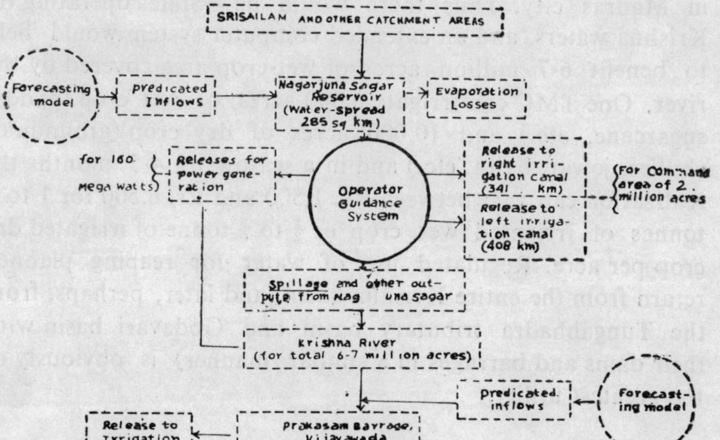

FIG. 11.2 : *Computer-aided operator guidance system for Nagarjuna Sagar*

It is contemplated to extend the above control and monitoring system to cover gradually the following objectives :

(a) To put data, collected manually through rain-gauges and flow-gauges located on the Krishna river, at various State-run and Centre-run measuring stations ;

(b) To fill up the reservoir sufficiently early in the season for timely release of water for purposes of irrigation, power generation and flood control ;

(c) To provide 6 to 8 hours' advance warning for release of water from the reservoir, whenever needed ;

(d) To release water economically during the drought-prone years (when the rainfall is less than 25 inches for a specified year), normally for 3 out of every 10 years.

The Krishna river has an inter-State basin involving Maharashtra, Karnataka and Andhra Pradesh with 12 catchment areas (contributing water to the Krishna basin) distributed over these States. At Nagarjuna Sagar and Srisailam, there is a demand for irrigation. Besides, it has recently been proposed to withdraw water, downstream of Srisailam, for use in Madras city. Thus there would be 4 States operating on Krishna waters, and an extended computer system would help to benefit 6-7 million acres of wet-crop area covered by the river. One TMC can irrigate 6,000 acres of wet crop (paddy, sugarcane, etc.) and 10,000 acres of dry crop (groundnut, chillies, jowar, bajra, etc.) and in a season of 4-5 months the realization can vary between Rs. 1,500 and Rs. 6,500 for 1 to 3 tonnes of irrigated wet crop or $\frac{1}{2}$ to $\frac{3}{4}$ tonne of irrigated dry crop per acre. Regulated use of water for reaping planned return from the entire Krishna basin (and later, perhaps, from the Tungabhadra tributary basin and Godavari basin with their dams and barrages in a similar manner) is obviously of the greatest utility.

11.10 Banking management

Time was when banks used to advance loans only to big industrialists and in a metropolitan city like Calcutta, this could have meant just 13 credit operations for the State Bank of India (SBI) each involving crores of rupees. Developmental banking has now changed the scene completely going for lakhs of creditors for each region and advancing Rs. 400-500 to each of such underprivileged persons as landless labour, physically handicapped or unemployed youth, small farmers, small traders, handcart pullers, small-scale or tiny-sector manufacturers of agarbattis, masalas, shoes and chappals. In the SBI's integrated rural development schemes, a few other sectors are also covered like medium industrialists, big farmers, grocers and traders, doctors and chemists. Under the Bombay Circle, for instance, the SBI operates 20 branches in 24 villages, and has financed 1,500 households to the tune of 50 lakhs, in the Vidarbha region alone.

Developmental banking places a high priority on the social obligation of Indian banks offering loans and advances at differential rates of interest (4½% or so) to the weaker sections of the community. So far, the proportion of "secured" loans in India has been 95 per cent of a bank's portfolio, in contrast to only 33 per cent in the USA. Such a high degree of availability of "collaterals" had given the Indian banker a feeling of complacency, to which could be attributed his lack of interest in a comprehensive credit investigation, covering all operating aspects of a borrower's business. Dispensing with securities substantially now and lending, in principle, to "socially accepted business" with a production or employment orientation makes inquiries into credit-worthiness very necessary before giving bank loans. Such inquiries can comprise survey of skills and training ; assessment of trustworthiness ; investigation on business status ; insistence on the maintaining of accounts ; probe into financial statements for the past 3 years (especially in relation to outside borrowings and the business stake for its own responsibility) ; survey of market-competitors and employment potential ; satisfaction on past performance ; availability of personal guarantee (usually two) ; and need for further counselling and educating (often at bank's cost) on how to start a business and run it profitably.

The above one-time data base can help fix a repayment programme based on the regular profit from business. In order to exercise continuous control and supervision over a borrower's operations, the bank must watch a client's business, and the debits and credits to his account. Apart from automatic debiting the clients' interest accounts and sending notices to defaulters, there has to be inspection of the client's books, units and performance on such items as its sales, its credits and creditors, its outside borrowings and its order-book position. Monthly stock statements on stock of goods for small business and on stock position of raw material, semi-finished and finished production for industrial concerns, and annual profit-and-loss statements have to be insisted upon. Linkages may have to be established with lending on bills, e.g., discounting of the clients' outward bills for credit-supplies and collecting money from its customers; and less frequently, buying its inward bills and enhancing its bank loan. Periodic advices on diversification, etc., for more sales and more profit may hence be called for.

There is evident scope in the above one-time and recurring banking operations of using a computer to log the relevant data, to maintain updated information and to use simple logic and rules, in order not only to analyse and understand the client's business, but also to decide where, when and for whom to expand (or contract) the bank loans and in what manner. The Administrative Staff College has submitted to the Punjab National Bank (PNB) a proposal for computer-based loans and advances, data-logging and control system, to be centralized at each of the PNB's regional offices for all its branches operating loans above Rs. 2,000. An important feature of implementing such a proposal anywhere would, of course, be first a dialogue with the employees for explaining how such mechanization would help to improve the bank's efficiency to discharge its social obligation and to achieve expansion of banking operations, so that eventually there is increased labour employment rather than any labour displacement.

Benefits from such a control system would be as follows :

(i) better recovery of bank loans, due charges and capital ;
(ii) better watch on over-drawals and regularization of borrowings ;
(iii) Re-circulation of bank money for more frequent usage and to more sectors of the weaker economy.

11.11 Conclusion

The crucial assumption in all the above socio-economic applications of computer-based control and monitoring systems is the acceptance of the new technology and a realization of its tremendous use-potential particularly when hardware costs are plummetting down and distributed computing and data-processing has become feasible.

Major limitations and the likely ways to overcome them are as follows :

(a) *Quick collection of reliable data and information* : Human operators, placed at various key points, should have facilities to collect and send data about progress and performance at all convenient times. There should be sufficient user instructions to log data on input formats, to use codification and to operate terminals, where necessary.

(b) *Fast communication of data* : Prompt collection and communication (at a distance, if need be) of data should be commensurate with their processing which is usually quite fast. Timeliness and relevance of processed decision from rough data can be good indicators of utility of the whole approach.

(c) *Data handling, storage and analysis* : Modern computers, with tapes and disks for auxiliary data-storage, are well equipped to handle, store and analyse information at easily accessible points. Further, as events are reported, the tape or disk-based data can be kept continuously uptodate for both operator guidance and reference by planners.

(d) *Rapid feed-back and evaluation* : The speed and ability of computers to process logical problems enables a fast response to situations requiring in-depth analysis. When diversions and unexpected charges occur and are reported, computers can be used by the planners to rapidly evaluate the situation ; to determine alternative courses of action ; and to communicate decisions and instructions for operator-guidance. Such a response can be achieved in a matter of seconds or minutes.

To summarize, computers have come to stay as management tools. They can function as control tools of the management for achieving optimal levels of performance in key result-areas of the socio-economic environment. The corrective decision, however, is furnished for human operator's guidance and needs implementation in the social system commensurate with the response time for processing. Unless control of social resources is at the same speed as the evaluation and analysis, the whole control process is meaningless especially for a tardy implementation. Sensing data from the social system and monitoring the control process continuously is the only means to ensure that the control is effective and yet responsive to social changes. On the other hand, it may be necessary to detect the out-of-phase conditions of control where decision-algorithms themselves may have to be changed, in phase with the social change.

CONCLUSION

12

INFORMATION MANAGEMENT PLANNING

12.1 General

Good-quality data are usually hard to come by. The following two illustrations will help to illustrate the point :

(a) The Estimates Committee of the Lok Sabha found the National Sample Survey Organization's (NSSO) data on the unemployment situation in the country inadequate for decision or carrying out time-bound employment schemes. In its twentieth report, the committee pointed out that in view of the Government's determination to solve unemployment in the next ten years, it was important to have a clear picture of the problem "from season to season and year to year".

(b) The Reserve Bank asked the nationalized banks to set up cells for monitoring the health of the sick industries to which they offer loans. It also asked the banks to have similar cells for small units as well. The detailed constitution of the monitoring cells would be decided by the respective banks. The nationalized banks thought of placing technical personnel and experts in finance on the monitoring cells.

12.2 NIC approach

The approach followed while setting up the NIC is typical of planning for large information system in government. This may be illustrated as follows :

(i) financial provision as under UNDP assistance programme ;

(ii) installation of a large host computer at a central location and connection of terminals placed at the user-sites. These terminals may vary from dumb terminals through intelligent terminals up to slave mini-computers as studied by the Department of Electronics ;

(iii) installation of a number of on-line terminals from the above slave mini-computers for use of senior executives of the Government ;

(iv) first-phase implementation of the following systems ;

    (a) Agricultural Information System ;
    (b) Science and Technology Information System ;
    (c) Manpower Information System ;

(v) Overlap of common data as follows :

    (a) The farmer and the industry interested in fertilizers, pesticides, tractors, etc. ;
    (b) Data on manpower essential to ascertain the impact of planning on various quartiles of population ;

(vi) commissioning of system studies (phases) of activities to be computerized by user departments (within 3-4 years by a team of Systems Analysts), with recruitment/re-training of staff as Systems Analysts over 6 months to 1 year ;

(vii) possibility of the Department of Personnel and Administrative Reforms recommending a task-force consisting of inter-disciplinary specialists to study and suggest on activity plan in order to integrate a 5-year planning machinery, performance budgeting mechanism and organization of NIC hosting the large computer, in the context of the performance budgeting concept launched by the working group of the Administrative Reforms Commission in 1966-67.

12.3 Skeleton model

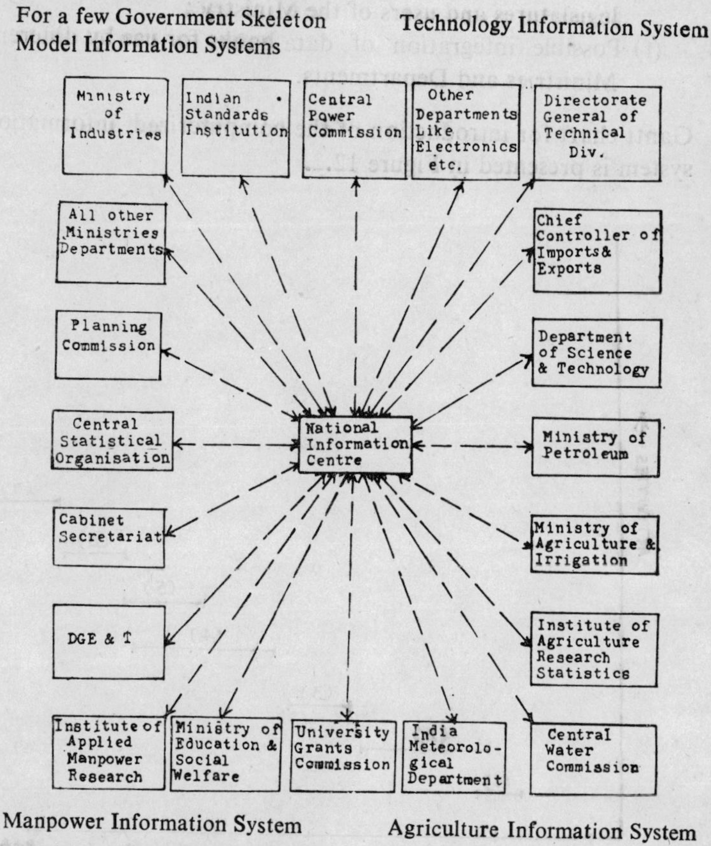

FIG. 12.1 : *Reflects a skeleton model for a few government information system*

12.4 Generalized approach

In general to set up a computerized information centre for a ministry or department, the following steps are needed :

(a) Storage or large volume of historical data for purposes of analysis facility ;
(b) Building and study of realistic models ;
(c) Monitoring of information at various points of time ;
(d) Very fast updating of data ;

(e) Fast retrieval of ad hoc queries as demanded by legislatures and users of the Ministry ;

(f) Possible integration of data banks for use by different Ministries and Departments.

Gantt chart for introduction of the computerized information system is presented in Figure 12.2.

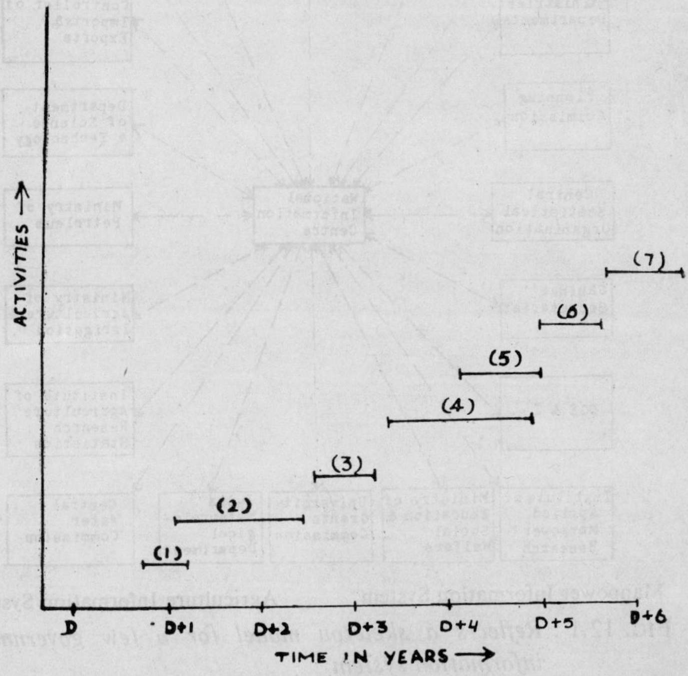

FIG. 12.2 : *Gantt chart for introducing computerized information system*

LEGEND

(1) Setting up of task-force
(2) Task-force deliberations and recommendations
(3) Recruitment of staff and re-training
(4) Background analysis and system analysis
(5) Parallel running of systems
(6) Modification to programme suits
(7) Cut-over and live system run.

12.5 Illustrative exercise

The blue-print for a programme of implementation of an information system for the Ministry of Industry can be visualized as follows :

General

Since a considerable data base exists in the Industry Ministry in the basic records and documents, a beginning can be made for developing their information system for industry straightway. This development is likely to be helped further with the considerable effort that has already gone in codification and classification in the manufacturing sector both for major products (along with raw materials and components) and for manufacturing aspects.

MIS activity selection criteria

Currently, the main need is to develop management ratios, economic performance factors and other information indicators in the field of industry. For this purpose, certain figures of merit have been suggested in Chapter 7.

At the next stage, it is desirable to develop information analysis on industry interfaces. This includes input-output relationships amongst various industries and linkages between established industries and the basic applied research carried out in the CSIR and other laboratories.

At the final stage, it is possible to build mathematical models for planning and control in different industrial sectors using optimization techniques.

Industry selection criteria

It is hardly possible to develop an information system for all industries at a time. It is, therefore, very necessary to begin with certain selected industries especially in the large and medium sectors where a large volume of data exists already. Gradually, one can switch to industries in the small-scale sector, after carrying out the groundwork of data-capture and data-cleaning. With the above end in view, the following criteria can be visualized for selection of industries : (i) scarcity; (ii) crucial importance to national economy ; and (iii) mass consumption.

The entire large and medium industry sector can be divided into six blocks, of 33 industries each, by applying the above criteria. The proposed first block of 33 industries is given at Table 12.1.

TABLE 12.1 : **Proposed list of industries for initial data base**

1. Cement
2. Paper and Paper Board
3. Newsprint
4. Caustic Soda
5. Soda Ash
6. Aluminium
7. Auto Tyres and Tubes
8. Calcium Carbide
9. Copper
10. Zinc
11. Industrial Machinery (for chemical, printing, rubber, paper, sugar, cement)
12. Commercial vehicles
13. Tractors
14. Scooters
15. D.M.T.
16. Caprolactum
17. Insecticides and Pesticides (BHC, DDT)
18. Polythelene (HD & LD)
19. Synthetic Detergents
20. Soaps
21. P.V.C. Resins
22. Polystyrene
23. Rayon-Tyre Cord
24. Nylon-Tyre Cord
25. Industrial Gases, e.g., Oxygen Dissolved Acetylene, Carbon-Dioxide
26. Anodes/Cathodes (for alkali industry)
27. Razor Blades
28. Hurricane Lanterns
29. Dry Cells
30. Matches
31. Bicycles (complete)
32. Milk Products (Baby Milk food)
33. Drugs (Antibiotics, Sulpha-drugs; Hormones, Vitamins, Analgesics, Anti-malarial drugs, Anti-dysentery.)

Aspect selection criteria

There are certain common features in the development of industry in India, which have been dealt with in the main report. In order to initiate an information system, these common aspects can make a very desirable starting point, as they relate to a large number of industries and as information on them is needed by many Ministries and Departments in the Government of India. Selection criteria among these common aspects are : (i) importance ; and (ii) data availability.

Applying the above criteria the following gradation is made :

First phase

(1) Capacity creation
(2) Target setting
(3) Industry licensing
(4) Production

Second phase

(5) Investment
(6) Import
(7) Export
(8) Foreign exchange allocation

Third phase

(9) Planning
(10) Inventory control
(11) Research and development
(12) Manpower

Once the common aspects are taken care of for most industries the specific aspects ought to be taken up for the features and problems peculiar to each industry.

Time schedule

Keeping the above selection criteria in view for MIS activity, industry and common aspects, the available data should be arranged for codification and incorporation in the data base. Historical time-series data have a good deal of significance for industry, since most of the first-stage MIS activities can be accomplished with the help of such data. As one proceeds to inter-face types of problems and eventually to mathematical model-building, a priority has to be assigned to obtain the current status data.

The proposed time schedule for development of the information system for industry can be visualized as a 3-dimensional matrix with the following faces :

(i) industry versus common aspects, as shown in Table 12.2 ;
(ii) industry versus MIS activities, as shown in Table 12.3 ;
(iii) MIS activities versus common aspects as shown in Table 12.4.

The volume of primary data available on all industry basis and for the DGTD are shown in Table 12.5 and 12.6 respectively. For the common aspects, most of these data should be stored in the NIC for the large and medium industries. When the specific aspects for each of these industries are taken up, and also when the MIS activities are extended beyond the first 200 industries, primary data are to be stored in the NIC only on a selective basis.

A schematic representation of the 3-dimensional matrix (used for deriving the time schedule) is given in Fig. 12.3.

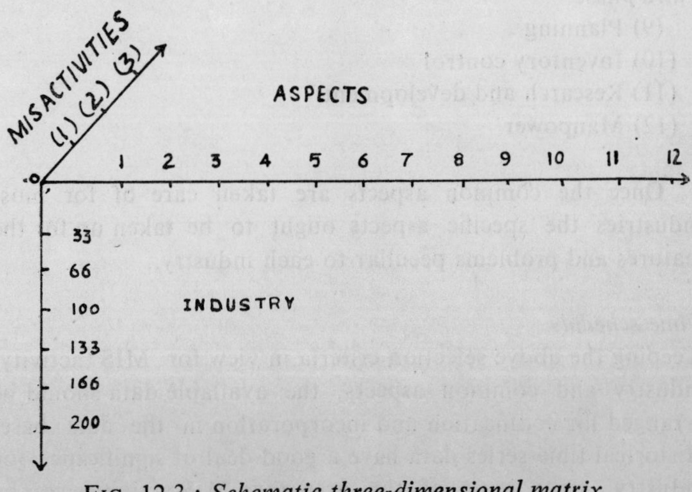

FIG. 12.3 : *Schematic three-dimensional matrix*

TABLE 12.2 : Time schedule matrix on industry versus aspects

Aspects → / No. of Industries ↓	Common Aspects 1 2 3 4	5 6 7 8	9 10 11 12	Specific Aspects
	Months	Months	Months	Months
33	1-4	5-8	9-12	13-24
66	5-8	9-12	13-16	17-28
100	9-12	13-16	17-20	21-32
133	13-16	17-20	21-24	25-36
166	17-20	21-24	25-28	29-40
200	21-24	25-28	29-32	33-44

TABLE 12.3 : Time schedule matrix on industry versus MIS activity

MIS Activities→ / Industry ↓	Management Ratios, Economic Performance Factors & Other Information Indicators	Industrial Inter-Face Activities	Mathematical Model Building
0	Months	Months	Months
33	1-4	5-8	9-12
66	5-8	9 -12	13-16
100	9-12	13-16	17-20
133	13-16	17-20	21-24
166	17-20	21-24	25-28
200	21-24	25-28	29-32

TABLE 12.4 : **Time schedule matrix on MIS activities versus aspects**

Aspects → / MIS Activities ↓	Common Aspects 1 2 3 4	5 6 7 8	9 10 11 12	Specific Aspects
	Months	Months	Months	Months
Management Ratio, Economic Performance Factors and other Information Indicators	1-4	5-8	9-12	13-24
Industrial Interface Activities	5-8	9-12	13-16	17-28
Mathematical Model Building	9-12	13-16	17-20	21-32

TABLE 12.5 : **All-industry information system**

1. *Basic Facts:*
   No. of Industries : 200
   No. of Products : 2,000 (@ 10 products/industry)
2. *Data Availability & Generation :*
   (In terms of equivalent punched cards)
   Average figures per industry :

Aspects	Data generation rate (card/year)	Compression ratio	Net Input rate (Card/Year)
(A) *Common* :			
Phase 1			
(i) Production			
(ii) Licensing			
(iii) Target setting	4000	50%	2000
(iv) Capacity creation			
Phase 2			
(i) Investment			
(ii) Imports			
(iii) Exports	7000	25%	1750
(iv) Foreign exchange allocation			

Phase 3			
(i) R&D			
(ii) Manpower			
(iii) Inventory	2500	50%	1250
(iv) Planning			
(B) *Specific*	2500	50%	1250
Total			5250

Average input rate/industry = 5,250 cards/yr.
Total input rate for all industry = 1.05 million cards/yr.
= 75 million character/yr.
Date available in 1975 = 300 million
(last four years' record)

3. *Cumulative Data* :

	Existing base in 1975	Annual inflow rate in next 5 years	New base in 1980
Documents	6.0 m	1.50 m.	12.0 m
Punched cards	1.0 m	1.05 m.	8.0 m
Tapes	.10	5	40

TABLE 12.6 : **Data base for industry within DGTD**

	Existing base in 1975	Annual inflow in next 5 years	Expected base in 1980
Documents	1,60,000*	1,60,000	8,00,000 to 9,00,000
Punched cards	60,000	1,20,000	6,00,000 to 7,00,000
Tapes	8	16	80 to 90

*1972 Annual Report

Note : To get the cumulative figure for the entire industry sector, the figure needs to be multiplied by a factor of 5.

APPENDICES

*APPENDIX 'A'**

MANAGEMENT INFORMATION SYSTEM FOR THE DEPARTMENT OF CHEMICALS AND FERTILIZERS

1. Scope and objectives of MIS

The Department is essentially responsible for planning, regulating and monitoring of development in the fertilizers, chemicals, drugs, pharmaceuticals and pesticides sectors, the most important function being planning and monitoring of production of essential items. The Ministry is also interested in sales, distribution of products, exports, imports to meet internal shortages, manpower employed in the industry and so on many of which are also monitored by other agencies. Three other critical areas of responsibility are : (i) performance of public sector undertakings in financial and physical terms, (ii) progress of projects in the organised sector for setting up capacities for production of major items, and (iii) pricing of fertilizers, drugs and chemicals under various statutory regulations.

The MIS should be directly relevant to the major objectives of the Department such as monitoring of formulation, approval and implementation of new projects to ensure that planned targets of capacity and output are achieved on schedule, optimum utilisation of capacity and ensuring availability of products in adequate quantities. The system has to be so devised that the major activities can be regularly reviewed at appropriate levels in physical and financial terms. It will not thus consist merely of data reporting, but will necessarily have a monitoring bias to enable identification of problems or bottlenecks, timely decisions and corrective action being taken where necessary. In particular, in regard to the public sector undertakings under the administrative control of the Department, the system should enable proper monitoring and

*Reproduced, with permission, from the Report of the Sub-Group of Advisory Committee on Management Accountancy in Government as the Proposed Management Information System for the Department of Chemicals and Fertilizers, New Delhi, 1978.

evaluation of their performance against laid-down targets. The scope of the MIS should primarily relate to improving performance within the government except to the extent that information relating to the private sector is essential for decision and policy making at government level and to help remove constraints on production such as power, transport, etc.

2. Input forms

Input Form No.	*Name of the Report*	*Frequency*	*Submitted by*
1	2	3	4
0-00	Weekly telex on production	Weekly	Production units in the organised sector
0-01	Production Statement	Monthly	-do-
0-02	Sales, Despatches & Stocks	Monthly	P.S.Us.
0-03	Plant Maintenance/ Operations	Quarterly	-do-
0-04	Manpower Statement	Quarterly	-do-
0-05	Industrial Relations	Quarterly	-do-
0-06	Profit & Loss Statements	Quarterly	-do-
0-07	Internal Resources	Quarterly	-do-
0-08	Cash Flow Statement	Monthly	-do-
0-09	Plan Expenditure Summary	Monthly	-do-
0-10	Management Ratios	Yearly	-do-
0-11	Supply of bulk drugs to Non-associated Formulators	Quarterly	Production units in private sector
0-12	Progress on Drugs Projects by holders of Letters of intent/industrial licences	Quarterly	Holders of letters of intent/industrial licences in private sector
0-13	Import and Stocks of Canalised Drugs and Pharmaceuticals	Monthly	Production units

1	2	3	4
PC-1	Pre-construction activities	Quarterly	Project authorities (PSUs)
C-1	Physical Progress of construction	Quarterly	-do-
C-2	Physical Progress Explanatory Sheet	Quarterly	-do-
C-3	Financial Progress Projects	Monthly	-do-
C-4	Progress of Interrelated Activities	Quarterly	-do-
C-5	Manpower Position Report	Quarterly	-do-
C-6	Scarce Resources Position Report	Quarterly	-do-

Note: Forms C-2, C-4 and a simplified version of C-1 may also be extended to selected private sector projects desired to be monitored.

3. Output returns

Weekly reports

MIS-1 : This brings out production information in regard to fertilizers in terms of nitrogen (N) and phosphorus pentoxide (P_2O_5). It will form the basis for weekly review meetings to be conducted by the Joint Secretary (F).

Monitoring of production in the drugs and chemicals sectors is not being undertaken on a weekly basis ; hence no weekly output return from these Divisions is called for.

Monthly reports

MIS-2 : This is a format to bring out monthly production in different sectors. Two variants have been proposed. Form MIS-2 (Fertilizers) will bring out production performance of large units in both public and private sectors of fertilizers in terms of N_2 and P_2O_5. Form MIS-2 (PSUs) which has essentially the same format as the previous one may be used for bringing out production performance of public sector units under the Drugs and Chemicals Divisions of the Department. In this form should be included all production units for the concerned product including those which are scheduled to go into production during the year and for which annual targets have already been fixed.

MIS-3 : This is a summary of financial progress of projects in the public sector. Each Division will prepare its own report in respect of projects undertaken by PSUs under its control.

Quarterly reports

MIS-4 : This is a format designed to reflect on a quarterly basis production of selected bulk drugs. The same format is also suitable for the Chemicals Division.

MIS-5 : This is designed to keep track of action taken on project proposals received by the Department from the PSUs. This return will include all proposals requiring approval of the EFC/PIB. The intention is to ensure that there are no delays in receiving proposals for new projects in relation to targeted Five Year Plan capacities.

MIS-6 : This indicates physical progress on critical milestones pertaining to major projects undertaken by PSUs. For effective monitoring of physical progress, it is considered essential that—

(i) only a few major milestones which are critical to keeping the project on schedule should be taken up for monitoring and these should be determined in consultation with the project authorities.

(ii) a Master PERT chart related to these milestone should be obtained from the project authorities and kept updated in the Department.

MIS-6 together with the corresponding monthly return on financial progress of projects (MIS-3) and the Master PERT chart will be among the background material for Quarterly Review Meetings to be conducted at Secretary/Jt. Secretary's level. Since the projects as a rule do not adopt 'PERT costing', it is not possible to relate physical and financial progress towards each milestone. The two forms—MIS-6 and MIS-3—together would, however, enable the Department to monitor progress to a reasonable extent. Format MIS-6 can, if required, also be extended to cover selected projects undertaken in the private sector.

MIS-7 : This is designed to reflect the financial performance of PSUs in significant areas.

MIS-8 : This has been devised to monitor supply of bulk drugs to non-associated formulators. It may be necessary to add a column to indicate the obligation of the concerned company to supply bulk drugs to non-associated formulators in terms of quantities as stipulated in the licence documents.

MIS-9 : This is devised to enable monitoring of progress achieved by holders of letters of intent/industrial licences in setting up of production facilities for drugs. This form should be prepared on the principle of "exception reporting" and should exhibit only such cases where critical delays have developed at some stage or other.

Annual Returns

MIS-10 :
MIS-11 : These formats reflect the health of each PSU and would also provide a measure to the Department to assess comparative performance of PSUs in each sector.

4. Benefits

The MIS is relatively simple and is capable of being implemented within the existing resources of the Department. It will enable relevant information being gathered and made use of in respect of the key sectors of fertilizers, essential drugs and chemicals, and pesticides. In respect of these sectors, the system, if implemented, will :

(i) draw attention to phasing of activities in each sector from the stage of formulation of plans onwards, to ensure that plan targets are achieved on schedule;

(ii) focus attention of the Department on the timely receipt and processing of project proposals, in respect of both public and private sectors where investment is required to meet Plan targets ;

(iii) indicate slippages in progress of projects in critical areas and enable corrective action being taken ;

(iv) draw attention to the rate of utilisation of existing capacities in relation to what was anticipated and identify action required by the Department and by Government for achieving current Plan targets ;

(v) enable the Department to monitor expenditure against Plan outlay and to forecast likely shortfalls and overruns ;

(vi) indicate likely achievements in relation to targets, both short-term and for the five year period ;

(vii) enable close monitoring of physical and financial performance of PSUs, individually as well as in comparative terms ;

(viii) indicate likely increases or reductions in the internal resources of PSUs against projected figures and budgetary provisions ; and

(ix) enable monitoring of supply of selected bulk drugs by major producers to non-associated formulators.

*APPENDIX 'B'**

MANAGEMENT INFORMATION SYSTEM FOR THE MINISTRY OF STEEL AND MINES

1. Main functions

The Ministry of Steel and Mines comprises of two Departments—Department of Steel and Department of Mines.

The Department of Steel is responsible, inter-alia, for the planning and development and regulation of the iron and steel industry including electric are furnace units, re-rolling mills, alloy and special steels and ferro-alloys, as also for the concurrent development of input industries such as iron ore, manganese ore, chromite, limestone and other minerals used in the steel industry. The implementation of Iron and Steel (Control) Order, 1956, distribution, import and export of iron and steel also falls within the ambit of its functions.

The Department of Mines is responsible for the survey and exploration of all minerals, other than natural gas, petroleum and atomic minerals ; for mining and metallurgy of non-ferrous metals like aluminium, copper, zinc, lead, etc. ; and for the administration of the Mines and Minerals, Regulation and Development Act, 1957 and the Rules framed thereunder for all mines other than coal, natural gas, petroleum and atomic minerals.

2. Objectives of the MIS

As the Ministry is essentially responsible for planning, regulating and monitoring developments in the Iron and Steel, mining and metallurgical sectors, the MIS has to enable it to :

(a) Monitor production of essential iron and steel items, non-ferrous metals and mineral items ;

(b) Monitor sales, distribution exports, imports of these items so as to ensure adequate availability of these critical industrial raw material ;

*Reproduced, with permission, from the Report of the Sub-Group of the Working Group in Review and Redesigning of Management Information System for the Ministry of Steel and Mines, New Delhi, 1981.

(c) Monitor (as the owner and the Administrative Ministry) the performance of Public Sector Undertakings under its control ; and

(d) Monitor the progress of projects undertaken in the organized sector for setting up additional capacities for production of major items in the sector.

3. Summary (output) reports

S.01	Production Summary (Main Products)	Monthly
S.02	Production Summary (Ores)	Monthly
S.03	Sales and Stocks	Quarterly
S.04	Summary of Financial Performance	Quarterly
S.05	Status Report on action taken on project proposals	Quarterly
S.06	Critical Milestones pertaining to Major Projects	Quarterly
S.07	Construction Projects Summary (Public Sector)	Quarterly
S.08	Construction Projects Summary (Private Sector)	Quarterly
S.09	Comparative Corporate Data	Annual
S.10	Performance of PSUs Plant-wise	Annual

The salient features of the Summary Reports are discussed below :

S.01 and S.02—Production summary—Monthly

This is designed to provide information by individual plants to facilitate monitoring of monthly production of iron and steel items and non-ferrous metals, as also iron ore, etc. At present, the Planning Commission does not get information on iron ore and manganese ore. A separate format (S.02) has, therefore, been designed to give the total picture of ore production, both in public and private sectors. The Indian Bureau of Mines will be required to give the monthly production information in regard to private sector.

S.03—Sales and stocks—Quarterly

This is designed to monitor the sales and stocks position. This will also give the total picture of the public and private sectors. The position analysed in this output format can be used for locating bottlenecks in sales and problems in clearance of stocks.

S.04—Summary of financial performance—Quarterly

This is designed to monitor the performance of PSUs against the approved project costs, annual plan provision, etc.

S.05—Status report on action taken on project proposals —Quarterly

This report is to include all the proposals requiring approval of EFC/PIB. The intention is to ensure that there are no delays in receiving proposals for new projects in relation to targeted Five-Year Plan capacities. This would be used both as an input format to be filled in by the concerned Section/Division and as an output format to be made use of for QPR meetings, reporting to outside agencies, etc.

S.06—Critical milestones pertaining to major projects —Quarterly

This report confines itself to critical milestones (a) delayed ; and (b) those likely to be delayed. For effective monitoring of physical progress, it is considered essential that—(a) only a few major milestones, which are critical to keep the project on schedule, should be taken up for monitoring and these should be decided in consultation with the project authorities ; (b) a Master PERT chart relating to these milestones should be obtained from the Project authorities and kept updated in the Departments.

This summary, together with corresponding monthly summary on financial performance (S.04) and the Master PERT chart would serve as background material for the Quarterly Performance Review Meetings.

S.07—Construction project summary (public sector)
S.08—Construction projects summary (private sector) } *Quarterly*

These will facilitate monitoring of progress of projects under construction. The proposed MIS has not provided for corresponding input format for S.08, covering private Sector. The Sections/Desks will have to devise appropriate formats for this purpose.

S.09—Comparative corporate data } *Annual*
S.10—Performance of PSUs plantwise }

These formats reflect the health of each PSU and would also provide a basis to the Department to assess the comparative performance of each PSU.

4. Use of MIS in formulating development plans

An area of vital importance to the Department is the formulation of development plans for creating capacities in critical products on the basis of projections made for the Five Year Plans. On the basis of these projections, the Departments should, at the beginning of the Plan period, work out detailed proposals and identify organisations which will be responsible for creating or expanding production capacities to the required extent. It would then have to work backwards and determine, in broad milestones, such as, dates by which feasibility reports should be received, the Government approval accorded, project construction and commissioning, etc. While Form S.05 will enable the Department to monitor action on feasibility reports already received, the activities prior to receipt of feasibility reports can most conveniently be monitored on the basis of simple control charts to be maintained in each Division against which receipts of project proposals/feasibility reports may be watched. The control charts should also cover project proposals to be received from the private sector and subsequent action regarding necessary clearances from financial institutions, FIB, PIB, etc. A watch on this would be kept through review meetings taken by the Secretary where the concerned Joint Secretary will make an oral presentation of progress in formulation of plans and receipt of project proposals. Additionally, a quarterly status report covering each sector should also be prepared by the Joint Secretary and submitted to Secretary, suggesting such corrective action as may be called for.

5. Input formats

Report No.	Name	Frequency
1	2	3
	I. Pre-Construction	
PC.1	Pro-Construction Progress	Quarterly
	II. Construction	
C.1	Physical Progress	Quarterly
C.2	Physical Progress Analysis	Quarterly
C.3	Financial Progress Analysis	Quarterly
C.4	Inter-related and Major activities Analysis	Quarterly
C.5	Manpower Position	Quarterly
	(For Completed Projects)	
CP.1	Project Description	One year after formal completion of the project costing more than Rs.5 crores.
CP.2	Pro-Construction Information	
CP.3	Physical Construction	
CP.4	Analysis of cost Variation	
CP.5	Brief Narrative Report	
	III. Operation	
0.01	Daily Production Report (for Steel only)	Daily
0.02	Daily Position Report (Important raw materials and inputs)	Daily
0.03	Weekly Production Report (trimonthly for aluminium)	Weekly
0.03-A	Weekly Report on Coking Coal	Weekly
0.03-B	Weekly report on Power Position	Weekly
0.04	Production Report (Ferrous & non-ferrous)	Monthly
0.05	Production Report (By-products)	Monthly
0.06	Production Report (Ore and Mine Development)	Monthly
0.07	Production Report (Drilling) MEC only	Monthly
0.08	Production Report (Mining) MEC only	Monthly
0.09	Report on installed, available and utilised capacity of drilling MEC only	Monthly Monthly

1	2	3
0.10	Report on Sales and Stocks (Main Projects)	Monthly
0.11	Report on Sales and Stocks (By-products)	Monthly
0.12	Major Contracts/Orders Position	Quarterly
0.13	Plant Maintenance/operation	Quarterly
0.14	Drills/Rigs Maintenance/operation	Quarterly
0.15	Manpower Position	Quarterly
0.16	Industrial Relations	Quarterly
0.17	Profit and Loss Statement	Quarterly
0.18	Summary Information Report to accompany Profit and Loss Statement, namely, 0.17	Quarterly
0.19	Internal Resources	Quarterly
0.20	Cash Flow Statement	Quarterly
0.21	Summary of Plan Expenditure	Quarterly
0.22	Inventories Position	Quarterly
0.23	Management Ratios	Annual

Index